As In The Days Of Noah

David Powell
with
Paul Keith Davis

Includes The Book Of Enoch
& Testament Of Moses

Unless otherwise indicated, all Scripture quotations are taken from The New American Standard Bible. Copyright © 1960, 1962, 1963, 1968, 1971, 1972, 1973, 1975, 1977, 1995 by The Lockman Foundation

ISBN 978-1-908154-01-9
Printed in the United Kingdom

www.freedompublishing.org

CONTENTS

Dedication

To Jacqueline and Wanda
Your beauty and purity shines as a bright light to many and we would not
be who we are today, or be able to do what we are called to do, without
your love and endless support.

ACKNOWLEDGEMENTS

Writing a book is rarely ever a single-handed project and this one is no exception!

My thanks must start with Paul Keith, who trusted me with his insight and teaching on The Days of Noah, and allowed me to build on it. Your friendship, advice and support over the years has encouraged and helped us through the challenging season of preparation for what is God is about release across the world.

Thanks to Carol Clarkson who spent many days transcribing Paul Keith's teaching for the first part of this book. I am glad you were challenged and forever changed in the process!

To Jason Hooper for your invaluable advice, insight and challenges, as we worked though each chapter to ensure accuracy and improve the flow of the message for the reader.

Thanks to my mother for her initial review and edit before she left us for heaven. Her legacy has

I am delighted to have had Justyn Hall design an amazing cover that captured the message of the book even before we had finished writing it.

And finally to my friends, students and partners, who have encouraged me in the process and constantly asked when it would be printed! Well now it has been and I hope it was worth the wait.

PREFACE

by David Powell

In February 2006, I hosted our first advanced training school in London, England – an event that was so nearly cancelled. This was the first time I met Paul Keith Davis and it was one of the most impacting meetings I have ever attended.

Through a culmination of interlinked events, spread over the preceding twenty months, my destiny and calling was released in the first twenty minutes of the opening session. It seemed that, until then, our ministry had been conceived and was growing, but now we would would finally see the promise of a "plan and purpose" (Jeremiah 29: 11) become a reality.

The Lord had given Paul Keith a prophetic word that morning. As a result we changed the name of the ministry, turning it into the *School and Company of Overcomers*, with a calling to train, equip, release and support groups of believers around the world who were answering the call of heaven to do what Jesus did whilst on the earth.

Since then we have heard a number of other phrases used to describe this movement, such as "the Sons of the Kingdom", "The Overcomers" and "the Bride of Christ". Each describes a different characteristic and facet of the same emerging group of people – those who are totally sold out, unwavering in their commitment and dedication to the Lord. A group willing to pay whatever price is necessary in order to have a part in what the

Lord is going to do, as we approach the close of the time of the Gentiles and see one last, great harvest come into the Kingdom.

Within ten months of the call and commission being released by Paul Keith we entered an intense season of preparation that lasted over four and a half years. Now it seems worth it, even if like most of us, we never want to go that way again!

I have been privileged to spend a lot of time with Paul Keith over the last eight years, travelling with him at times and attending conferences and meetings in different nations. The message he carries continues to change my life and shapes the message we carry to the nations. My hope is that it will have the same impact on your life as you read the following pages.

Part One of this book is based on a transcript of Paul Keith's revelation about the Days of Noah and how this relates both to the end time move of God, as well as the season we are now entering. It is taken from his CD and DVD teaching series, along with additional insights released by him since then. There have been some changes made to make it read more easily and some of the teaching has been turned into separate chapters.

"The Days of Noah" is the first of three teaching series that Paul Keith has released. I would highly recommend listening to the other two: "The Feast of Tabernacles" and "Sonship and the Sevenfold Spirit of God". Paul Keith's ministry resources and other information can be found at www. whitedoveministries.org

Part One

By Paul Keith Davis
The Days of Noah Series

As In The Days of Noah

"For the coming of the Son of Man will be just like the days of Noah; for as in those days before the flood they were eating and drinking and marrying and giving in marriage until the day that Noah entered the ark, and they did not understand until the flood came and took them all away, so will the coming of the Son of Man be."
(Matthew 24:37)

The Spirit of Understanding is one of the most important ingredients and profound spiritual anointings we can have, because it will separate being fruitful from unfruitful. In the Parable of the Sower (Matthew 13:19) it says that those who would not receive the words are those who did not understand it. The people who had thirty, sixty and a hundred fold returns were those who had the Spirit of Understanding. There was a revelatory release in them to recognize the revelation they needed in order to become fruitful; and that is the way it is today.

"By faith Noah, being warned by God about the things not yet seen, in reverence prepared an ark for the salvation of his household by which he condemned the world and became an heir of the righteousness which is according to faith." (Hebrews 7:11)

If Noah had not had the Spirit of Revelation he would have died with everybody else in the flood. Enoch was a man known by everyone as one who walked with God and he named his son Methuselah because he said, "When he dies, it will come!"

In ancient Jewish writings, it records that just seven days after Methuselah died, the flood came. Noah kept an eye on him and as long as they were keeping Methuselah on life support they were alright – but the moment he died, they knew it was time to get in the ark. How long was Noah in the ark before the flood came? Seven days and I suspect that the day Methuselah died Noah went into the ark.

A revelatory anointing was essential here, because the Bible says that there had never been rain before the flood. Can you imagine building a three hundred foot boat when no one had seen rain, and the conversations Noah would have had with those in his community? "Why are you building a boat, Noah?" "Because it's going to rain." "What's rain?"

Similarly, we are teaching things today and people are asking, "what's that?" There are revelatory insights coming that are going to be essential – that will be like an ark to people. Our ark is not being built in the natural, but I have been seeing and experiencing how the Lord is building an ark in the Spirit. It is an ark of truth and as long as we are in that ark of truth nothing happening in the world is going to touch us. We need to be in this ark of truth because we need the Spirit of Understanding. We are about to hear a lot of truth spoken in the coming years; there will be things that we may never have heard before, but that should not surprise us. It does not mean that we are going to accept everything that people say. If something is not consistent with the Bible, then do not accept what those people are saying. You may say, "How do we know one person's interpretation of certain things is true?" There has been infallible proof given about certain things. For instance, the message that came through William Branham in 1963 gives us the "seed form" revelation of what we need to understand in Revelation 2 and 3. That revelation concerned the white horse rider, the red horse, the black horse and the pale horse being the Spirit of the Anti-Christ. If anyone tries to release a revelation contrary to that, I believe their whole revelation is wrong.

I believe with every ounce of my being that it is the very nature of God to be ever increasing. Can you imagine God doing something with a really big bang and it just fizzling out toward the end? That is the doctrine that a lot of people believe – that Christians are just barely going to hang on at the end. NO! God is going to end things in a better way than He started them. There is going to be a victorious Bride that emerges without spot or wrinkle and she is going to shake the heavens. It will happen and we may as well be a part of it, because the preparation and the refining and the grooming we have been through is to prepare us for that purpose.

Angelic Realm
There is the Spirit of Truth that has been given in our day that declares, "For the coming of the Son of Man will be just like the days of Noah." That phrase is much more significant than we realize. We need to understand that there are clear historical documents about the things that took place in creation from the time of Adam to the flood. If you study the life of Noah you can see that, as much as Noah was a plumb line, he was also a dividing line. For example, we are hearing a lot of talk about angels and a lot of people are being critical of those who are talking about angels. But what we should understand is what Jesus said in Acts 3:21:

"Heaven must retain Him until there has been the restoration of all things."

Do you know that there is absolutely clear historical evidence that exchanges with the angelic host were so common that people did not consider it to be extraordinary? For example, in Acts 12 when Peter knocks on the door to enter and the men inside believe it is his angel and not him.

I do not worship angels, but I am really glad when one comes because they are messengers from heaven. I want to be so acclimated with the realm of the Spirit, that I am not overwhelmed when an angel comes or when we see them. When we begin to recognize them, we begin to cooperate with heaven.

There has been this incredible message spoken about that I agree with: *there must be divine alignment between heaven and earth*. How can we cooperate with that if we shield our eyes from that realm? On some level we have to see into that realm in order to align ourselves with what is going on there. Jesus said that He only did what He saw the Father do (John 5:19) and He only said what He heard the Father saying (John 8:28).

As we read the book of Genesis, we look back to a day when some angels left their spiritual habitation and, somehow, if you read the historical evidence, had the ability to manifest themselves in the natural realm. We do not know how they did that, but see the consequences of it. In Genesis 18:2 two angels came with the Lord to visit Abraham and Sarah and to check on Sodom and Gomorrah. These are the same caliber of angels mentioned in Genesis 6.

Genesis 6:4 says that these angels:

"...left that domain, they saw the daughters of men and they co-habited with women and produced an offspring."

The English translation says *"they produced giants"* which is a mistranslation. The Hebrew word means, "they produced fallen ones". Their offspring were a hybrid, a spiritual being mingled with flesh. God got so upset about it that He cast those original fallen angels into hell.

"For if God did not spare angels when they sinned but cast them into hell and committed them to pits of darkness reserved for judgment and did not spare the ancient world but preserved Noah, a preacher of righteousness and seven others when He brought a flood upon the world and the ungodly." (2 Peter 2:4-5)

"And the angels who did not keep their own domain but abandoned their proper abode He has kept in eternal bonds under darkness for the judgment of the great day." (Jude 1:6)

What happened to their offspring, the Nephillim?

Someone I have a lot of respect for, who was a very conservative preacher in the United States and a scientist, said that there are estimates of somewhere between several hundred million people, right up to several billion people on the earth at the time of Noah. The majority of them had had their blood line polluted with the offspring of this crossbreed race that was born because of the fallen angels.

That is why God had to destroy the whole earth. The Bible says that Noah's genealogy was pure, meaning that he did not have the mixture of this fallen race of humanity called "giants" in his blood line. You may say that this is just an old, ancient part of the Bible, but it is in the New Testament too, and Jesus references it himself in Matthew 24: *"For the coming of the Son of Man will be just like the days of Noah."* The Lord told me that He, "dealt with the fallen ones; you are going to have to deal with their offspring." All of a sudden our understanding of spiritual conflict goes to another level.

COVERS OF HELL

One night, a few years ago, I just could not sleep and so I prayed and prayed until I could not pray any more. Around midnight I went to bed and the minute my head hit the pillow I went into a revelatory experience. The only way to describe it is that immediately I was looking into the bowels of hell. It was sulphuric in nature, ugly, dark and smoky.

I saw what appeared to be a manhole cover and the moment it opened darkness began to flow up. All these evil beings were coming up and I was thinking, "We have to get the lid back on." One of these things looked like Adolph Hitler and another looked like Joseph Stalin. I saw several tyrants I knew that were hideous in nature coming up from hell. It was not their spirit, but the evil being that was occupying them whilst they were on the earth. These evil beings occupying the earth are looking for someone to manifest themselves through. I watched as they manifested in the bedrooms of different people, teaching them how to walk in realms of darkness that would stagger the imagination. They are somehow directly related to the race of people that existed during the days of Noah. As Jesus said, *"For the coming of the Son of Man will be just like the days of Noah."*

At the point where I felt that I could not watch this any more, all of a sudden a voice from heaven came booming down: "And the sons of light must respond in like fashion." I watched angels coming down from heaven, meeting in the bedrooms of people and teaching them how to walk in realms of glory never before so easily accessed.

We need to know the truth and what is going on in the spirit realm. What

I am interested in is not emphasizing the darkness, but that which is coming from heaven. This is part of the mandate of WhiteDove Ministries. You and I are some of these sons of light who are going to respond in "like fashion". I believe that we are being prepared to access those levels in the Spirit.

I had this experience on a Friday night and on Monday morning the Lord said to email Neville Johnson about it, a prophet in Australia. With the time zone differences it normally takes three or four days to get a reply back, but before the end of the day one came back. He said that very morning he'd had exactly the same experience. He even saw the same evil beings that I had seen.

Neville had told a couple who were with him in Australia what he had seen at breakfast and then my email came through 12 hours later. Out of the mouths of two or three witnesses let the word be established! It is abundantly clear that we are in a place right now where things are being released from hell, but what we should really be interested in is what is being released from heaven.

We should not be surprised by this. Isaiah 60:2 says that, *"darkness shall cover the earth and deep darkness the people, but the Lord shall arise over you and His glory will be seen upon you."*

MESSENGERS OF HIS FACE

What is coming out of hell is not demons but evil beings. What is coming down out of heaven is not just angels – they are messengers. They are "Angels of His presence" and come directly from standing in the presence of Almighty God. They have been reserved for this hour and this generation, and are being released from heaven carrying in them, and through them, the glory of God.

Isaiah 63:9 shows us it is going to be exactly the same way today.

"...in their affliction He was afflicted and the angel of His presence saved them. In His love and in His mercy He redeemed them and He lifted them and carried them all the days of old."

The word "angel" here is more accurately translated "messenger" and the word "presence" is more accurately translated "face". It says in Jewish literature that the Angels of His Presence are a special, unique angelic company of the heavenly host that carry the glory of God. It is literally saying that the Lord represented Himself to Israel as a messenger sent from the face of God.

Exodus 23:20-25 describes this very angel:

"I am going to send my Angel before you. He will go before you to bring you to the place that you are going to inherit... My name is in him, do not be rebellious towards him for he will not pardon your transgression, but if you do all that he says then I will be an enemy to your enemies and an adversary to your adversaries. You'll serve the Lord your God and I will bless your bread and your water and I'll remove sickness from your midst."

This is the "Angel of His Presence" and under his jurisdiction there are angels that stand in the presence of Almighty God. They are coming down to train people to walk in levels of revelatory light. Remember when Gabriel came to Zacharias, an old man wanting an impossible desire fulfilled in Luke 1:19? He said, *"I am Gabriel who stands in the presence of Almighty God."* How many of us want an angel to come and stand before you and say, "I am sent from the presence of the Almighty God"?

The greatest revival ever released in modern Church history was commissioned by an Angel of His Presence. On May 7th 1946, William Marion Branham went into the woods of Louisiana by himself and prayed and prayed until he could not pray any more. Around 3.00am a pillar of fire came into the cabin deep in the woods and he heard footsteps walking across the wooden floor.

An angel came and said, *"Fear not for I am sent from the presence of Almighty God."* He was commissioned that night and literally ignited a revival that changed a generation. When these Angels of His Presence come they are going to ignite something in a body of people that will begin to change our generation.

The Lord has been talking to me about Him picking a fight and that this is an old war that has been going on for millennia. In Ezekiel 28 it says that Lucifer was in the Garden of Eden and then God put Adam right under his nose and breathed the breath of life into him. Who picked the fight – Lucifer or God? It sounds like God did! God made Adam a son of God and then He put him in the very spot where Lucifer was.

This is the very thing Lucifer wanted, to be a son of God. Now you know why Lucifer is so angry with all of us, because we are all sons of Adam, we are all derived from him. Our invitation is be the Bride of Christ and to sit on His throne for eternity (Revelation 3:21).

This conflict goes way back and God was forced to annihilate an entire generation of people, perhaps hundreds of millions of people, because of the rebellion and sin that existed in Noah's day. Now there is a bridal company of people emerging across the world and this battle is about to escalate to a level that we have not seen before.

THE BRIDE OF CHRIST

It is most likely that we have another decade or two, three perhaps, before the Lord comes back, because we still have millions of people to get into the Kingdom and we have a lot of sick people who need to be healed. Eventually we are going to have to do some of this *en-masse* because we cannot fast for forty days to get one person healed! We must have an anointing that operates in a corporate environment where people are healed and delivered in very large numbers in order to bring in the level of harvest that we have been promised.

I believe a billion or more people are coming in between now and the end of the age. They are going to come to God through the Sons of Light who have responded to this invitation to be equipped and trained; a group of people who carry an anointing in and of themselves, where they are not dependent upon a building or a place to be anointed.

"Gather for Me seventy men from the elders of Israel, whom you know to be the elders of the people and their officers and bring them to the tent of meeting … and I will take of the Spirit who is upon you, and will put Him upon them." (Numbers 11: 16-17)

They are going to carry the anointing and governmental authority like Jesus. *"And the government* [dominion authority] *will rest on His shoulders"* (Isaiah 9: 6).

The Tutor, the Holy Spirit (John 14:27; 1 John 2:20, 27) is preparing a body of people, the friends of the Bridegroom, who are rising up right now. They are ministers and ministries who are becoming known as friends of the Bridegroom who will help prepare a body of people for Him.

There is an increase and accelerated sense of purpose and importance. This not time to play around, we need to get focused. It is time to "grow up", to get over our silly offenses and all the things that are keeping us from where we need to be. It is time to remove the parameters we have lived under and cross-pollinate with other Christian streams, because others have things that we need and vice versa. We will be like Cornelius and the Jews, we are going to co-mingle and bring our cultures together because we have a common vision.

There is a place of companionship with God, a bridal paradigm. Noah is not a type of the Bride, but Enoch is. Enoch walked with God, he was caught up and "was not". If you want to know what the Bride of Christ is going to look like, study Enoch and study John. John was allowed to emulate a portion of what the Bride of Christ will be like. I believe Elijah is actually one of the ones that will be a prototype of what is coming and he was caught up in a chariot of fire.

There is this realm in heaven that is being accessed right now. We cannot go flippantly there, but the door is open and we can begin to press into that. Many people are encountering that realm for the first time in their life, more than at any time in the last five years. As we pray for people and release the purposes of God into their life, that same night some of them are having angelic visitations.

I was in Arizona where there were probably two thousand people in the building. I had finished preaching and praying for a lot of people when I saw a pastor I knew. He had planned to go home to prepare for his own service, but the Lord told him to stay as He had something for him. As I looked at him I saw an arm extend out of the spirit realm and into this earthly realm, just the forearm, with a staff in his hand. I leaned over and said to him that the Lord was giving him a staff. I put my hand on him and he went out in the Spirit.

The next day I heard from him that he had an angel show up in his bedroom that night and he told me that he had received another word during the conference that the Lord wanted to give him a staff.

These realms are accessible now to us all.

HISTORICAL BOOKS

In the days before the flood, people were eating and drinking; they were marrying and giving in marriage right up until the day Noah entered the ark. They did not understand until the flood came and took them all away. *"For the coming of the Son of Man will be just like the days of Noah."* We need to know what went on in Noah's day that was so traumatic.

The Bible says that no word may be added to Scripture and not one word may be taken away from it. God has put His seal on the Bible and made it infallible. We go to the Greek and Hebrew at times because the English language is sometimes weak, in order to get a more complete understanding. But it is still the Word of God.

One of the greatest enemies of this generation is our 21st century mindset. Our way of thinking is so far removed from the first century Christian mindset, that we do not even really understand what was being spoken when the Epistles or the Gospels were written. We do not understand what was in their mind when they heard the words we read today.

For example, Peter said in the Acts 2 that what the people saw was a fulfillment of something spoken by the prophet Joel, which was emerging now. No one had ever seen tongues of fire come down on people. They had never seen people spilling out onto the streets prophesying and speaking in languages that they had no way of knowing by natural means.

In the book of Jude, the author is trying to make an analogy regarding a new spiritual conflict. The Pentecostal outpouring had occurred and already in the Church there were counterfeit anointings. The Bible calls these false apostles – those who were preaching a gospel contrary to the one that the apostles were delivering at that point in time.

Jude was trying to get the Jewish people of that day to understand something about this conflict and about the two spirits that were working simultaneously within the context of the Church. So he wrote about the two spirits that were present in the Garden of Eden – the tree of the knowledge of good and evil and the tree of life, which is the Lord. These two run concurrently through history and will reach maturity at the end of the age. Jude was trying to prepare the people for this because of a central belief that these things could happen in their day.

We now know that this is the last generation, because since 1948 Israel has been back in its homeland and Jerusalem is back in the hands of the Jewish people for the first time in 2,600 years. This is a prophetic fulfillment that no other generation can point to. Many believe that you and I will see the Lord return, or that our children will see it. I know people who are not young who have been given the promise that they will live to see the Lord return.

So Jude, alerting believers to those operating under a false anointing, took something that his readers would definitely know about and understand. He said this conflict is very much like the day that Michael contended with Satan over the body of Moses. He delivers this in a matter of fact way, assuming that everybody reading his epistle will know what he is talking about.

But two thousand years later we read this and ask, "What conflict? When did Satan fight with Michael over the body of Moses?" There is no other reference to the event in the Bible, but Jude refers to it as fact and now expression is a part of the eternal Word of God. Why would God put it in there if He does not want us to understand what that is all about? When the apostles wrote the epistles, what had been ingested came out in the letters they were writing to the churches, then God directed these people to make that the canon of Scripture.

Starting in 325AD we entered a season that was known as the times of apostasy, when an organizational spirit entered the Church and where man was set over it. At that time there were senators in Rome trying to govern through politics and Constantine who was trying to unite his two kingdoms. Constantine saw the power of Christianity and the traditions of the Senate, so he decided to take some of the realities of Christianity and mingle them with the traditions of Rome, to create a man-made political structure. Most of us have come from a system that still has elements of that in it.

In that century things that had readily been accepted as Bible truth, going back to the days of Noah, were suddenly considered heresy and people began to say that everything in the Bible was not to be interpreted literally. When the Church went into apostasy and was no longer functioning in the supernatural realm they had a real problem – because how do you explain away the book of Acts or the miracles of the gospels? In order to "explain" this contradiction, theologians created the doctrine known as Cessationism, saying that such miracles were only given in order to establish the early Church – and so they tried to explain away the supernatural.

Things that were considered basic biblical principles were completely removed from the faith of the true Christian Church. Not only that, tens of millions were martyred because they would not believe it. Millions died because they refused to believe that Genesis 6 said anything other than what had been taught for thousands of years.

The false leaders of that day demanded that the teaching be rescinded that pointed back to the activity of angels on the earth, even though the Septuagint (the Greek translation of the Old Testament) literally translates those words as, *"**the angels of God** saw the daughters of men."*

The people who held to this literal, accurate translation of the scripture were accused of worshipping angels and were killed as heretics. Millions died for the truth that I am teaching today. Hebrews 12:1 says we are surrounded by a great cloud of witnesses – people who gave their lives so that somebody could stand up and say, *this is the way it was*. Today more and more people all over the world are teaching about the fallen angels and the Nephilim. This is encouraging, because it is important to understand and we are going to have to deal with it.

Historical books

Much of the history that people were acquainted with in that day was removed by the organized Church in the third and fourth centuries and so throughout Church history, we have had no clue what that is all about.

The Dead Sea scroll discovery in 1948 was the single greatest archaeological discovery of modern history. It gave authenticity and validity to fragments of documents that had been found during the eighteenth century and they are still finding things that we do not even know about. God supernaturally preserved those documents in the Dead Sea area, knowing that they would be pertinent to the end time generation who would need to understand what went on in the days of Noah.

In Israel, they have recently found a human femur bone that was three feet long. Should that really surprise us? The Bible says that once there were giants living and people are now discovering the evidence. They have found documents and scrolls in an old house in Cairo that dates back to the first century. We know that not one word can be added to or taken away from the Bible, but dictionaries and commentaries have also been discovered and we use them to gain further insight.

In the same way, I believe that God has given us some of the commentaries of the first century Church that have been preserved so that we can begin to read them and adjust ourselves to the first century mindset. We have books that have the DNA of that generation and we can read them to more fully understand the truth. That is how it was for the Jews and in the lives of the early Church. These are documents that many staked their lives on!

We will have to do that to fully understand what Peter was talking about in 2 Peter 2:4 when he said God did not spare the angels who sinned, but cast them down to hell and delivered them into chains of darkness, to be reserved for judgment.

JANNES AND JAMBRES

In the day Jude was written, all Jewish families had a book called *Jannes and Jambres*. It is an historical story telling of a confrontation Moses and Aaron had with two magicians. Every Jewish believer had this book, just like every Jewish believer of that day also had the book of Enoch and the Testament of Moses. Sadly no copies of this book exist today.

TESTAMENT OF MOSES

The Testament of Moses is a historical document which contains the exact quote that Jude used in the book of Jude.

In the Testament of Moses we discover this confrontation between Satan and Michael over the body of Moses:

"But at the end of the same year in the twelfth month of the seventh day, Moses, the servant of God, died and was buried on the fourth of the month on a certain mountain by the archangel Michael. For the devil contended with the angel and he would not permit his body to be buried saying, 'Moses is a murderer. He slew a man in Egypt and buried him in the sand.' Then Michael prayed to God and there was thunder and lightning and suddenly the devil disappeared but Michael buried Moses with his own hands."

In another part of the book it tells about when Moses died on the mountain and Michael is sent to change the place of the body:

"Then when the devil blasphemed against Moses and proclaimed him a murderer again on account of his striking the Egyptian, the angel, not bearing the blasphemy against him, said towards the devil, 'The Lord rebuke you.'"

THE BOOK OF ENOCH

The Book of Enoch is a valid historical document, but it does not carry the authenticity of Scripture. In some nations they include the Book of Enoch within Scripture, but I do not believe you can. I believe we have all 66 books we are supposed to have.

The Book of Enoch was not written by Enoch. It was written two hundred years before the Lord's birth by someone who had accumulated the oral traditions of Enoch. In those days history was not written down but passed orally from generation to generation and they had to tell it exactly the way it was. By the second century BC those oral traditions were put into a book.

Every believer in the early Church would have had the Book of Enoch, which is nothing but supernatural. Here was a man who walked with God and who went to heaven like we go to the store. He saw and read things, he encountered angels, he even had the fallen angels come to him and ask him to go to God and ask Him for forgiveness on their behalf, and the Lord sent him back to tell them, "I will not forgive you; not only that, I am sending you to prison."

Around 1750, Dr James Bruce went to Ethiopia and found the Book of Enoch in its complete form and brought it back to Britain where it was viewed by various museums. Scholars began to study it and discovered that this was indeed a true historical book. The scholars that studied it, who were brilliant theologians, first thought the Book of Enoch was written after the Bible because there are so many similarities in it.

When the Dead Sea scrolls were discovered almost 200 years later, we found out that the book of Enoch predated the Lord Jesus by two hundred years. The scholars' conclusion was they could see similarities in the book of Enoch with what the King James Bible said. One hundred phrases in the New Testament directly relate to the book of Enoch and the Lord Himself in the gospels quoted the Book of Enoch twenty four times. Of course, Enoch got it from Him to begin with! God sovereignly protected it for our benefit and the book of Enoch tells us exactly what went on in Genesis 6.

The Book of Enoch is just a historical document, but the Bible is inspired. The people who wrote the Bible did not have the gospels like we have now. Jude was just a believer writing a letter to some Christians and he had, like we have, a library of things like the Jewish history, the Testament of Moses, and the Book of Enoch.

In the seventeenth century, Sir Isaac Newton, prophesied that there is coming a generation of people who will insist upon the literal interpretation of the prophecies, and they will do so amidst great turmoil and persecution. That is us. We are insisting upon the literal interpretation of the Scriptures.

I do not believe that the Bible put all of these things into the Millennia. I literally believe what the Bible says, that we are going to taste the good word of God and the power of the Kingdom age this side of eternity (Hebrews 6:5). We are insisting upon that literally and we have seen it in some measure in the people who have gone before us.

A copy of the Book of Enoch and The Testament of Moses have been included in the appendices at the end of this book.

THE FALLEN
ANGELS

The Lord told me about the spiritual powers that overcame in Noah's day, that we are called to overcome in ours. We are going to have to defeat what defeated them in that day. The Lord is not going to let the devil have the last word. A company of people is emerging in this generation who have encountered heaven, who have seen the Lord on some level, and who will have been endued with virtue and power in order to be able to stand before these forces and overcome them.

There is a restraining force in the world today. Holy Spirit is keeping at bay certain evil spirits that have been held back and hidden for a season of time. There are other things coming in the Great Tribulation, but these evil beings I saw are coming before that. They are being released right now, but the good news is, heaven is responding!

I have a great respect for Billy Graham and had hoped to meet him when we held a conference honoring the fathers of the faith, but it did not happen because of his health. He is one of God's great generals.

A while ago I was sitting and reading when I went into a vision and I saw what looked like a Billy Graham meeting. I saw the beautiful music and all the people around the coliseum. Everyone was dressed really nice and sitting very politely listening attentively to him preach. When it came time for the altar call people very politely got out of their seats and walked, single file, to the podium. Anyone who experienced these meetings knows what a great sight they were.

All of a sudden I heard a voice saying, "What is coming will not be like that" and I saw was another meeting where the whole altar area was filled with gnarled bodies; twisted, mangled bodies with distortions that I did not realize were even possible. There were wheelchairs everywhere and the people at the back were manifesting demons of the most foul nature I have ever seen. Families that had never been in church were coming into the back of the church bringing people who were so demented, tormented and demonized that they made *The Exorcist* look like kindergarten! These people were out of their natural minds. Others were coming to these meetings saying, "Please can you help this person?"

We are supposed to be a mature body of believers and I am prophesying that we need to get some serious authority from God, because what is about to come is going to be far beyond anything we have seen so far. I saw curses being hurled at people; things that we had thought were relegated to India and Africa are now about to come to America.

KINGDOM AUTHORITY

My wife, Wanda, and I recently spent six hours with a white man called Paul Dell and a black man called Elijah Maswanyhatti who were missionaries in Africa, both highly esteemed men of God. Their mandate was to go into a village and drill a water well. Most of the people in that region walk miles each day to fetch water, so you are a hero if you can produce water for someone in Africa. But their real motive was to win the village for Christ.

Once the water is there and the village has confidence in them, they then take on the local witchdoctor. You are not going to win the village until you first bind the strongman. You have got to deal with the spiritual authority in the village first and then plunder the village for God.

"How can one enter a strong man's house and plunder his goods, unless he first binds the strong man?" (Matthew 24:29)

In some cases it did not take long before the demons manifested. At that point either you are backed up by heaven or you are in trouble! In most cases they could deal with the witchdoctors, but in other cases they had trouble. They said that it was fairly common to see the witchdoctor wither up on the ground like a snake. It sometimes shocked Paul when a 16-year old girl would turn into a tiger before his eyes!

I would not recommend anyone doing this unless they are backed up by heaven, but we need to be prepared for this because these things are happening increasingly.

Another time Paul went into a village and had a hard time breaking through, so he got some of the ladies that he had won to the Lord and they went into a little grass hut, sat around the fire and prayed. They were interceding and praying in tongues when all of a sudden something came falling through the roof of the hut. There in front of them was a naked man who had been flying over the hut. He flew "through" their prayers and it broke his power and he went tumbling through the roof.

That is a very extreme case, but I am telling you this because we need to get ready. This is not bizarre, weird stuff, it is already happening in places and I believe that we will all have at least one person in our family who will need to get free, whether a cousin, aunt, uncle, or distant relative. The good news is there is an opportunity from heaven for a body of people to be anointed to know a realm of authority that we have never seen before. We will be able to speak to these things and there will not be one ounce of fear in this group of people, because we will have seen the Lord face to face.

The story is told of John. G. Lake that he was called in to pray for a little girl who was so demonized that she could not be restrained by chains. It is reported that she would beat up everybody who came in the room. They said that five or six people would also go in with him to try to hold her down while he prayed for her. Eventually he went in by himself, shut and locked the door behind him, and declared that one of them was going to win! You either have it at that point or you do not. We should not be presumptuous, but there is a realm of Kingdom coming that is of that magnitude.

Mahesh Chavda was once in a meeting in Africa and people brought pregnant women to him. Because the witchdoctor had put a curse on them, it was as though they were carrying their baby on their backs, twisted from the front to the back. Some of these women had been carrying their babies for eighteen months and couldn't give birth because they were under a curse. When Mahesh prayed and broke the curse, the women went into labour.

We have been pretty well protected in the western Church from things like this, though there have been some things happening in California and other places. But we are now in the end times and have crossed a threshold in the realm of the spirit. We can no longer bury our heads in the sand and pretend that this stuff does not go on. If we do, then we are not going to be prepared for it. All of a sudden someone will burst in through the back doors of your church and it will be right in your face. The good news is, the anointing to contend with this is coming; a special grace; a realm of heaven. We need to be prepared.

I believe that there is an awakening going on all over the world amongst a body of people who now realize that these are the end times. We can access things that we could not access before. Like Joseph, we are coming out of the dungeon, out of the pit, and are going to begin to sit on the throne with delegated authority to change nations.

There are people who have been prepared, who have gone through the dark night of the soul. Many leaders I know have been through a phase where the dealings of God bore on them so heavily that they felt like they were going to die. That is how severe it can be. But then all of a sudden you come out the other side and all of those issues you had before are gone!

The Lord is raising up a body of people who are just like He was on the night before He was crucified, when He stood before the disciples and said,

"For the ruler of the world is coming and he has nothing in Me." (John 14:30)

He is going to come to us and we will have to deal with the fears, the tares of the soul, ambition, personal agendas, etc. All the things that have derailed every outpouring in history will have to be extracted. Paul writes the same in his letter to the Galatians:

"I have been crucified with Christ; it is no longer I who live, but Christ lives

in me; and the life which I now live in the flesh I live by faith in the Son of God." (Galatians 2:20)

REPLICA DAYS

Why do we need to know all there is to know about the days of Noah?

"For the coming of the Son of Man will be just like the days of Noah."

Jesus said "just like" and in English the word "just" is very weak. The Greek word here is much stronger. It literally means, "for the coming of the Son of Man will be *a replica* of what happened in the days of Noah." It is not just that there will be *some similarities* facing the generation that sees the Lord return, it is going to be *the very same* level of spiritual confrontation that existed in the days of Noah.

If the Lord has given us this key to understanding the coming confrontation, we are going to need to learn it. If we are going to have the same level of conflict, then we have to think about the days of Noah. Noah lived amongst a generation of people who were much more numerous than most of us think. In Genesis 5 and 6 the Hebrew says that, *"man began to multiply greatly on the earth"* and that *"evil permeated the generations"*.

Something went on that was so grotesque and offensive that the loving Creator of Heaven and earth, the merciful God, had to destroy hundreds of millions of people and wipe out every breathing creature on the face of the earth, with the exception of Noah and those in the ark. Just as it was in that day so shall it be in these days. Something equally grotesque and offensive is going to be in the earth.

God won the victory on the cross but He wants to delegate authority to His Bride. He is calling His bridal company to carry that level of authority. We have not yet walked in the level of authority He has purchased for us. The full appropriation of the blood is going to be released in this generation and the fullness of His power.

Once we are in eternity we do not need all of those things – we need them now. We need the blood now, the power now, the authority now, because this spiritual battle is about to heat up to a level we have never seen before.

We have to respond. The angel in the encounter I mentioned earlier said "the sons of light will respond in like fashion." That is what we are. We have to respond and open ourselves up to the realm of the spirit. Just like God did with Joshua, He is coming to demonstrate himself as the Captain of Hosts.

His Manifest Presence

"For the coming of the Son of Man will be just like the days of Noah."

The word translated "coming" is *parousia* in the Greek and is very significant. The *parousia* is the manifest presence of the Lord. There is another word in the Greek that talks about the appearing: *epithinia*, which means "the manifestation", from which we get the word "epiphany".

At some point the Lord Himself is going to come down in His glorified physical form and set His foot on the Mount of Olives and it will split the North and the South. This is going to connect the seas and when that happens, this battle is over. But this verse is not talking about that appearing.

This *parousia* is a season of time when the manifest presence of GOd appears, like the pillar of fire shown to the children of Israel. Everything that happened in the wilderness will be magnifed as though multiplied by one hundred, because that was the former rain and we will experience the former and latter rain together. He is the Alpha and Omega; what He started He will finish even grander than before. It will be more powerful and I am already hearing reports that some of this is starting to happen.

Dave and Cheryl Bryant are pastors in America. Cheryl told me about a woman who walked into her church one day. The Lord spoke to her and told her that the woman was very gracious and loving and He wanted Cheryl to take her into her own house and treat her as part of her family and set her free. Cheryl walked over to this lady and introduced herself and said what she had heard the Lord say. The woman had heard the Lord say the same thing.

It turned out that she was Anton LaVey's biological daughter and was born to be the bride of Satan. If you don't know, Anton LaVey wrote the satanic Bible and had a satanic following that was probably the most heinous America has ever seen. For two years this lady had been ministered to by her church and some followers of LaVey's cult had turned up at the church because they'd been able to set her free.

One day Dave and Cheryl took her out for dinner and when they came out of the restaurant, they found that Dave had locked the car keys in his Cadillac Escalade. You do not attempt break into an Escalade as they have one of the best security systems. Dave could see through the window that the keys were in the ignition, so he started calling an automobile recovery service on his phone.

The woman asked why he was doing that and then walked over to the car and began staring that the door locks. Dave told me that within a matter of seconds all four door locks popped up. The lady then turned to Dave and Cheryl and said, surprised, "Can't you do that?" "No," Dave replied, "and don't you ever do that again!"

KINGDOM CLASH

"But know this, that in the last days perilous times will come: For men will be lovers of themselves, lovers of money, boasters, proud, blasphemers, disobedient to parents, unthankful, unholy, unloving, unforgiving, slanderers, without self-control, brutal, despisers of good, traitors, headstrong, haughty, lovers of pleasure rather than lovers of God, having a form of godliness but denying its power." (2 Timothy 3:1-5)

"Now as Jannes and Jambres resisted Moses, so do these also resist the truth: men of corrupt minds, disapproved concerning the faith; but they will progress no further, for their folly will be manifest to all, as theirs also was." (2 Timothy 3: 8-9)

In these days, the same spirit that was on Jannes and Jambres will once again rise up to withstand the anointing, but because of the anointing on us their folly will be made obvious.

A few months ago Bobby Connor was walking through an airport going to the gate to catch his plane when he noticed, about thirty yards ahead, a group of people gathered around somebody. He could tell they were very attentive and thought that someone might have fainted or something was wrong. He went in that direction thinking that maybe he could pray for them. When he got there he found a guy sitting on the floor with his legs crossed and his hand up in the air. He had his boarding pass and his pen levitating off the floor and he was moving them around with his hand.

Bobby asked the Lord what he wanted him to do and the Lord said to bind his power. Without saying one word audibly, just whispering it to himself, he said, "In the name of the Lord Jesus Christ I bind that power of darkness." As soon as had he uttered that to himself the boarding pass and pen fell to the ground.

Immediately the guy knew that someone had broken his power and of all the people gathered around him in the airport, he took one glance around and snarled straight at Bobby. He looked at Bobby with this hateful glare and he picked his stuff up and started walking towards him. Bobby said to the Lord that if he came up to him he would cast the devil out of him, but the man walked right past him and gave him another snarl as he went.

That is the type of confrontation that is coming and we had better have the goods to deal with it! We had better be able to respond. The *parousia* and the Angels of His presence are releasing an impartation that we need, for the coming of the Son of Man will be just like it was in the days of Noah. The *parousia* we are after is the one that is going to prepare the Bride, the one that is going to enter into the Bride, to bring us into a union experience with Him. The forerunners we have seen in prior generations who were the most significant in their day all carried this level of manifest presence. People like, Maria Woodworth-Etter, Katherine Khulman, William Branham, A.A. Allen – every one of them had a personal encounter with the *parousia* of God.

There were many people who were effective in the last generation; many of them had gifts of healing; but every one of these that I have mentioned, the ones that stand out head and shoulders above the rest, had an encounter and came out of it living and functioning in a realm way above anything we have seen before. They were the prototypes of this commissioning of the bridal company that will carry this level of authority.

I want to be one of them. I want you to be one too. We have come this far towards obtaining it; let us go ahead and ask the Lord to do it in us and then through us.

NEPHILIM

All this is important because it begins to give us a little bit more understanding of Genesis 6:1:

"Now it came about, when men began to multiply on the face of the earth, [in the original language it talks about "accelerated multiplication"] *and daughters were born to them, that the sons of God saw that the daughters of men were beautiful; and they took wives for themselves, whomever they chose."*

There are two theories in regard to the sons of God. The one that I do not believe is that the sons of God symbolically represent the sons of Seth and the daughters of men symbolically represent the daughters of Cain. Seth was the second son of Adam and Eve; Cain was the reprobate son who killed his brother Abel. Proponents of this view believe that, due to this conflict, the Hebrew phrase used in Genesis 6 – *bnei ha-'elohim* – should be understood to mean "the sons of Seth" and not "the sons of God".

But the Bible does not say that and you have to violate biblical principles to make the text mean that. There is no evidence in the history of mankind to suggest that if a believer married an unbeliever they would produce offspring who were over ten feet tall! There is nothing, medically or scientifically, to prove this. Noah lived 2.5 millennia before the time of Christ and for over 2000 years the Seth theory was not even considered. It only came into existence in the fourth century AD, around the time when men were denying the supernatural.

When the scripture says that they "took themselves wives" it means by compulsion, not by choice. These women were taken rather than given in marriage. Jewish believers would read this and know exactly what was meant. They knew that in the days of Noah these marriages were of a very unusual nature. It says, "the sons of God" (*bnei ha-'elohim*) saw the "daughters of men" (*benot ha-adam*), so the daughters of mankind were taken by the sons of God, which we find out was perverted and unusual.

Jude said that the days of Noah were like the days of Sodom and Gomorrah, where they were taking "strange flesh". If Jesus said that we are going to have to confront the very things that existed in that day, we need to understand who were the sons of God and the daughters of men.

The Bible says there were "men of renown" – men of great valor, but in an evil way. They devoured all the natural resources of the land and became evil and corrupt.

"Then the Lord saw that the wickedness of man was great on the earth, and that every intent of the thoughts of his heart was only evil continually." (Genesis 6:5)

Bnei ha-'elohim – the sons of God – are angels who saw the daughters of men. They left the domain of the spirit and came into the natural realm. These fallen angels broke covenant with God. We do not know if those angels were part of the fall with Lucifer or if there was a second rebellion. I tend to think that these were a company of the original rebellion. They were called "watchers" who came down on Mount Hermon during the days of Jared, Enoch's father. Jared means "the time of descent".

They were in the spirit realm but crossed into the natural and brought to mankind the knowledge of everything that is evil and perverse – the taking of roots for the making drugs; sexual perversity; witchcraft; how to take iron out of the earth and make weapons of war; and they released bloodshed on the face of the earth. Some historical documents go so far as to say that men were hungry for the knowledge that these fallen angels possessed about the universe, the stars, astrology, and how to illegally alter the natural realm.

In John 10:8 Jesus put it a bit differently when He referred to Himself as the "sheep-gate". Everyone has to go through Jesus to enter the realm of the spirit, so those who attempt to enter via the side are referred to as "robbers and thieves" In other words, there are ways to get into the spirit realm "illegally". These fallen watchers were introducing people to witchcraft and the divination that we see referred to in the book of Acts.

When they took the daughters of men and had children, a new type of being was born. We were not born a son of God, we were born a son of man.

Every person born after Adam was born a son of man, except Jesus because He was born as the Son of God. He was born *bnei ha-'elohim.* We are now the sons of God because we are born again. God Himself came down and took up residency in us and made us a new creation. We are born again and therefore can be called sons of God, but before God's intervention through Jesus, no one else could.

God told Satan His plan, that the seed of Eve was going to crush his head, and he would bruise his heel. He told Satan that the Redeemer, the Messiah, was coming through a woman, so the enemy tried to pollute all of humanity through this fallen race by multiplication until it had spread throughout the earth. Satan attempted to abort the coming forth of the Messiah by trying to pollute mankind so He could not be born, but God was bigger than that and He saw to it that Jesus came!

Every Jewish writer of every book of the Bible understood this. This is New Testament theology. When Jesus said, *"For the coming of the Son of Man will be just like the days of Noah"* His hearers knew that the bloodline of all humanity was polluted, with one exception, Noah. In the Hebrew language it says he was pure in his genealogy. His bloodline was pure, right back to Adam. These fallen angels did not manage to influence Noah's life and therefore the Messiah had to come through him.

During the flood, Almighty God struck the earth so hard in His fierce anger, that the earth which was in its perfect orbit was knocked out of its axis by 23 degrees. He split open the continent. It rained for 40 days and 40 nights. Water came out of the deep until the water went higher than Mount Everest and killed every living creature on the face of the earth. All of our storms and all the weather patterns we have now are the result of the days of Noah. The ozone layer would have been seven times thicker than it is now. It was the most cataclysmic event in the history of the earth since Lucifer fell along with a third of the angels.

"...for the windows from on high are open, and the foundations of the earth are shaken. The earth is violently broken. The earth is split open. The earth is shaken exceedingly. The earth shall reel to and fro like a drunkard and shall totter like a hut. Its transgression shall be heavy upon it, and it will fall, and not rise again." (Isaiah 24:1;4-6;18-20)

Evil was so widespread that God had to kill everybody. Have you ever wondered why the Lord had to totally destroy Sodom and Gomorrah and kill every man, woman and child? When we understand that there was something so evil in them you realize why He did that. The kingdom was taken away from Saul because he refused to destroy the Amalekites and all their possessions, so Samuel wiped the rest of them out (1 Samuel 15:10-33).

If all the giants were killed in the flood how did some, like Goliath, appear after the flood? Some believe it was through genes carried by the wives of Noah's sons or, like today, for medical reasons caused by increased growth hormones from childhood.

Peter and Jude tell us that the fallen angels who came into the earthly realm were imprisoned, so we do not have to deal with them any more. The Lord said something to me a long time ago that did not make a lot of sense at the time, but it is making a lot more sense now. The Lord said that He took care of the fallen angels and we are going to have to deal with their children.

Their offspring were called the Nephilim and were up to twelve feet tall. There were hundreds of millions of them, maybe billions. In fact, every family line upon the earth was polluted with their genes. The Nephilim, the offspring of the fallen angels and their descendants, died in the flood, but because they were a hybrid, a cross between a spiritual being and flesh, their spirit remained in the earth. That means that we are going to have to deal with those spirits.

"We wrestle not against flesh and blood but against principalities, powers, rulers of darkness in this earth and spiritual wickedness..." (Ephesians 6:12)

Some are looking for people to possess. Something has been opened up in the bowels of hell that is releasing this evil on a level we have never seen before and it is about to get really, really dark. That is exactly the condition that existed in the days of Noah. Darkness covered the earth, wickedness and perversity covered the earth, and deep darkness covered the people. The difference is in this day God is going to have a victorious host. He is going to have a group of people who have the authority over that realm.

People are going to come beating our door down when they know we have some authority over what is killing their family; when their children are so gnarled and twisted and mangled. Somebody is going to have to deal with this and raise these children up, because this will be demonic in nature. It will be the spirit of Hell released in these people and we need to be ready for this.

There is a realm of anointing and impartation coming and we have started to experience some of it recently. I have not yet had an angel of His presence come, but some people have seen things in our meetings that make us feel as though we could take on a lion. I have never felt or experienced such a measure of strength and impartation before in my life. We are coming out of this oppressive, preparatory mode as a body of people prepared and ready.

Our generation is called to overcome the same level of spiritual conflict that existed in the days of Noah. In Mark 5 Jesus dealt with legion and all those demons could do was negotiate the terms of their surrender! You and I are commissioned by heaven in John 14:12 to the same and greater works that Jesus did.

Understanding The Word

We are entering a new season of the Spirit. In September 2001 I wrote an article which specifically identified September 17th 2001 as the closing out of a season. I did not call it a season of war and, to give credit where credit is due, Chuck Pierce prophesied at the same time that we were entering a new season and that it was a seven year cycle of war, which ended September 29, 2008 on the biblical Holy Day of Rosh Hashanah

From 2001-2008, in the natural and in the spirit, there was a season of waging war upon the Church. The problem was, most people in the Church did not realize it. We need eyes to see and ears to hear; if we do not realize that we are in a fight, then we are going to get beaten.

In ancient Israel there were feasts that identified the times and seasons of God. Although we no longer live under the Law, we still keep a watchful eye on those feasts as there are significant prophetic events that still happen surrounding them. Rosh Hashanah (which is also known as the Feast of Trumpets) begins at sundown one day until sundown the next day.

Ten days later is the Day of Atonement, which is the day that the High Priest would prepare himself with special garments, engage in a ceremonial washing, and then go into the Holy Place. The veil into the Holy of Holies was around three feet thick and once a year the High Priest had to bow low, and humbly enter the presence of Almighty God.

45

Some believe the High Priest had a supernatural encounter with the presence of God and I am starting to believe that too. We are going to live in the realm of the supernatural and so we need to cultivate a mindset for that realm. If we someone, as Jesus did, walks through a wall, we won't have any problem believing that could happen. I have had experiences where I have been able to see through walls. It is not science fiction; it is what we are going to move in and the Lord is setting it in front of us so that we can contend for it. If Philip can be "translated" from one spot to another, or Elijah outrun a king's chariot and horses, how much more will you and I be capable of in the last days? We need to recognize that we are living in very significant days.

Since Rosh Hashanah 2008 we have shifted into a cycle of acceleration in the Spirit and a time of fruitfulness. I believe that we are going to see a wave of harvest quite possibly like the seven years that Joseph prophesied when he interpreted Pharaoh's dream – where there are seven years of plenty followed by seven years of famine.

We need to recognize that as a generation we are going to go through some stuff. If we are expecting escapism, which has been taught in a lot of places throughout the Church, it is not going to happen. Does that mean that we are going to go through the Great Tribulation? I believe we will escape that, but we will face difficulties and challenges in the days ahead.

We can see that right now. Just turn on any news channel and you will see the darkness covering the people and deep darkness in the earth. Isaiah prophesied it when he said:

"The people who walked in darkness have seen a great light; those who dwelt in the land of the shadow of death, upon them a light has shined. You have multiplied the nation and increased its joy; they rejoice before You according to the joy of harvest, as men rejoice when they divide the spoil. For You have broken the yoke of his burden and the staff of his shoulder, the rod of his oppressor." (Isaiah 9:2-4)

We see in the midst of the darkness a body of people emerging who have an anointing that is so brilliant that they are illuminated like a bright light in a dark room. That is you and I. We are literally seeing light beginning to radiate out of people. I believe that we will walk into Wal-Mart, illuminated with the brilliance of God.

"You are the light of the world. A city that is set on a hill cannot be hidden. Nor do they light a lamp and put it under a basket, but on a lampstand, and it gives light to all who are in the house. Let your light so shine before men, that they may see your good works and glorify your Father in heaven." (Matthew 5:14-16)

We do this by spending time with God and in His Word, because this generation will be Word and Spirit orientated.

A few weeks before he went to glory on March 12, 1947, Smith Wigglesworth released a prophetic word about three coming moves of God. The first two of these have occurred over the last 60 years validating the prophecy. The third and final move he saw was a combination of the first two – a coming move of both the Spirit and the Word!

We are going to understand the Word of God like no other generation. No matter how deep they go into to it, people's hunger is going to compel them out of complacency, out of lukewarmness and out of organizational religiosity, into the place where they are going to eat the deep meat of the Word and mature rapidly.

I believe that this is the transition we are going through at the moment. The battle we are going to be engaged in requires that we have great strength – and we can only get that from meat, not milk. We are going to need to teach and demonstrate the full gospel of the Lord Jesus Christ. We are going to contend for the full measure of our inheritance.

For those of us who are pressing into maturity, John 16:13 says that the spirit of truth is given to us to guide us into all truth. If it is in the Bible then we have a right to understand it. We have a spiritual deposit from heaven to allow us to do that and the fullness is going to be released at the time appointed by the Father (Galatians 4:2) to all those who are mature sons.

I want to be like the crusty old dog Caleb. I named my son Caleb and did not realize it meant "crusty old dog". It also means "the one who takes the mountain"! I want to say, "I do not care how many giants are between me and them, that mountain is mine!" It does not matter if you are eighty years old like he was, we are going to see something that is so real to us that we do not even recognize what stands between us and it; it is going to be paramount for us.

We are already starting to see it. The revelations that are coming during this important season have already begun, so my encouragement is to get yourself before the Lord, open your heart and say, "Lord, here I am, talk to me, tell me the secrets of the Kingdom. Tell me what's on your heart." That sometimes means just sitting before the Lord without asking or contending for anything or engaging in intercession, but simply giving the time to Him. That is what you have to do to discipline yourself, because life has focused us on *doing* rather than *being*.

"Be still, and know that I am God; I will be exalted among the nations, I will be exalted in the earth!" (Psalm 46:10)

I once got so desperate for the Lord that I told Him I would stay in bed until He spoke to me. 10 o'clock came and I was doing alright. 11 o'clock and I was getting a little hungry and thirsty. By 12 o'clock I needed to go to the bathroom. I sat there until 3 o'clock in the afternoon before I finally got out of that bed. The Lord started talking to me after I got out of the bed!

I believe there is something of that determination growing in us all — that we are going to get before the Lord and, like Jacob, not let go of Him until He blesses us. That is what the Lord is looking for. That is not going to weary Him; He is looking for something to be awakened in us, so that we begin to do that.

We are entering a season that is going to require maturity. It is going to require a mature body of people emerging with a real, tangible anointing to be able to deal with what is coming. I believe in the Spirit of Revelation and Holy Spirit who leads and guides us into all truth. I believe He still gives revelation in all the ways that He did in the Bible by visions, dreams and revelation from His Word. In 1992 the Lord spoke to me and said that what came illegally in the days of Enoch, will come legally by the sons of God in this day as an end time release of supernatural insight, revelation and power.

FIRST AND SECOND TEMPLE

Solomon built the first temple after David secured the land. David was a giant slayer and slew Goliath. When he did that he was, like many of us, a young man of substance but not YET of significance. That changed forever the day Goliath fell face down before God. It seemed like every time David turned around Israel was having a battle in the "The Valley of Rephaim". His whole ministry centered around his anointing, which was given to him to allow him to deal with giants that still existed in the earth after the flood of Noah.

David prepared the land but it was Solomon who built the temple. When it was complete he dedicated it to the Lord and something significant happened at the dedication. Moses dedicated his temple during Passover, but Solomon dedicated his temple during the Feast of Tabernacles, which is the spiritual season we are about to enter into – a season where the fullness of the Spirit of God will dwell, or tabernacle, in us.

"And when the priests came forth from the Holy Place, for all the priests that were present had sanctified themselves without regard to divisions, and all the Levitical singers Asaph and on down the line..." (2 Chronicles 5:11)

"And in unison when the trumpeters and the singers were to make themselves heard with one voice to praise and to glorify the Lord; when they lifted up their voice accompanied by trumpets and the cymbals and instruments of music and when they had praised the Lord saying 'He indeed is good for His loving kindness is everlasting', then the house of the Lord was filled with a cloud so that the priests could not stand to minister because the cloud of the glory of the Lord had filled the house." (2 Chronicles 5:13)

This is a type and shadow of this generation, because we are the temple of God. We are not looking at temples made of bricks and mortar or a house made by hands. We are entering the season of time when some people are going to begin to experience God's glory. The dedication of Solomon's temple is symbolic of this generation.

What we have been through is a season of pruning, refinement and preparation, so that the glory of God can come and dedicate our temple to

Him to such a degree that many people will not be able to stand when they come into the company of this group of people.

"'And the Lord, whom you seek, will suddenly come to His temple, even the Messenger of the covenant, in whom you delight. Behold, He is coming,' says the Lord of hosts. 'But who can endure the day of His coming? And who can stand when He appears? For He is like a refiner's fire and like launderers' soap. He will sit as a refiner and a purifier of silver; He will purify the sons of Levi, and purge them as gold and silver, that they may offer to the Lord an offering in righteousness.'" (Malachi 3:1-3)

I believe wholeheartedly that we are entering into that season when the glory of God is going to be revealed on a body of people. We know it is going to happen because it is in the Bible, but I believe that it is going to happen in our lifetime. I used to say that my children would most likely see the return of the Lord, but now I am thinking that I am going to see it. The more I receive from God, the less time that I feel we have. I am not setting dates, but am simply saying that the more God talks to me, the less time I realize we have.

We know that the temple that Solomon built was destroyed when Nebuchadnezzar came into Israel and took the Jewish people into Babylonian exile (2 Chronicles 36:19-21). They existed there for seventy years and somewhere around 538BC there was a decree given to the Jewish people to go back into the land of promise, where they found nothing but burnt stones (Nehemiah 4:2).

They were called to restore the temple that had once been built by Solomon. This is a picture of where we are. We saw in the early Church that there was a temple that existed, a Pentecostal Church, but it fell apart. It was eradicated by Babylonian confusion. Now what is being built today is the restored temple.

"'The latter glory of this house will be greater than the former,' says the Lord of hosts." (Haggai 2:9)

It does not say the house is going to be better, just the glory. As in Nehemiah's day, God is using burnt stones to rebuild this temple at the end of the age, in order to bring in the harvest.

The second temple was the one that was in existence at the time of the Lord's ministry. It was the temple in existence at the time when the disciples penned their epistles. This is important, because during that period of time, much of what had been committed to oral tradition was now being committed to pen and parchment.

The enemy has tried to get this generation to be so naturally minded that we do not see anything of a spiritual nature. We need to realize that we are spiritual beings and what goes on in the spiritual realm should be more real to us than what goes on this natural realm. We must switch our perspective.

The enemy would very much like for you and I to have our heads stuck in the sand, unprepared for what is coming, but the Lord is not going to allow it. He is going to have watchmen on the wall who are going to declare this message to let you and I know that we are about to enter into a conflict that is going to be so severe, the only thing that we can compare it to is the days of Noah.

Sometimes when I teach this it is so foreign to the minds of many people that they cannot grasp it and it needs to be the other way round. We need to be able to see something in the Word, no matter how obscure, and be able to wrap our spiritual minds around it. We must be able to see the reality and the application of it for our generation, because we are not to be children of darkness or ignorant of the enemies devices (2 Corinthians 2:11).

"Now as to the times and the efforts of the times and seasons, brethren you have no need of anything to be written to you, for you yourselves know full well that the day of the Lord will come just like a thief in the night. For while they were saying peace and safety..." (1 Thessalonians 5:1-3)

He says for those that have understanding, those who have a spiritual mindset to grasp the day and who have embraced the preparation. They are going to be ready and it is going to be a time of great victory. It is literally the parable of the ten virgins. There will be some who are wise and some who are foolish. The wise virgins are hearing the message, preparing themselves for what is coming, carrying a deep, mature love in their hearts and retaining their focus only for the bridegroom.

"For while they were saying peace and safety then destruction will come upon them suddenly like the birth pains upon a woman with child and they shall not escape. But you, brethren, are not in darkness that the day should overtake you like a thief for you are all sons of light and the sons of day." (1 Thessalonians 5:3-5a)

It is not to overtake us like a thief because we are sons of light. We are not of the night, nor of the darkness. We are at a time when there is a spiritual illumination that is being given to prepare us.

CREATION

"In the beginning God created the heavens and the earth. The earth was formless and void and darkness was over the surface of the deep and the Spirit of God was moving over the surface of the waters." (Genesis 1:1-2)

These are two very interesting verses. I believe it is going to take thousands of years just for us to understand, *"in the beginning God"*.

Transliterated into Hebrew it reads, *Bereishit bara Elohim*. The literal meaning of *bereishit* is "in the dateless past". *Bara* means "brought out of nothing". So the literal translation of Genesis 1:1 is,

"In the dateless past, Elohim brought out of nothing the heavens and the earth."

Now we have to understand something about the nature of God, because when He does something it is always perfect.

"...everything God does He does in perfection." (Deuteronomy 32:4)

"He has made everything beautiful in its time." (Ecclesiastes 3:11)

Isaiah was a prophet and he saw in Genesis 1:1 that God created something out of nothing. It is totally contrary to the nature of God to create something formless and void, so Isaiah says that He intended it to be habitable; it was not created to be a waste place.

"For thus says the Lord who created the heavens. He is the God who formed the earth and made it. He established it and did not create it a waste place but formed it to be inhabited. I am the Lord and there is none else." (Isaiah 45:18)

Jeremiah also saw what took place in the beginning. He was taken out of the natural realm, into the spirit, where there is no time, space or distance and where time is happening simultaneously as far as God is concerned. He saw earth in the condition that it existed in Genesis 1:1. He was also able to look back and see the earth as it existed in Genesis 1:2:

"I looked on the earth and behold it was formless and void [Genesis 1:1] *and to the heavens and they had no light* [Genesis 1:2]*, but then I looked on the mountains and behold they were quaking and all the hills moved to and fro."* (Jeremiah 4:23-24)

But he goes on to see it before it became formless and void:

"I looked and behold there was no man and all the birds of the heavens had fled. I looked and behold the fruitful land had become a wilderness and all its cities were pulled down before the Lord before His fierce anger. For thus says the Lord, 'the whole land shall be desolate, yet I will not make a full end of it.'" (Jeremiah 4:25-27)

God said, "I am going to bring planet earth to the brink of annihilation but I am going to leave a little piece of it there to restore it." The Jewish translation of Jeremiah 4:23-27 says,

"I looked at the land and it was formless and void and the sky had no light. I looked at the mountains and they shook and they moved back and forth and I looked and there was no human being and all the birds of the air had fled. I looked and the fertile fields were a desert and all the lands where cities were, were razed to the ground at the presence of Adonai because of His burning anger. The whole land will be desolate although I will not destroy it completely."

So Jeremiah saw it as formless and void in the dateless past *and* when there were cities and some form of humans; when there were birds of the sky, when there were mountains. Then God got so upset at Lucifer's rebellion that the mountains quaked and the land disappeared. There was some form of man back then, but not as there was in the days of Adam. Have you ever wondered where Neanderthal man came from? No one can say that he did not exist because we can look at the evidence in museums. I don't believe that this contradicts the Bible. Rather, it completely proves it.

"Out of the mouth of two or three witnesses let a word be established." (Matthew 18:16)

So in Genesis 1 we see the great, perfect, Creator of the Universe at work and the way in which He created planet earth. It was habitable, it was beautiful, and it was fruitful. It was not formless and void as described in Genesis 1:2. So what happened between Genesis 1:1 and 1:2?

The Lord's number one man, the one who was in charge of the very throne room of God, who walked on the coals of fire before the throne, who was the leader of the orchestration of the worship in heaven, who saw the glory of God with his own eyes for eons of time, rebelled against God and wanted to become God.

I do not know how it happened, but there was a war in the heavens and you know who won – it was not Lucifer! He was kicked out of heaven and brought a third of the angels down with him. God was so angry that He smote the earth and everything that existed on planet earth was destroyed in an instant.

The Lord covered the sun and refused to allow the light of the sun to touch planet earth. He turned it into a block of ice, which was the ice age. Science tells us that without the light of the sun hitting the earth it would freeze solid in a matter of seconds. There were news reports from Siberia a couple of years ago that said that a mammoth had been found which had died with food in its mouth. It was frozen instantaneously whilst it was still eating its food. Science is telling us that, but they can't explain how it could happen, so they are trying to imagine all kinds of things. One theory is that a meteor hit the earth and all the dust it threw up blocked the light of the sun from the earth. No, I believe God just said, "No more sun."

"It is God who removes the mountains, they know not how when He overturns them in His anger. He shakes the earth out of its place and its pillars tremble. He commands the sun not to shine and He sets a seal upon the stars. Who alone stretches out the heavens and tramples down the ways of the sea." (Job 9:5)

At no other time in history was the sun commanded not to shine upon the earth. When the flood came in Noah's day the sun still shone, but in

Genesis 1:3, permission was given for the sun to shine again. The words "Let there be..." are not creative words, but words of restoration.

Now we do not know how long it was between Genesis 1:1 and Genesis 1:2, but most scientists say it was billions of years.

We do not know how long earth existed in that condition, but it was a long time. Have you ever wondered why Lucifer is kind of angry? He sat out on a block of ice in darkness for millions of years and then in that very place God takes a pile of dirt, fashions the form of a man, breathes His life into him and then gives him everything Lucifer wanted. That is why we are in such a battle!

This battle that we are about to be involved in, front and center, goes all the way back to those days and God says that *you* are part of the generation that will appropriate His victory and do what has not been done in over 6,000 years. Now you understand the magnitude of the battle and the importance of your life. You see now why the devil has tried to wipe you out, because he has known by the prophecies of the Bible that there would be a generation who would carry the Lord's victory to its fullness.

We need to understand everything we can about the spirit realm. The Bible says, *"My people perish for lack of knowledge"* (Hosea 4:6). The anointing is limited in its effectiveness by our lack of knowledge and the anointing alone is not sufficient because it must be mingled with an understanding of the Word. This is what it will mean to be Word and Spirit orientated. I want the anointing, but I want the Word too, so that I can understand this domain.

ACCESSING THE GATES

I can tell you this for a certainty: that the generations that existed up until the times of Noah were the most brilliant that ever existed in the history of mankind. Science has proven that. When Nimrod and others were building a tower, God Himself said, "If we do not go down there and stop them they are going to achieve their mandate."

I used to think *poor guys*, no matter how high they build that tower they are not going to get to heaven, but just the opposite was true. They knew something about the secrets of the universe and they were trying to build a portal. Read for yourself in the Bible how God said that they were just about to do it. He needed to come down and scatter them and confuse their language, or else they would achieve what they were trying to do. You may think that that is too farfetched.

But remember what Jesus said – that those who try to access the spirit realm apart from Him do so as robbers and thieves. New Agers, Occultists and Satanists are trying to get into the realm of the supernatural illegally. They love for us to open up the heavens and then not occupy them, because they will! In the places that have known the greatest revivals, if that revival was lost, that place would often become the darkest place of any, because a portal is established in the realm of the spirit.

For many years in England the Muslims have had a policy of buying up old churches and turning them into mosques because they are a thin spiritual place. Smith Wigglesworth's house and chapel are both owned by Muslims. In Moline, Illinois, there is still a thin spiritual place on the land where Maria Woodworth-Etter used to hold her crusades and conducted water baptisms in the pond, a hundred years ago.

Remember what Jacob said: this is none other than the house of God, the very gate of heaven. The ladder was touching earth and angels were ascending and descending. In other words, what Adam did by handing over to the devil his inheritance, we have done also. God gives us revival and we cannot hold the ground long enough to man the gate, so the devil takes it and brings in seven times more evil than was there before the revival ever happened. That is the truth and that is why I believe that revival has been delayed.

However, a group of people who love God enough is emerging that will see something so much greater than themselves. They are willing to find a company of folks who are going to love no matter what. They are going to begin to occupy a little piece of ground, then all of a sudden, if we can be trusted with that, He will give us more. That is where we are headed.

For millions of years there was darkness over the earth until finally the Lord came back in Genesis 1:2 and began by saying, *"Let there be light."* He was allowing the restoration to begin.

"God is light and in Him is no darkness at all." (1 John 1:5)

When God made Adam there was no darkness in him. He was made in the mirror image of God, the fullness of the Father, the fullness of Jesus and the fullness of the Spirit of God. If there had been a mirror in the garden in Eden, then when Adam looked in it, he would have seen God in his own reflection.

The Bible calls Jesus the Second Adam and it is the perfect description. He clearly tells us that He and the Father are one (John 10:30; John 17:21-23) and He even prays that you and I would be one with Jesus just as he and the Father are one (John 17:21). Jesus was the light of the world (John 8:12) and in Him there was no darkness either. And he was filled with the Spirit of God, making Him the mirror image of God on earth.

There is emerging from these years of preparation a company of people who will be bright lights in darkness, carrying the fullness of the Spirit of God in them, and who look like Jesus and have the miracles, signs and wonders following like He did. That level of relationship only comes through death to our own agendas and a surrender of our free will – just as Jesus did. It comes out of the place of union with Christ at a level few have achieved since the Acts of the Apostles.

"I do not pray for these alone, but also for those who will believe in Me through their word; that they all may be one, as You, Father, are in Me, and I in You; that they also may be one in Us, that the world may believe that You sent Me. And the glory which You gave Me I have given them, that they may be one just as We are one." (John 17:20-22)

Enoch

Enoch was the seventh in the line of Adam and when he saw the destruction on the earth coming he named his son Methuselah, which means "when he dies it is going to come." Everybody knew that Enoch walked with God. They kept one eye on what they were doing and one eye on Methuselah because the day he died was the day it was coming.

We are told by Jewish tradition seven days after Methuselah died the flood came. How long was Noah in the ark? Seven days! It sounds like the day Noah saw Methuselah die, he headed for the ark because he knew Enoch prophesied it.

If Enoch prophesied the flood of Noah and it came to pass, then I am confident in this promise, when he says that at the end of the age he saw the Lord coming with ten thousand of His holy ones with Him. That is you and me. Every generation of prophets and patriarchs saw this day that we are in right now. They saw the confrontation.

All of the spiritual conflicts that have existed from the days of Adam to this present hour are culminating right now. What David dealt with, you and I are going to deal with. What Joshua dealt with in the promised land, you and I are going to deal with. And there is going to be something uniquely given to us to be able to overcome it!

SIGNS OF
THE TIMES

I was in Wisconsin and started teaching a little about William Branham. Often I find that if I honor someone from the past, the atmosphere breaks and it allows a realm of heaven into a meeting. Branham used to crawl into a cave and spend two or three days by himself, laying on a piece of rock and praying until the angel of the Lord showed up and told him what he needed to do.

One day he went out into the middle of the woods by himself and prayed until 3.00am, until there was no more prayer left in him. A pillar of fire came into the cabin and he heard footsteps coming along the wooden floor. An angel appeared and said, "Fear not, for I am sent from the presence of Almighty God."

We need to understand that angels such as these are coming. One came into our meeting in Wisconsin. People saw the outline of a man standing behind me with their natural, open eyes. I did not see it, but I felt it. I am not trying to elevate myself by recording this, I share it to tell you that they are here and they are coming.

There was a misty, white cloud that also came into the church that day and went right over the people. I saw it with my natural, open eyes and others saw it, but almost everybody knew the anointing was there. I could see it and I just felt that it represented a small token of what is coming –

that we will soon get to the place where God's glory will come on a house.

"And in unison when the trumpeters and the singers were to make themselves heard with one voice to praise and to glorify the Lord ... then the house of the Lord was filled with a cloud so that the priests could not stand to minister because the cloud of the glory of the Lord had filled the house." (2 Chronicles 5:13)

What we are after is the *parousia* that is coming to the Bride of Christ. Christ in me is the hope of glory. There is a *parousia*, a manifest presence promised to a bridal company, where the Lord Himself will come and manifest Himself in a body of people. Do I deserve this? Absolutely not! Do I ask for the grace to do it? Yes, every day!

The manifest presence of God is coming. Do not settle for anything less. I know we need the gifts of the Spirit, but there is something beyond the gifts. There is a *parousia* presence promised to the Bride and we must set our face like flint to receive it.

There is a big resistance against certain spiritual things. One of them has been the principle of honoring the fathers. Something significant happens in the heavenly realms when we begin to honor someone. The enemy does not want people to know that this kind of supernatural life is achievable in God, so he tries to shame people and disgrace their testimony, even if it is because of one single mistake.

The Bible says that, *"Noah was a friend of God. He walked with God."* Noah made a big mistake and was not supposed to get drunk and embarrass himself in a tent. It wasn't a good thing to do, but didn't alter the fact that he was still a friend of God. Ham saw the nakedness of his father and told his two brothers. But Sham and Japheth walked backwards and covered the nakedness of their father. They did not tell anybody about the incident. But as a result of his lack of honor, the entire genealogy of Ham was completely cursed and polluted.

I believe the enemy is trying to put the same spirit that was on Ham on people today, so that we would not honor the testimony of those who have gone before us, see how they achieved the anointing, and understand what they did to get before God and receive what they needed to change their generation. So they have been obscured and when we have tried to honor these men and women of God it has created a stir.

It is the same with this message that is coming forth now. There is a resistance the enemy is releasing to keep us from understanding our Judaeo-Anglo-Christian heritage. The spirit of anti-Christ does not want us to know the appointments of God's times and seasons.

"Now as to the times and epics brethren, you have no need of anything to be written to you, for you yourselves know full well that the day of the Lord will come just like a thief in the night. While they are saying peace and safety, then sudden destruction will come upon them suddenly like labors of a woman with child, and they will not escape..." (1 Thessalonians 5:1-3)

If we stop there, there is no hope.

"...But you brethren, you are not in the darkness. This would overtake you like a thief but you are sons of light and sons of day and we are not of night nor darkness." (1 Thessalonians 5:4-5)

Clearly the Lord is saying that we can know when He is coming back to do something. In fact, if we do not, then we have missed our commission. If we are not aware of what is going on in the heavens and in the spirit realm, then the Bible says we are not functioning as a son of light.

JEWISH FEASTS

"The Lord spoke to Moses saying, 'Speak to the children of Israel and say to them the feasts of the Lord which you shall proclaim to be holy convocations, these are my feasts.'" (Leviticus 23:2)

We mistakenly say sometimes that these are the feasts of Israel. The Lord said that they are *His* feasts. I do not believe that we are to return to the Old Testament observance of the feast because we live in a different dispensation. But just as the Lord Jesus came and perfectly fulfilled the Feast of Passover, and just as surely as the Holy Spirit split the heavens and came upon the hundred and twenty to fulfill the Feast of Pentecost, just as those two feasts were literally fulfilled, so also will the Feasts of the seventh month be fulfilled. They will literally be fulfilled and we have not seen that yet. There is no place in history that you can point to and say that those feasts have been fulfilled, as we can with Passover and Pentecost.

In Leviticus 23:2 the Hebrew word for "feasts" is *mo'ed* which literally means "divine appointments". Somewhere at the end of the age, which I believe we have crossed into, God said, *"Do two men walk together unless they have made an appointment?"* (Amos 3:3). In some translations it says, *"can two walk together unless they agree?"* I think that is true in spirit but it literally says, "Do two men walk together unless they have made an appointment?" The Lord has made an appointment and He is going to show up to fulfill His side of the deal, so we had better be ready to show up.

That is why we are sons of light and we need to be aware that we have changed season. We are no longer in a "Pentecostal Age", in a season where God can bless leaven. He blessed leaven for a while but He is not going to bless it in a new season. That means we have got to be very careful what we teach. Just a little bit of leaven, a little bit of man-made process, and traditions will leaven the whole loaf.

We have come out of that into a place of revelation and it is up to us to align ourselves with His message. We have to make the adjustments because His word is eternally true and He has given us the Spirit of Truth and will guide us into all truth (John 16:13) if we follow His lead.

The other Hebrew word for "feasts" is *miqra* in Hebrew, which means "dress rehearsal". Every year at Passover for centuries Israel went out and found a lamb without blemish, they examined it for four days and then did all the rituals that belong to Passover. They sacrificed the Passover lamb. Then Jesus showed them that He is the Lamb of God. What they had done for centuries was a dress rehearsal for everything He literally did the day He walked into Jerusalem in 33AD. He was examined by the leadership of Israel exactly on the day of Passover, while they were still in dress rehearsal. We are told by some historians that, literally, as they were nailing Him to the cross, they were singing Psalms 22:16 in the synagogue: "Thou hast pierced my hands and my feet." Like the Jews of that day, we too can miss our day of visitation, which is why I am teaching this.

There was also a dress rehearsal for Pentecost when Moses received the Ten Commandments. Moses instituted Passover the night before they escaped from Egypt and then they went through the wilderness for fifty days. Moses goes up onto the mountain for a period of time and there the Lord gives him the Ten Commandments. When Moses comes down he finds Israel having built a golden calf and Aaron leading them in worshipping it. Moses got so upset that he took the Ten Commandments and threw them and they broke on the ground.

That day was the 17th of Tammuz, which begins a twenty one day season of time in Israel called Dire Straits that is historically tragic:

- Nebuchadnezzar came into Jerusalem that day, ransacked Jerusalem and tore down the temple on the 9th of Av.
- Prince Titus, Prince of Rome, came into Jerusalem on the 17th of Tammuz, ransacked it for 21 days and burned down the temple on the 9th of Av.
- It was on the 9th of Av that Ariel Sharon ordered the evacuation of the Jews out of Gaza and America paid a price for that and we're still paying. As long as we stand with Israel everything is going to work out alright.

It is believed in Judaism that Rosh Hashanah is the day that the world was created. The first day in the Bible could be interpreted as the first of Tishri. Rosh Hashanah is the same day that Abraham offered Isaac before he offered a ram.

FEASTS OF SEVENTH MONTH

We have entered into a new season of the spirit that is typified by the feasts of Israel that are in the seventh month.

"All the men of Israel had assembled themselves to the king at the feast, that is the feast of the seventh month." (2 Chronicles 5:3)

Pentecost was the third feast of Israel and another feast followed in the seventh month called the Feast of Tabernacles. Here is what is important: Pentecost was the only feast that allowed leaven, so that means we are coming into a leaven-free period of time. Leaven means "the doctrine of man". There has been a measure of blessing on some of the things where we have had truth mingled with opinion.

I am in the place now where I do not want my own opinion or my own thoughts entering in at all. My opinion is wrong but His opinion is everlasting. We need to find out what He thinks about something. I will often ask the Lord what He thinks and how are we doing. You would be amazed how often you get a response as to whether something is pleasing or not, whether you yielded to the fear of man, whether you pulled on some of your own traditional understanding. Did you present the manna, the Rhema word of God, the revelation of the hour?

This was a picture of a company of people who would exist at the very end of the age, that when we would begin to sanctify ourselves, a message of truth would come forth. It does matter what you believe. We are sanctified in truth. I can tell you unequivocally that we are entering a season when the leaven in us has got to come out.

On February 25, 2007, my wife had a dream in which she heard a voice say, "I am going to bring a hurricane on Rosh Hashanah and it will mark the cleansing of the land." When she hears that voice it is always accurate. On September 12-13, 2007 we were in Texas conducting a meeting with Chuck Pierce and Peter Wagner and I had forgotten about the word and that it was the day before Rosh Hashanah.

I noticed Wanda watching the weather and there was no hurricane in sight the day before, but later in the day a hurricane formed off the coast of Houston, off Belmont, Texas. It was the fastest forming hurricane in recorded history. Never before had a little thunderstorm turned into a hurricane in just eighteen hours. That hurricane was called Humberto which from its German root means "Famous Giant". The land is being cleansed of the spiritual "men of renown", the giants of darkness in this day!

Hurricane Katrina which hit New Orleans on August 25-26, 2005 was one of the first signs. Katrina means, "pure", or "to cleanse and purify", marking the cleansing of the land. We are made out of dirt, we are the dust of the earth, and I believe that we have been in this purifying process for seven years now. The seven year war season has been a season of cleansing and preparing a body of people. If God had given us what we were asking Him for seven years ago, we would already have lost it by now.

I am convinced there is a remnant group of people who are allowing the Lord to remove whatever is not of Him from within them. Who of us wants to be at the pinnacle of their ministry, only for the enemy to come and sink a hook into the depths of our soul, to pull us down so that we lose the anointing, embarrass ourselves and the Lord and everything else that goes with that? We want to be able to perpetually steward what is coming and I believe what is coming is the essence of God.

I believe the Feast of Tabernacles is symbolic of where we are heading and I am going to contend for this with all of my heart.

"Speak to the sons of Israel saying 'in the seventh month...'" (Leviticus 23:24)

Every time you see the "feasts of the seventh month" in the Bible it is talking about the last day generation and these are our feasts. Passover was in the first month and Pentecost was in the third month. Then there was a three month season before the feasts of the seventh month. What we have had, in essence, is two thousand years since the Day of Pentecost which could be interpreted as a dry season. We have been coming out of that season through the Great Reformation, but now we are at the brink of crossing over into the observance, spiritually speaking, of the Feast of Tabernacles.

In the context of the Feast of Tabernacles, there are three feasts. The first is the Feast of Trumpets, which also falls on the first day of the civil calendar and is called Rosh Hashanah. There are some very clear prophetic implications concerning this feast.

In the New Testament, have you ever wondered about 1 Corinthians 15:51?

"Behold I show you a mystery. We shall all not sleep but we shall all be changed in a moment in the twinkling of an eye at the last trump."

The Feast of Trumpets in the days of Israel was a divine appointment. Three times a year all the men of Israel had an appointment with God at Passover, Pentecost and Tabernacles. The blowing of the ram's horn began the Feast of Trumpets, which is an emblem of God's mercy. On the Feast of Trumpets they would blow a series of blasts followed immediately by another series of blasts, immediately followed by another kind of blast on a Shofar.

Each series was nine blasts consisting of three segments of three blasts: the Tekiah, the Sheravim and the Teruah. They would do that eleven times on the day of the Feast of Trumpets. At the end of the eleventh series of nine blasts, the hundredth blast was called the "last trump". The one, long, final blast was to let everybody know that the Feast of Trumpets had come to an end.

When Paul wrote that, everybody in the first century Church knew that he was talking about the Feast of Trumpets.

"But of that day and hour no one knows." (Matthew 24:36)

Although commonly understood to apply to the second coming of Christ, this phrase is also related to Rosh Hashanah, the beginning of the New Year. When Israel went into Babylonian captivity their whole existence centered around these feasts. They had to know when the beginning of the New Year was, so they had two priests who went out and watched the horizon. When they saw the first emblem of the new moon they knew it was time. But the moon would look different in Babylon than the priests in Jerusalem were used to seeing, so they extended Rosh Hashanah over two days and formed a series of signals. Across a series of mountains big piles of wood were built and as soon as the priests in Jerusalem saw the beginning of the new moon they notified the people who lit a fire on the first mountain. The people on the next mountain saw it and lit theirs, all the way from Jerusalem to what is now Iraq.

The Jews in Babylon were looking not to the east but to the west, so that they knew they had seen the new moon in Jerusalem and they could observe Rosh Hashanah. The problem was it took them a whole day to get the fires across. So no man knew the day or the hour that the beginning of the New Year came, but they observed it over two days.

Some very rare celestial occurrences are taking place. Some of them, I think, are most encouraging signs and some of them are a cause for concern. In 2008 there was a solar eclipse on Av 1 and another on Av 1, 2009 (the longest recorded in history) followed by another on Av 1, 2010. In other words, there was a solar eclipse on the same day of the year three years in a row, which is unprecedented.

Historically, a solar eclipse has meant judgment on gentile nations. Based on our calendar, Av 1 occurred August 1, 2008, July 22, 2009 and July 11, 2010. The current economic collapse started just after August 1st 2008 and has lasted multiple years! But as long as we are part of His kingdom that cannot be shaken then we will be alright.

Noah is a type of the Church and Enoch is a type of the Bride. Noah went through the tribulation, even though he was in the ark. Revelation 7 mentions the foolish virgins that go through the tribulation, but they are in the ark, they are in God.

I was praying one day and I felt that I went up in the Spirit. I saw what looked like open space, but saw something travelling down and moving towards me. As it got closer it appeared to be a double door that had stones around the outside. I was not moving or else I would have gone through the door, the door was coming to me. There are things in the Spirit that are heading this way and it is up to us to get in front of them. I saw one of the doors open and I moved myself to be in front of the door and it came right to where I was and stopped. As I stuck my head in I saw these beautiful streets in bright colors. I saw Mount Zion.

Of all the nations of the earth God picked Israel and within Israel He narrowed it down to Jerusalem. Within Jerusalem He narrowed it down to Mount Zion. There is a company of people who will be known as the Bride of Christ and I believe that we are entering into a season for their emergence. I want to be one of them and I hope you do too.

REVELATORY TRUTH

In 2003 I wrote a book called *Engaging the Revelatory Realm of Heaven* and in the process of that the Lord had me stumble across Sir Isaac Newton. I knew he was a brilliant scientist and I found a few things that he had said. This is one that is both critical and beautiful:

"I do not know what I may appear to the world, but to myself I seem to have been only like a boy playing on the seashore and diverting myself now and then finding a smoother pebble or prettier shell than ordinary, whilst the whole great ocean of truth lay undiscovered before me."

This describes how we have been with God's truth – we have only found a nugget here and a nugget there, but we have a whole ocean out there available to explore. I have been studying Sir Isaac Newton and in the process I have rediscovered some teachings, because they deal directly with the days of Noah.

Newton was a seventeenth century scientist who made some brilliant discoveries, but in his generation he was known as a theologian more than a scientist and was fluent in Hebrew, Greek and Latin. He had incredible prophetic insights about the ways of God.

For instance, in a day when it was very unpopular to write it, he wrote that the 1666 Great Fire of London was God's blessing! In May 1665 the Bubonic Plague broke out in London and an estimated one hundred thousand lost their lives, about twenty percent of the population. On September 2, 1666 the fire started in a bakers and quickly spread, with thousands of homes lost. But had it not been for the fire, the numbers dying of the plague would have been much greater. The fire killed most of the rat population that caused the plague to spread. It was the mercy of God in the midst of what looked like certain tragedy.

That might give us a little encouragement right now with all the economic shaking across the world. I do not like people having trouble and Christians are having hard times now, but I am not overly concerned because my faith is not in this kingdom but in another Kingdom.

I think it is like the London fire – that on the other side of this economic shaking we are going to say that it was a blessing, because it is making us do things that will position us to be able to steward what is coming.

Sir Isaac Newton also had a theory, which he wrote about extensively, on the book of Daniel and the book of Revelation. He had a belief, a theory, which had to come by revelation because he had no opportunity, in his own generation, to prove it. He believed Jerusalem was the center of the timepiece of God – that you could take major crossroads in human history and measure them according to the temple mount in Israel.

David Flynn recently wrote a book called, *The Temple – the Timepiece of God*, taking Newton's theory and testing it out. It was not capable of being examined in any other generation but ours, because for the first time we have appropriate satellite technology. It is now possible to measure the distance from the temple mount in Jerusalem to where, say, Babylon is from an elevated point of view. You cannot take a map and draw a straight line because the distance has to be measured in nautical miles, taking into account the curvature of the earth. For example, David Flynn proved that it was 539BC when Nebuchadnezzar fell and it was exactly 539 nautical miles from Nebuchadnezzar's palace to the temple mount. It was 1022 nautical miles from the temple mount to London, England, and London was founded in 1022AD. These are just some examples which tell us that we have entered a new day.

One fact that really caught my attention is that on the 08.08.08 the opening ceremony of the Beijing Olympic Games was held. This was also the date that Russia invaded Georgia. David Flynn measured the distance from the temple mount in Jerusalem, Israel, to the very spot where the armies of Russia crossed into Georgia and it was exactly 888 nautical miles. Then he found out that it was not by accident this happened, because exactly 888 years ago there were secret organizations formed that were sponsoring that war. The Illuminati was formed 888 years ago, on August 8. The point is, this was a "chosen" date and not a random one. It was very specifically appointed for Russia to cross over into Georgia.

888 years ago there was a man who had a revelation that he was something like King David. He called himself King David 2nd after the King of Israel, and felt that it was his commission as the King of Georgia to run all of Islam out of Georgia, which he did. This was quite a righteous thing to do. The president of Georgia at the time of the Russian invasion, President Mikheil Saakashvili, felt he had a commission like that of David 2nd 888 years ago, and as a result of that, he opened up the borders of Georgia to Israel so planes could land in Georgia, because Israel was planning on bombing Iran. According to Smith's Dictionary, and according to Josephus, what is now known as the land of Georgia was once known as Gog.

What does that mean to us? It means that this is a new day. I do believe that 08.08.08 was a new beginning and I find that there is infallible evidence.

Do you know that Jesus represented in Greek is 888 and that America was founded in 1776 which is 888 + 888!

THE COMING YEARS

I believe we have come into this new season of time where there is a shift in the realm of the Spirit and I am going to highlight some things that are going to happen that I believe will encourage you to begin to press into God for the harvest.

People are being equipped and prepared and there will be an anointing coming for us to rise up. Governmental or political battles may be pawns in the overall battle, but this is a spiritual battle between light and darkness. Nothing surpasses the power of a praying Church. The battle is teetering in the spirit realm and everything from now on is going to be put in the hands of the Church.

"The sun will turn into darkness and the moon into blood before the great and awesome day of the Lord and it will come about that whoever calls upon the name of the Lord will be delivered." (Joel 2:31)

In Revelation 6 there is a similar verse at the breaking of the sixth seal on the scroll that John sees in heaven, but the reaction of the people it talks about is the is opposite to the one Joel saw:

"I looked when He broke the sixth seal, and there was a great earthquake; and the sun became black as sackcloth made of hair, and the whole moon became like blood; and the stars of the sky fell to the earth, as a fig tree casts its unripe figs when shaken by a great wind. The sky was split apart like a scroll when it is rolled up, and every mountain and island were moved out of their places. Then the kings of the earth and the great men and the commanders and the rich and the strong and every slave and free man hid themselves in the caves and among the rocks of the mountains; and they said to the mountains and to the rocks, 'Fall on us and hide us from the presence of Him who sits on the throne, and from the wrath of the Lamb; for the great day of their wrath has come, and who is able to stand?'" (Revelation 6:12-16)

Two groups of people crying out: one for life and the other for death, when the sun is turned to darkness and the moon to blood

In 2014 and 2015 something will happen that hardly ever occurs. In 2014, on Passover, there is a lunar eclipse when the moon turns to blood red. Then on the Feast of Tabernacles that same year, there is a second lunar eclipse. In 2015, on Passover another lunar eclipse happens and then on the Feast of Tabernacles another lunar eclipse.

Two years in a row on Passover and the Feast of Tabernacles you have a lunar eclipse, which is extremely rare. The last time it happened was in 1967 and 1968 when Jerusalem came back into the hands of the Jews. The time before that it happened was 1948 and 1949, when Israel became a nation after centuries. Then we have to go back to 1492 and 1493 when the Jews were expelled from Spain and America was discovered by Columbus.

This rarity is called a Tetrod and will not occur again the entire twenty-first century!

In the Jewish calendar, 2015 is the sabbatical year 5775. It is the seventh year of the seventh season and everything Israel does is in seven year cycles. At the beginning of that religious year there is a lunar eclipse and then, that same year at the beginning of the civil year, Rosh Hashanah, the Feast of Trumpets, there is a solar eclipse. In the year 2015, on four Jewish holidays, the sun will be turned into darkness and the moon be turned red just like it said in Joel and Revelation.

There is more. I discovered a Messianic Jewish believer called Mark Blitz, from El Shaddai Ministries, and he has done some research concerning times and seasons for Israel and Jerusalem.

Jerusalem was recaptured on June 7th 1967. Seven years times seven seasons equals 49 prophetic years. There are two beliefs about when the Jubilee season started. Did it start in 1948 when Israel became a nation again or did it start when Jerusalem was liberated and went back into the hands of the Jewish people?

That debate is still going on today, but if we look at the year 1998, the Jubilee year based on 1948, not much happened that I know of.

My belief is that June 7th 1967 is the start of the Jubilee season because, as the book of Daniel records, everything God deals with is to do with

Jerusalem. As we know, a Sabbatical year is seven sessions of seven years, a total of forty-nine prophetic years. The Jewish calendar consists of 360 days. So 49 years x 360 days comes to 17,640 days.

Starting at June 7th 1967 and going forward 17,640 days you come to September 23rd 2015, which just happens to be the Day of Atonement. It was on the Day of Atonement that they declared the Jubilee and every slave could stop work and go home. It does not fall the day before Atonement, not a week after the Day of Atonement, but on the exact day.

The years 2014 and 2015 are pivotal.

"They will fall by the edge of the sword and will be led captive into the nations and Jerusalem will be trampled underfoot by the gentiles until the times of the gentiles are fulfilled. There will be signs in the sun in the moon and in the stars and on the earth, dismay among nations, perplexity at the roaring of the sea, men fainting from fear, for the powers of the heavens will be shaken. Then they will see the Son of Man coming on a cloud." (Luke 21:24)

If you research this you will probably find a lot of people saying that the Lord is coming back in the year 2015. I do not see a Bride without spot or wrinkle, I do not see the harvest coming in, and I do not see all these things happening by then. I think we have many years left, but I believe this is an infallible sign. Just as something significant happened in 1948, just as sure as it happened again in 1967, something cataclysmic is going to happen in 2015.

I have no idea what it will be, but I am trying to encourage to see that we have a few years to get some harvest in. We have a short span of time left and we need to get before God day and night and ask Him to give us what we need to bring in the harvest. We need to contend for God, for the *parousia* presence to fall on us and that every gift in us would be awakened; to ask him to remove everything that is standing in the way, whatever stumbling block is before us, and that He would send the *"angels that gather"* (Matthew 13:41) to pull it up and remove it from out of our way. We need to be about our Father's business. We must not focus on the world or focus on what is going on in the economy, because we have a harvest to gather. I believe that over the next few years there will be a harvest of "harvesters". Joseph gathered wheat and he locked it in barns, in a place of safety and security. I believe the wheat is representative of the Sons of the Kingdom that you and I are going to bring in.

That is why I lead an equipping centre, to give people something practical to take back to their churches. We need to be focused not only on bringing the people in, but getting them ready. I do not think we have a lot of ministries that are geared to be able to train up and raise up militant, front line warriors. God has promised us that we will have the ability to raise up a body of people and will be able to teach them in one year what it took us ten years to grasp. I am going to feed them meat and trust God to give them the ability to digest it, because they have got to be raised up.

Could it be that we will have seven years of famine? I do not mean a literal famine, but seven years of some really tough stuff. When there is nothing but darkness out there and you are the only one in town with light, they will beat your door down. That is the great harvest.

My belief is that the Bride of Christ will be taken out before the Great Tribulation, but that does not mean that we will not go through some stuff and some hardship, because how can darkness be covering the earth and deep darkness the people, unless we are arising and shining? We need to expect that it is going to be pretty rough out there, but we are not going to live in fear about it because we are in a different Kingdom.

Heidi Baker, from Iris Ministries in Mozambique, has told us privately that on a number of occasions when they were feeding the hungry, they would have something like twenty-five loaves of bread to feed a hundred people, and she would say, "Give everyone a whole loaf." Somehow all one hundred got a loaf of bread. We are not going to put limitations on God, we are going to keep on pulling out loaves of bread until everybody has one. I believe there will be miracles of multiplication. I believe that we are going to see creative miracles in the coming days. It is going to be necessary.

But right now we need to get on the road. Some people are holding their lives together on a wing and a prayer, but if you take your eyes off your circumstances and put them on this destiny, then God will take care of everything else. If we begin to focus on this incredible destiny, all of a sudden these things seem smaller and our faith can be elevated. I know people are going through hard stuff and we have some things ourselves because we are not immune, but I just know and I believe that God's going to come through.

Part Two

By David Powell

WHY NOAH?

"Since all these things are to be destroyed in this way, what sort of people ought you to be in holy conduct and godliness, looking for and hastening the coming of the day of God."
(2 Peter 3: 11-12)

When I first listened to Paul Keith's teaching in the preceding chapters, Holy Spirit asked me a simple question which has shaped much of my life since then. Like so many of heaven's questions' its simplicity hides its impact.

"What was it about Noah that qualified him to save humanity from destruction?"

Over the following months I began to see characteristics in Noah that qualified him in his day to be strategically used by God. Over time I realized that this was also the call of the Father to an end time generation.

Noah was a pre-covenant Gentile who lived before God established His promise and the El Shaddai blessing with Abraham and his descendants. So shall it be at the coming of the Son of Man. Like Noah, there will be a group of believers living totally free from the constraints of religion and legalism, because of an intimate face-to-face relationship with God; with a deep love-based relationship with Jesus, as any bride has for her bridegroom, rather than a passing acquaintance with Him based on religious duty and Law.

Centuries later, God established a new covenant with Moses sealed with the blood of bulls and goats. He continued to love His chosen people, protecting and prospering them. In a single night, the Children of Israel plundered Egypt, the richest nation on the earth, and in doing so recovered all that was stolen in four hundred years of slavery. For forty years God appeared to them every day as a cloud and fire, provided quail and manna, and stopped their clothes from wearing out and kept their eyes and teeth from failing.

Today, the Jewish people are some of the most prosperous people on the earth because of the blessing given to Abraham and passed down his generational line. Solomon's wealth was so incredible that people would marvel in awe at the favor on his life. Yet Paul writes that you and I, as Gentiles, will have so much more favor and blessing – that we will provoke the Jews to jealousy:

"I will provoke you to jealousy by those who are not a nation, I will move you to anger by a foolish nation." (Romans 10:19)

"I say then, have they stumbled that they should fall? Certainly not! But through their fall, to provoke them to jealousy, salvation has come to the Gentiles. Now if their fall is riches for the world, and their failure riches for the Gentiles, how much more their fullness!" (Romans 11:11)

HEROES

Most of our heroes of the faith in the Old Testament lived supernatural lives with heavenly and angelic encounters that many today long for. They were not perfect, yet talked face to face with the Lord. Some were caught up into heaven for incredible experiences; many met and talked with angels; many performed incredible miracles and signs and wonders – all out of a pre-covenant or Law-based relationship. I find this both irritating and motivating! Deuteronomy 29:29 contains a promise that quickly made it my favorite verse in the Bible. It offers this generation an opportunity to experience the same things as our Bible heroes and the forerunners of the faith from prior generations:

"The secret things belong to the Lord our God, but the things revealed belong to us and to our children forever."

Jesus was a transitional leader who lived under the Law, but taught and ushered in a new covenant of grace. He prospered to the point where Judas could steal from the money that was given and He went to the cross in a seamless robe, a designer garment of its day. He moved in the fullness of the Sevenfold Spirit of God years before there was a corporate release. He saw healings and miracles happen every time and everything was subject to Him, even death. His relationship with His Father was on a level few people I know experience.

How much more you and I who live under a covenant sealed with the blood of His own Son? What was possible for these Old Testament heroes in their day should be easier for us under the covenant we have with the Father. Even if we are not operating in the fullness of it yet, we have Holy Spirit living in us.

But "the things revealed" opens a door that makes it possible for you and I to access the same spiritual encounters and live at the same level they did. Their ceiling is now our floor, whether we squander that inheritance or not. We should start our Christian walk where they finished building and not have to start at the same point they did.

For the Lord's return to be "just like the days of Noah" I believe there has to be modern day "Noahs" on the face of the earth who will lead many to righteousness.

PROTOCOL

However, there is a protocol for participation in what the Lord is going to do on the earth before His return. Each of us needs to meet His criteria in order to do the same works, never mind the greater works. I am not talking about religious works or even "duty", but about living in the fullness of all that grace has given us. I am not talking about striving, but the ability to live totally surrendered and yielded to Him. Paul summed it up by saying that he no longer lived, but Christ lived in him (Galatians 2:20).

I am challenged by the fact that in Antioch when people looked at Paul and the other believers there, they saw them saying what Jesus said, doing what He did and having signs and wonders following. That is the true standard for apostolic ministry. For that reason they called them "little Christs" or Christians. They were a mirror image of the original.

Religion has made everyone who prays a two minute prayer a "little Christ", even when they do not sound like Him, do not live like Him and have no signs following. As I search the New Testament I see four different levels of relationship revealed. Different words are used to describe each level and are mirrored in both the parable of the sower (Luke 8) and the four stages of the river flowing out from the throne in heaven (Ezekiel 47).

- **Believers** – those who repent and are baptized. Their spirit is born again but there is little or no spiritual growth in their lives. In the parable of the sower they would be the ones where the birds of the air come and ate up the seed that was sown. In the river which flows from the throne of God, this would be an ankle deep level of commitment.
- **Followers** – many followed Jesus until His teachings became too hard for them and then they deserted Him. In the same parable they spring up quickly but there is a shallowness to their roots that often means they wither when challenges come along, or they are choked by the thorns of life. It is the knee deep impact of the river of God.
- **Disciples** – those who accept the discipline of the Gospel. The commission the Lord gave was to make disciples of all nations, not church members or even just converts. In Luke 2 we see Jesus confounding the scholars and leaders in the temple, yet returning home, submitting to Mary and Joseph and from that place growing in wisdom until the time appointed by the Father. Waist deep water does not just signify sanctification, but also the point of no return. Once we yield control, take our feet off the ground, the Spirit of God moves us whereever He pleases.
- **Little Christ's** – those who are the mirror image of Jesus, doing what He did whilst on the earth. This is my goal, to live as a "mirror image of Jesus" so non-believers see that in my life and ministry! This is the fullness of the river encounter – an abundance, a fast flow of the Kingdom of God in and through our lives.

I recently found out that the Jews believe there are four levels of reading of God's Word, with each one taking the reader to a different level of relationship and insight:

1. *Peshat*, the plain (simple) or literal reading.
2. *Remez*, the allegorical reading through text hints or allusion.
3. *Drash*, the metaphorical reading through (a rabbinic sermon's) comparison/illustration.
4. *Sod*, the hidden meaning obtained by reading through text's secret or mystery.

There is a preparation needed for us to handle the release of the power of the Sevenfold Spirit of God which abided in Jesus and the hundred and twenty on the day of Pentecost. If it were possible for those in the Upper Room to have the fullness of Holy Spirit abide in them, then it is possible for us too. A similar era of habitation is starting, not just with the one or two, but on a company of people across every nation of the world. In order to be the habitation of God each one of us is required to live at a higher level.

Psalm 24:3-6 describes two levels of encounter with heaven: *"Who may ascend into the hill of the Lord?"* and *"Who may stand in His holy place?"*

As I studied these verses I began to see a requirement and a blessing for those who ascended, or visited, the hill of the Lord:

"Who may ascend into the hill of the Lord?

He who has clean hands and a pure heart,

He shall receive blessing from the Lord."

Some have a "Sunday only" friendship or experience with God, going to church more out of a duty or for the social side of church life. As believers they are able to ascend the hill of the Lord and receive blessings from God just like any child does from its parents.

But there is a greater blessing reserved for those seek to stand or abide in His holy place:

"Who may stand in His holy place?

(He) Who has not lifted up his soul to an idol, nor sworn deceitfully.

(He shall receive) righteousness from the God of his salvation.

This is Jacob, the generation of those who seek Him, who seek Your face.

Selah." (Psalm 24:3-6 NKJV)

Moses knew God personally, but Aaron only knew His acts. The Apostle

John knew the Lord on a deeper level than the other disciples, but Judas only knew his acts. Jacob wrestled God for a blessing, whereas Esau sold his inheritance for a pot of stew. The door is open to all for a deeper, more intimate relationship with Jesus. Both Aaron and Judas had the opportunity for a closer relationship, but both turned down their chance. Many today seek the hand or acts of God in order to meet their needs, without taking the time to know and experience the person of God.

Character has always been a fundamental criterion for the Lord using anyone, even when believers have pursued the blessing of God in order to have their needs met. Many have followed an anointed man or women of God rather than pursue a personal relationship with him. Many pursue the presence of God without the same desire for the persons of Father, Son or Holy Spirit.

In 2004, Tim Hughes wrote a song called *Consuming Fire* which for many has become a prayer, a cry from people's spirit to the Lord:

There must be more than this, O breath of God, come breathe within
There must be more than this, Spirit of God we wait for You
Fill us anew we pray, Fill us anew we pray
Consuming Fire, fan into flame, a passion for your name
Spirit of God fall in this place, Lord have your way
Lord have your way in us. (Copyright © Thankyou Music 2009)

A few years ago, around 5:35am, I had an encounter where I stood outside the doors to the throne room of heaven. A few years before I'd had a similar experience, so knew what the doors represented. Like the first time, I pushed open the door and went to enter, but this was a different expereince. Instantly, it was as if every cell in my body was screaming out in agony because of the overwhelming holiness in that place. As I awoke I was trying to claw my way through the mattress to hide between it and the base of the bed. In the hours that followed, one of many questions I asked the Lord was why I could visit the first time but not the second time.

The answer I received was that on the first visit I was shielded, but this time God wanted me to experience the fullness of the holiness of heaven. It was an encounter that changed me forever. As I wait for an invitation to return to throne room, like many others, it has been a journey of dealing with issues that would stop His presence and the Spirit of God fully abiding in me.

At the start of John 15, Jesus talks about both the fruitful and unfruitful branches of the vine that are pruned. For the fruitful branches it is done so that they can bear more fruit. Having gone through the process more than once in my life, it is anything but pleasant. Throughout the Bible those who would impact nations and hold significant leadership office were pruned the most and multiple times during their life.

Joseph was given a great anointing along with many gifts and talents by God, but what was lacking was the wisdom to steward them. Insight without understanding is of little value to anyone. He started a journey that would change his character into a man who could be used by God to save His people from destruction. Not only did he gain his personal destiny and see his visions fulfilled, but he also built a legacy that four hundred years later would be released to Israel as they left Egypt.

Today, much is spoken about regarding our personal destiny, but few are focused on building a legacy. Destiny can easily become about *my life*, whereas legacy is focused on laying our lives down for future generations.

Moses spent forty years being taught he was "somebody" in Pharaoh's palace. He then spent the next forty years in the backside of the desert learning that he was "nobody", before seeing what God could do with "a nobody" in his final forty years. Having allowed the change to take place, God would visit and speak to him, lip to ear, in a deep, close relationship. He fulfilled his calling and destiny and left a legacy for the Jewish people for generations to come.

From a young age David was incredibly gifted and was anointed king over Israel. But it was in the years of waiting to take the throne and hiding in caves, being hunted down like a criminal, that his character changed and he became a man after God's own heart and someone who knew how to worship and celebrate God in all situations. His legacy was psalms and songs, plans for a great temple and fathering one of the wisest men to ever live.

"One thing I have asked from the Lord, that I shall seek: that I may dwell in the house of the Lord all the days of my life, to behold the beauty of the Lord and to meditate in His temple." (Psalm 27:4)

More pursue the anointing and power of God than pursue His character, yet we are called to be the reflection of the original. Character qualifies us to be used by God and the more our character is changed into the image of Jesus, the more we will see the plans and purposes He has for us revealed and released.

NOAH AND JESUS

As I pondered what qualified Noah, I saw seven characteristics in Genesis 6. What I had not expected to see was how these same seven characteristics also applied Jesus.

1. He was known by God
2. He knew the voice of God
3. He was a man of promise
4. He was a Tsaddiyq (righteous man)
5. He had a life of intimacy with God
6. He was obedient at all cost
7. He was faithful in face of opposition

Both Noah and Jesus saved humanity from destruction. Noah saved the physical man, whilst Jesus came to save the spiritual man from destruction. Noah built the ark, but Jesus came as the ark (John 15:4-5).

HE WAS KNOWN BY GOD

So it is Noah's character that gives us clues as to why God chose him to save humanity from destruction. Firstly, he was known by God.

"But Noah found grace in the eyes of the Lord." (Genesis 6:8)

In the Hebrew language the word for grace is *chen* and could also be translated as "attained favor and acceptance". As a noun it relates to the place or position that Noah held with God. He found a place of favor in the eyes of God and was acceptable to Him, which is why God made a covenant with him after the flood. As I write this, the farm we live on has a hundred mile an hour winds raging across it, driving rain and a valley flooded by the river in it. A lot of times there will be a double rainbow across the land, a promise that the land will never again be flooded in judgment. This coming move of God will be a downpour of anointing, authority, miracles, signs and wonders, even as dark storms engulf many.

Those who are "known by God" are being challenged and changed into His character ahead of a worldwide outpouring. Just weeks before his death in March 1947, Smith Wigglesworth prophesied three moves of God, two of which have already taken place. I believe we are in the early days of the third phase of this prophecy:

"During the next few decades there will be two distinct moves of the Holy Spirit across the Church in Great Britain. The first move will affect every church that is open to receive it and will be characterized by a restoration of the baptism and gifts of the Holy Spirit. The second move of the Holy Spirit will result in people leaving historic churches and planting new churches. In the duration of each of these moves, the people who are involved will say, 'This is the great revival.' But the Lord says, 'No, neither is this the great revival, but both are steps towards it.'

"When the new church phase is on the wane, there will be evidenced in the churches something that has not been seen before: a coming together of those with an emphasis on the Word and those with an emphasis on the Spirit."

"When the Word and the Spirit come together, there will be the biggest movement of the Holy Spirit that the nation, and indeed the world, has ever seen. It will mark the beginning of a revival that will eclipse anything that has been witnessed within these shores, even the Wesleyan and the Welsh revivals of former years. The outpouring of God's Spirit will flow over from the UK to the mainland of Europe, and from there will begin a missionary move to the ends of the earth."

In Genesis 6 the rainbow represents "promise" and in Revelation 4 it represents "the sevenfold Spirit of God". We are about to see a company of people who live and move in the promised Spirit of God poured out across the earth. The disciples were told to wait until the promise was released on the earth. Today many are waiting for the same fullness to come and dwell in them. Then, as happened in Acts 4, it will shake the buildings (chuches and organizations) we inhabit.

Time and again the Bible tells us that the favor of God rested on the heroes of the faith and they released it individually or across entire nations. In Exodus 33, God tells Moses *"I will also do this thing of which you have spoken, for you have found favor in My sight and I have known you by name."* Then Gideon said to Lord in Judges 6:17, *"If now I have found favor in Your sight, then show me a sign that it is You who speak with me."*

"For the eyes of the Lord move to and fro throughout the earth that He may strongly support those whose heart is completely His." (2 Chronicles 16:9)

What Noah, Moses and Gideon have in common is that their rise to prominence came at times of darkness and oppression. Noah saves humanity from destruction. Moses led God's people from under the hand of oppression and into the fulfillment of promises given centuries before. Gideon had to overcome his own fear, insecurity, inferiority and intimidation before he could be used to bring peace to a nation for the rest of his life.

All three had to live the life of an overcomer, a victorious one, and deal with the strongholds that kept them and others in bondage. They all had to overcome the principalities and powers that were on the earth at that time.

"For the coming of the Son of Man will be just like the days of Noah."

The favor we carry is not just to change our lives but the lives of those around us. Carrying favor and doing nothing with it is like the servant who buried his one talent in the sand (Matthew 24).

Those who use any gift of God see it grow, develop and mature. Take Samuel and Jesus as examples. The similarity in how the Bible describes their young lives is striking:

"Now the boy Samuel was growing in stature and in favor both with the Lord and with men." (1 Samuel 2:26)

"Jesus kept increasing in wisdom and stature, and in favor with God and men." (Luke 2:52)

Both Samuel and Jesus were children when this was recorded of them. When David killed Goliath and set a nation free from oppression, he was only there because he had brought his brothers lunch! None of them had the ability to earn favor and they had no powerful, transformational ministry at that time. There was nothing they were doing to earn favor other than being who they were. Like many of us today, all three young men were people of substance (favor) but not yet of significance. Sadly, so much of our identity has been established and conditioned based on doing or achieving. True favor flowing in and through our lives comes from us understanding that favor, like sonship, is a position we have.

A different Hebrew word is used to describe Samuel's favor. *Towb* means "morally good, prosperous, becoming, excellent". It is the same word used in Genesis 1 to describe God's reaction when He looked creation at the end of each day.

"God saw all that He had made, and behold, it was [morally good, prosperous, becoming, excellent]*..."* (Genesis 1:31)

Every aspect of creation, including Adam and Eve, had the fullness of the favor of God inside it and lived surrounded by that same favor. It is the reason why life flourished even after the fall of man. Favor is always fruitful because fruitfulness is the nature of God.

"The sons of God saw the daughters of men, that they were beautiful; and they took wives for themselves of all whom they chose." (Genesis 6:2)

The word translated here as "beautiful" or "good", depending on the translation you have, is also *towb*. In reality, the fallen angels saw the daughters of men carrying God's favor in their lives and wanted it for themselves. So they took them as wives and the Hebrew implies the women were "snatched, taken captive and carried away". Satan's plan of attack has always been against those who carry God's favor, because we have inside us the ability to be morally good, prosperous, becoming, and excellent.

Even before his rebellion in Heaven, Satan wanted God's favor for himself and when he could not get it he has consistently tried to steal it from those who do. His aim is to stop us experiencing the grace and favor of God in and through our lives. I am not surprised that there is a new depth coming to the core message of the grace of God at this time, as we understand more fully our true identity and position ahead of a global manifestation of Kingdom authority.

HE KNEW THE VOICE OF GOD

What both Samuel, Jesus and Noah also had in common was their ability to hear God's voice on a regular basis. Everything they did in ministry came from their ability to hear and obey the voice of God.

"And God said to Noah, 'The end of all flesh has come before Me, for the earth is filled with violence through them; and behold, I will destroy them with the earth...'" (Genesis 6:13)

Exodus 33: 11 gives us insight into the Lord's relationship with Moses:

"So the Lord spoke to Moses face to face, as a man speaks to his friend. And he would return to the camp, but his servant Joshua the son of Nun, a young man, did not depart from the tabernacle."

We will look at this in more detail later in the book, but an intimate walk with Father God and us remaining, or abiding, in His presence is a major key which qualifies current and future leaders for service. We cannot afford to be a generation that God says this of:

"Yet the Lord has not given you a heart to perceive and eyes to see and ears to hear, to this very day." (Deuteronomy 29:4)

Time and again Jesus told those that followed Him that the words He spoke and the things He did, were only what He saw the Father doing or heard the Father saying (John 12). If the Son of God needed to hear and accurately repeat the voice of God, then as imitators of Christ, we must do the same. There are other passages that promise you and me the same level of daily relationship. When Paul recounts his four-fold commissioning by God, he tells us: *"The God of our fathers has chosen you that you should know His will, and see the Just One, and hear the voice of His mouth. For you will be His witness to all men of what you have* [personally] *seen and heard."* (Acts 22:14-15)

Firstly, it is God's desire that we know His will and secondly that we see the Righteous One, as the New International Version translates it. Paul is told that he has been chosen to hear the voice of the Lord and then to be a witness of all that was revealed to him through supernatural encounters. The word used for "witness" is a legal term that literally means to only testify of what we have personally seen and heard. Our legal system would consider it "inadmissible evidence" for us to stand up in a court of law and recount someone else's experience or a second hand report.

Religion has made being a witness for Christ something completely different, empowering us to tell people what we know about, rather than what we have experienced. Whilst our spirits yearn for encounters with God and with heaven, and we long for adventures in faith, witnessing has become more about the theology of God than the demonstration of the Kingdom of God.

"But as it is written: 'Eye has not seen, nor ear heard, nor have entered into the heart of man the things which God has prepared for those who love Him.' But God has revealed them to us through His Spirit. For the Spirit searches all things, yes, the deep things of God." (1 Corinthians 2:9-10)

The Greek word translated as "revealed" is *apocalypto,* meaning an "unveiling; manifestation of; divinely granted appearance of Jesus". The promise to us is that through the work of Holy Spirit there will be an unveiling and manifestation of the things that God has prepared for those who love Him, even visitations from the Lord Himself.

Through all the noise and darkness on the earth in his day, Noah personally heard the Lord's voice. That opportunity is open to everyone today, not just through the voice of a church leader or an eloquent speaker, who tells us what to believe - but for ourselves, personally. That is a sign of maturity and qualification. It empowers us and is life-giving not life-taking. If Noah heard God for Himself, then so can each of us under the new convenant.

He was a man of Promise

In hearing God's voice Noah became a man of promise because one always leads to the other. It was a covenant based on a deep, personal relationship with God and not one based on works or performance. Long before Noah had a ministry or calling, he had a promise.

*"...I will establish My covenant with you; and you shall go into the ark –
you, your sons, your wife, and your sons' wives with you."* (Genesis 6:18)

After the flood subsides and the Ark comes to rest, God three times
repeats and reinforces that covenant with Noah in the early part of Genesis
9. This was a legal agreement made by God and the Hebrew word used
implies a divine ordinance with signs or pledges.

*"Of the birds after their kind, of animals after their kind, and of every
creeping thing of the earth after its kind, two of every kind will come to you
to keep them alive."* (Genesis 6:20)

In stark contrast to Moses, there is no record of Noah telling God he had
no experience or educational insight into animal husbandry. There is no
record of him heading off to college to study zoology, despite the fact that
he would be in the ark for almost a year.

Embracing the calling and commissioning of God always leads to an
enabling and empowering, even in the face of much opposition, natural
impossibility and isolation. When God looked out across the world the only
person he found through whom He could save humanity from destruction,
was Noah.

Many people I have met around the world are focused more on what
they cannot do than on what God will do through them. They have lost sight
of what God will do in and through a yielded life. Sadly, many never see God
do anything through them because of unbelief and self-disqualification.

In one of his newsletters a few years ago, Neville Johnson, a prophet
from Australia, wrote the following:

"Whenever God promises us something we are in trouble. We love the
promise, endure the principle, hate the problem, long for the provision.
Character is what happens between the promise and the provision. The
magnitude of the promise is matched by the magnitude of the problem."

In February 2006, Paul Keith gave me a prophetic word about the focus
for our ministry. It was far bigger than I had expected or ever asked for. My
spirit immediately embraced the word without question and got excited
about it coming to pass. Everything went well for the next ten months
and then, as Neville wrote, I hit the problem! That season lasted from 13

December 2006 until 27 May 2011 and when it quietly ended, my character had been changed through the trials and testing of that season in the blacksmith's fire (Isaiah 54:16) and of the refiner's fire and the launderer's soap (Malachi 3:2-3).

Like Noah, Abraham's promise of an heir and many descendants was given at a time when there was little he could do to make it come about and was on such a scale that it would have been hard for him to comprehend how it would be possible.

"May God Almighty bless you, and make you fruitful and multiply you, that you may be an assembly of peoples; and give you the blessing of Abraham, to you and your descendants with you, that you may inherit the land in which you are a stranger, which God gave to Abraham." (Genesis 28:3-4)

This is the first time that God reveals Himself as "El Shaddai". For a long time I took this to mean "the many breasted one" or "the all sufficient one" or "one who nourishes, supplies, and satisfies". A few years back a Hebrew theologian in Dallas gave Paul Keith a more complete meaning:

"The God of utter ruin and destruction who does for you what you cannot do for yourself."

Almighty God chose to covenant that He would do what Noah could not do for himself. He would bring two of every creature on earth to him at just the right time, and then make them all live in harmony inside a four hundred and fifty foot boat for a year. In itself that is incredible, but even more so because that same covenant is available to us today.

"By faith Noah, being divinely warned of things not yet seen, moved with godly fear, prepared an ark for the saving of his household, by which he condemned the world and became heir of the righteousness which is according to faith." (Hebrews 11:7)

"For the coming of the Son of Man will be just like the days of Noah."

There will be many who are known by God; who intimately know His voice; who live in the fullness of the promises of God in their day, and who move in godly fear.

It is our character that is THE key and Noah illustrates this perfectly.

TSADDIYQ

"Noah was a just [righteous] *man and perfect in his generations..."*
(Genesis 6:9)
"Then the Lord said to Noah, 'Come into the ark, you and all your household, because I have seen that you are righteous before Me in this generation.'"
(Genesis 7:1)

New Zealand is a nation that my wife and I both love and even though it is on the other side of the world, it is always the first thought when planning a vacation. I once told the Lord to never allow me to get invitations to minister there, as it would be almost impossible to discern if it was right! We spent Christmas 2007 in the spa town of Hanmer Springs and one Sunday the local church pastor spoke a message on character. In order to quickly illustrate his point he talked about the Hebrew word *tsaddiyq*.

This word is very rarely used in relation to a specific person. The Brown-Driver-Briggs Hebrew Lexicon gives the following meaning for the word:
- just, lawful, righteous
- just, righteous (in government)
- just, right (in one's cause)
- just, righteous (in conduct and character)

- righteous (as justified and vindicated by God)
- right, correct, lawful

It literally means a person who, by very nature, reputation and character is righteous. If you saw a Levite or Nazirite in Bible days, one would instantly know who they were by their appearance and what that implied about their character and lifestyle. The same was true of a Tsaddiyq. Their reputation and character would be widely known and it was first and foremost a radical lifestyle and an extremely high position to hold. "In thought or word or deed" they would always act in both the spirit and the letter of the Law.

In the whole of the Old Testament, the only person I can find among all the anointed and powerful men and women of God who was a Tsaddiyq is Noah. As God looked across the earth, what set Noah apart from everyone else was not just his pure DNA, as Paul Keith has mentioned, but every aspect of his character and reputation.

First Coming

If Jesus told us that *"the coming of the Son of Man will be just like the days of Noah"* it made me wonder if there was anyone with the same *tsaddiyq* characteristics at Jesus first coming. The Greek word for *tsaddiyq* is *dikaios* and Strong's concordance gives the meaning in a much more powerful way for us in the end times:

- in a wide sense, upright, righteous, virtuous, keeping the commands of God.
- approved of or acceptable of God
- used of him whose way of thinking, feeling, and acting is wholly conformed to the will of God, and who therefore needs no rectification in the heart or life

This is the level we are all being challenged to live at. It is beyond what is humanly possible to achieve and that is the point, because only God can create a person with a character like this. It is possible to achieve and many in Jesus' day lived there even before His death.

Sometimes *dikaios* is translated as "righteous" and other times "just" is used. Either way, to be an end time Tsaddiyq is going to take a major shift, so that our way of thinking, feeling, and acting is wholly conformed to the will of God, and who therefore needs no rectification in the heart or life; whose reputation and standing before God is wholly conformed to His will.

"There was in the days of Herod, the king of Judea, a certain priest named Zacharias, of the division of Abijah. His wife was of the daughters of Aaron, and her name was Elizabeth. And they were both righteous before God, walking in all the commandments and ordinances of the Lord blameless." (Luke 1:5-6)

The root word used for "blameless" could also be translated as "free from fault or defect". In the next chapter I will look at this in more detail, because as seemingly impossible as it is for us to achieve, righteousness is a position we occupy this side of the cross, even as we are going through a process of transformation to be able to live in the fullness of it.

Despite Elizabeth being barren and Zacharias's unbelief and rejection of a Messenger of His Face, God chose to entrust "the greatest prophet born to a woman" to Tsaddiyq parents (Luke 7:28).

"For John came to you in the way of righteousness." (Matthew 21:32)

Though the Bible does not directly say that John was a Tsaddiyq, it tells us he came in the way of a Tsaddiyq. It is clear to me that to hold the office of a prophet means living as one whose way of thinking, feeling, and acting is wholly conformed to the will of God, and who therefore needs no rectification in heart or life. I am not sure how many who are called "prophets" today would qualify for the office, based on this criteria. To desire any spiritual office in the days ahead will mean us becoming much more like Christ in thought, word and deed.

After their betrothal, when Joseph realized that Mary was pregnant, the Bible records:

"Then Joseph her husband, being a just man, and not wanting to make her a public example, was minded to put her away secretly." (Matthew 1:19)

Joseph was a Tsaddiyq and acted in keeping with his character. Way too often things that should be handled in private are aired publicly to friends and anyone else who will listen. With the advent of social media this has become easier and more damaging for us and others. The same people who want to prosper, too often shame and criticize, gossip and dishonor. Joseph represents those with a pure heart. His words and actions came out of a heart of love and compassion for Mary, not for himself. Here is a man who appeared to have been totally wronged by his wife, yet his response is to handle it quietly and in secret, not to publicly shame her. To maintain such purity requires the ability to forgive quickly and release the other person from all debts, as well as keeping a short account with God and with man.

"And behold, there was a man in Jerusalem whose name was Simeon, and this man was just and devout, waiting for the Consolation of Israel, and the Holy Spirit was upon him." (Luke 2:25)

As was the Jewish custom, eight days after His birth Jesus is taken to the temple to be circumcised. Simeon was a Tsaddiyq and, like Anna who was with him in the temple that day, was aware of the promises of God for Israel. They were waiting expectantly for the Lord's appearing.

There is a depth of expectation that comes to those who have both a revelation and understanding of the times we live in and the promises of God for us. Having an expectant heart allows each one of us to be prepared to receive the fulfillment of the promises and to pursue the release of it in and through our lives. The five wise virgins had expectant hearts for the Bridegroom to appear at any time and there is an expectancy and hunger for a more intimate relationship with Jesus that has His Bride focused on making herself ready.

Immediately before His crucifixion, Pilate's wife had a revelation of who Jesus was and the word use to describe him is a Tsaddiyq:

"While he [Pilate] was sitting on the judgment seat, his wife sent him a message, saying, 'Have nothing to do with that righteous Man; for last night I suffered greatly in a dream because of Him.'" (Matthew 27:19)

After Jesus is crucified, Joseph of Arimathea, who may have been a member of the powerful Sanhedrin, goes to Pilate and asks for Jesus body. He too was a Tsaddiyq:

"And, behold, [there was] a man named Joseph, a counselor; [and he was] a good man, and a just, who also himself waited for the kingdom of God." (Luke 23:50-51)

Like Simeon and Anna, and like many of us today, Joseph was also waiting for the appearance of the Kingdom of God. Expectation leads to positioning under the guidance and leading of Holy Spirit. It creates immoveable faith, that what seems impossible in the natural is easily possible with God. It creates a passion and a hunger like Jacob had when he wrestled God until he got his blessing. When we are consumed by such a desire we gladly pay the price of living the life of a Tsaddiyq.

TIME OF THE GENTILES

When it came time for the message of salvation and Holy Spirit to be released to the Gentiles, God finds a Tsaddiyq to use to as the release point:

"And they said, 'Cornelius the centurion, a just man, one who fears God and has a good reputation among all the nation of the Jews, was divinely instructed by a holy angel to summon you to his house, and to hear words from you." (Acts 10:22)

When he was writing the Psalms, David saw a future Tsaddiyq generation who had overcome the issues of the soul and whose way of thinking, feeling, and acting was wholly conformed to the will of God, and who therefore would need no rectification in their heart or life.

"For God is with the righteous generation." (Psalms 14:5)

Time and again when the Father chose to save humanity from destruction or to reveal Himself on earth, he used a Tsaddiyq. The men and women I have mentioned were forerunners, examples to us that it is possible to live the life of a Tsaddiyq in challenging times and amidst much darkness. *"For the coming of the Son of Man will be just like the days of [a Tsaddiyq]."*

As the time of the Gentiles now comes to an end, I believe we will see a worldwide company of Tsaddiyq arising.

A RIGHTEOUS
GENERATION

"For You, O Lord, will bless the righteous;
with favor You will surround him as with a shield."
(Psalm 5:12)
"The eyes of the Lord are upon the righteous,
and his ears are open unto their cry."
(Psalm 34:15)

On June 21, 2009 we were in a meeting in Singapore when the Lord interrupted the message I was listening to with this challenging question: *"What do you literally believe and why aren't you living it?"*

In trying to answer that question, so much of my life, beliefs and expectations have been challenged and it has been taking me to a new level of maturity and faith.

"As he thinks in his heart, so is he." (Proverbs 23:7)

So much of our belief system is defined by our thought life. Knowing something only changes our mind, but experiencing it changes our heart and lifestyle. As one speaker put it, "right believing causes right living." Yet too often our beliefs have been lowered to match our experiences (especially the negative ones) rather than requiring our experiences to match the Word of God. In order to bring ourselves into true alignment, we have to get beyond black ink on a white page and experience the truth of the Bible. At times we need to look to the original language for the fullness of truth to be revealed.

When the Children of Israel arrived at Mount Sinai they said to Moses, *"Speak to us yourself and we will listen; but let not God speak to us, or we will die"* (Exodus 20:19). They rejected the invitation to have a personal relationship with El Elyon, The Most High God.

In the third century AD, Constantine reinforced this by putting in place a structure that made communion with God about a man – the priest, pastor or preacher – who would tell people what to believe and expect them to follow what they were told. It was the Nicolaitan spirit mentioned in Revelation 2. Nico means "against" and Laitan means "the laity or people". It disempowers the laity from hearing God for themselves and over the centuries has held many captive to error, half-turths and dogma.

The vast majority of the Church still depends on their minister to provide fresh manna each week, rather than pursuing a personal relationship with Father or studying the Word for themselves. To see the fullness of God it is going to take more than a Sunday experience; it requires a total lifestyle transformation.

LITERAL WORD

"I pray that the eyes of your heart may be enlightened, so that you will know what is the hope of His calling, what are the riches of the glory of His inheritance in the saints, and what is the surpassing greatness of His power toward us who believe." (Ephesians 1:18-19)

There are four levels in this verse and we need to live in the experience of all of them. Paul prays that we will have (a) enlightened eyes in order that we might also (b) know the hope that comes from God's purpose and calling for us individually. As we transition into a Kingdom age we must see things as the Lord sees them and know our place in His plans.

Seeing and knowing His plans for us will be immensely challenging and will require us to change in many ways, but without that we cannot see the next two levels of Paul's prayer: (c) His inheritance in us and (d) the surpassing greatness of His power in us who believe.

I meet people around the world who hunger to experience and operate in His power, but have no understanding and revelation of their identity and position in Christ.

"These are in accordance with the working of the strength of His might which He brought about in Christ, when He raised Him from the dead and seated Him at His right hand in the heavenly places, far above all rule and authority and power and dominion, and every name that is named, not only in this age but also in the one to come. And He put all things in subjection under His feet..." (Ephesians 1:19-22)

Most believe that Christ is seated in heavenly places at this very moment, at the right hand of Father God, which is the place of authority and a place of rest. We rejoice in the fact that everything is under His feet and that He is FAR ABOVE ALL things.

But then reading on we come to Ephesians 2:6, which in the original manuscript flows seamlessly with no chapter break:

"[But God] raised us up with Him, and seated us with Him in the heavenly places in Christ Jesus, so that in the ages to come He might show the surpassing riches of His grace in kindness toward us in Christ Jesus." (Ephesians 2:6-7)

This is the position of the Bride of Christ. By overcoming the spirit of the last Church age (compromise and deception) she sits with Jesus on His throne for eternity. This will be a literal event when we enter heaven, but until then it is a spiritual position. Those who have made themselves ready get to enjoy it this side of death or rapture.

"He who overcomes, I will grant to him to sit down with Me on My throne, as I also overcame and sat down with My Father on His throne." (Revelation 3:21)

It means that right now the Bride of Christ is seated in heavenly places with Christ at the same time as reading this book! It means we are FAR ABOVE every sickness, disease, demonic principality or temptation. Alan Redpath, a British Bible teacher in the 1950-60's, wrote that a believer does not work up to the place of victory, but down from that place, because of the blood and name of Jesus. We so often try to do things to get victory without living in the reality that this is our position already. Graham Cooke recently put it this way: "We fight from victory not towards it. Therefore we are never staring defeat in the face; the enemy is, when he looks at us!" John had this revelation when he wrote that *"greater is He that is in me than anything and anyone in the world"* (1 John 4:4).

In John's first letter, more than once he writes that *"God is Love"*. This is not the *phileo* "brother" love that Peter said he had for the Lord in John 21,, but *agape*, a pure, deep love. God gave Jesus all authority and He went about doing what the Father was doing and saying what the Father was speaking. Jesus was telling His disciples and followers that all He was saying was what Agape was saying, and all He was doing was what Agape was doing – that it was Agape love that gave Jesus all authority.

Jesus goes further and tells them that He and Agape are one, and that if they have seen Him, then they have also seen Agape. If you and I are to be "little Christ's" as they were in Antioch (Acts 11:26) then we are going to have to experience and be transformed to be able to be the mirror reflection of Agape to a world and Church which are both chronically short of unconditional love.

"Truly, truly, I say to you, he who believes in Me, the works that I do, he will do also; and greater works than these he will do; because I go to the Father." (John 14:12)

"And there are also many other things which Jesus did, which if they were written in detail, I suppose that even the world itself would not contain the books that would be written." (John 21:25)

Jesus came as the Son of God. From His position as a Son He served and did everything the Father wanted doing. It was through His security in His Father's love and carrying the fullness of the Spirit of God, that He was able to see so many lives changed through miracles, signs and wonders. He was so secure in His identity and position that we were invited to live like Him and do the same works He did, since we now have access to the same source. Through salvation we became the sons of God and that is what we are, even if we never live in the fullness of that identity or position.

But Jesus then went further still and not only fulfilled His own destiny, He leaves a future generation a legacy, a promise, that they will do even greater works. Amazingly John also tells us that if everything Jesus did was written down the world could not contain the books, and yet you and I are called to the same and greater than he did. No wonder we have computers today, ready to store all the records of what we will see done in and through our lives.

Some, over the last two thousand years have achieved that, but never a worldwide company of people, never a single generation, until now. Jesus is effectively saying, "Go and achieve even more than I did!" This promise is ours by faith and by position. Paul confirms this when writing the book of Hebrews:

"For in the case of those who have once been enlightened and have tasted of the heavenly gift and have been made partakers of the Holy Spirit, and have tasted the good word of God and the powers of the age to come..." (Hebrews 6:4-5)

All of this is available to us this side of heaven and millennium reign of Christ. Paul describes a company of people on earth before Christ's return who will live just like Jesus in the fullness of Holy Spirit; in the fullness of the Word of God; and with a supernatural power that is available the other side of eternity. The world has not seen a move of power, miracles, signs and wonders on such a scale, and I for one want to be a part of it!

To live a life that does the greater works we need to overcome doubt as well as unbelief. Most of us could pray, "Lord I do believe, help me overcome my unbelief!" (Mark 9:24) Sadly, many have a "disappointment theology" rather than one of faith; a life of hope deferred than one of expectation.

Despite four hundred years of silence between the end of Malachi and the start of Matthew, both Simeon and Anna were in the temple each day with faith and the expectation of seeing the Messiah with their own eyes.

"I have come that they may have life, and that they may have it more abundantly." (John 10:10)

Jesus came so that you and I would experience life to the full and not simply exist like the rest of the world. He came that we would not settle for a measure of what is promised or possible, but to live in the fullness of all that is available.

He wants His sons and Bride to stand out from the crowd, to live differently, to be a sign and a wonder to all men. It is our difference that will attract many to God, not our conformity to the image of the world, or compromising truth so as not to offend, challeng or confront society. At the start of Malachi 3 we have the starting point for revival – that the Lord will come into His house as a refiner's fire and a launderer's soap to purify the ministers of the day, so He has those who will lead many to righteousness. It is through the process of purification that we are made different to those around us so the light that shines through us that will draw many to Him.

Though not a Christian, Marianne Williamson describes this in the famous passage from her book, *Return to Love*:

"Our deepest fear is not that we are inadequate.

Our deepest fear is that we are powerful beyond measure.

It is our light, not our darkness, that most frightens us.

We ask ourselves, Who am I to be brilliant, gorgeous, handsome, talented and fabulous?

Actually, who are you not to be? You are a child of God.

Your playing small does not serve the world.

There is nothing enlightened about shrinking so that other people won't feel insecure around you.

We are all meant to shine, as children do.

We were born to make manifest the glory of God within us. It is not just in some; it is in everyone.

And, as we let our own light shine, we consciously give other people permission to do the same.

As we are liberated from our fear, our presence automatically liberates others."

Noah understood this. He embraced his calling and talents, and was willing to be light in the darkness and to stand out from the crowd. The darkness of Noah's day was enough for Father God to repent he had ever made mankind (Genesis 6:6). Scripture tells us a day is coming when there will again be darkness over all the earth:

"For behold, darkness shall cover the earth and deep darkness the

peoples; but the Lord [the light of the world] will arise upon you and His glory wiil appear upon you." [emphasis added]

As is Noah's day there will be need for a company of people to carry a pure light in the world having overcome their fear of the darkness and being willing to uncompromising light:

"The people who walk in darkness will see a great light; those who live in a dark land, the light will shine upon them." (Isaiah 9:2)

"Let your light shine before men in such a way that they may see your good workds and glorigy your Father who is in heaven." (Matthew 5:16)

Sinner or Saint

In order to do this, we must realize the fundamental truth that:

"Anyone who is in Christ – the old has gone and the new has come." (2 Corinthians 5:17)

The old has completely gone and new has completely come, whether we see it or not. The truth is always the truth! We are already approved and accepted by God. To live in the fullness of these truths requires a transformation of our mind away from our upbringing and the influence of society, from incomplete Church teaching and training.

Many Spirit-filled, Bible believing people have an identity crisis and one of the biggest areas is that of righteousness. Sometimes in conferences or when teaching in Bible classes, I have asked for all the sinners in the room to raise their hands. I have yet to have less than eighty percent of the people raise their hands and most often it is close to a hundred percent of the people. How different this is from the reality of God's Word:

"If we confess our sins, He is faithful and righteous to forgive us our sins and to cleanse us from ALL unrighteousness." (1 John 1:9)

"Praise the Lord, O my soul, and forget not all his benefits – who forgives ALL your sins and heals ALL your diseases, who redeems your life from the pit and crowns you with love and compassion, who satisfies your desires with good things so that your youth is renewed like the eagle's." (Psalm 103:2-6)

When Jesus hung on the cross and said, "It is finished", He had overcome sin and restored a way back to a personal relationship with the Father. Death was defeated and eternal life was released to all who would believe in Him. Now we could eat of the tree of life that was in the Garden in Eden.

In the book of Romans, Paul uses the word "sin" forty-seven times, but only once is it a verb or action. The other forty-six times the word for sin is a noun, used to define a place or position. Yet over the centuries preachers and teachers have emphasized sin, the verb, until many are confused as to whether they are still a sinner or not, because they sin at times. The problem for many comes from being *sin conscious* rather than being *righteousness conscious*.

"How shall we who died to sin [place] *live any longer in it?"* (Romans 6:2)

"For the death that He died, He died to sin once for all; but the life that He lives, He lives to God. Likewise you also, reckon yourselves to be dead indeed to sin [place], *but alive to God in Christ Jesus our Lord."* (Romans 6:10-11)

We now live on the other side of the cross, no longer in a prison of sin but one of righteousness. Jesus came to take us from being trapped in a prison of sin to a place of righteousness though His death and resurrection. The word Paul uses for righteousness is also a noun! In this prison or place of righteousness we sometimes sin (verb), yet if we confess our sin (verb) He is faithful to cleanse us from all unrighteousness. When we get our clothes dirty they need to be washed to make them clean again. The same goes with our spiritual robes, but we wash them from the place of righteousness, not back in the place of sin!

In the Jewish betrothal ritual of Jesus' day, after the bride accepted a proposal she would call her friends together to celebrate her betrothal. At the end of the celebration she would have a *Mikvah* – a bath, which is where we get water baptism from and why Jesus taught the need to repent AND be baptized in order to be saved.

The Mikvah was a ceremonial cleansing and, as the bride left the water, she would be dressed in a new robe which had been provided by her husband, as she was now his responsibility. Symbolically this is you and I being given a robe of righteousness. She would then apply a veil across her face which symbolizes holiness and separation, because she was no longer available to the world. Like her, we are in the world but not of the world.

Time and again water is used to represent separation. Jacob wrestles God all night for a blessing and when he receives it everything changes for him and future generations. He then crosses the Jabbok river at the start of the new day and there is no way back to the old character or nature. The Children of Israel crossed the Reed Sea out of Egypt (representing captivity and sin) and there was no way back when the waters closed. Forty years later a new generation crossed the Jordan River out of the wilderness and into the promises of God and there was no way back for them. Jesus goes to the same river to be baptized and leaves filled with the Spirit of God at the start of His ministry.

It is the same for us. When we confess our sins at the time we are saved, He is faithful to cleanse us from all unrighteousness, both the sin and the fruit of it. Everything changes and there is no way back. We are moved from one place to another place and clothed in righteousness.

"I will greatly rejoice in the Lord, my soul shall be joyful in my God; for He has clothed me with the garments of salvation, He has covered me with the robe of righteousness..." (Isaiah 61:10)

Because righteousness is a place, it does not depend on how we feel or think, or about what lies the devil tells us. In fact, the more we know the truth and the Word, the easier it is to deal with the enemy. It is not about right doing, but about right believing that leads to right living!

Righteousness is like being given a brand new home but never enjoying the benefits or privileges of it. It is like having a mansion but living as a pauper or like being the ambassador to another country and sleeping in the cellar, not the private suite of the embassy or never using the status and authority the position gives us.

In the parable of the prodigal sons, the older brother had everything, but lived as a slave not a son. He had no revelation of his true identity and his wrong believing led to wrong living! Despite having everything possible around him, he failed to live life to full because of a poverty mentality and an orphan heart. Even within the place of righteousness these areas can rob us of fulfilling the promises and calling of God.

"Now Joshua was clothed with filthy garments and standing before the angel. He spoke and said to those who were standing before him, saying, 'Remove the filthy garments from him.' Again he said to him, 'See, I have taken your iniquity away from you and will clothe you with festal robes.' Then I said, 'Let them put a clean turban on his head.' So they put a clean turban on his head and clothed him with garments, while the angel of the Lord was standing by.'" (Zechariah 3:3-6)

Joshua has his iniquity removed from him and he is then clothed in "festal robes". The Hebrew word used for the new garments given to him actually means a robe of state. It signifies him holding a position of authority.

"And the angel of the Lord admonished Joshua, saying, 'Thus says the Lord of hosts, "If you will walk in My ways and if you will perform My service, then you will also govern My house and also have charge of My courts, and I will grant you free access among these who are standing here."'" (Zechariah 3:6-7)

There will be a generation that lives the life of a Tsaddiyq rooted in a place of righteousness and in our true identity as Sons of the Kingdom and joint heirs with Christ. They will walk in the fullness of truth and from that place fulfill God's call on their lives whilst having full access to God and heaven.

I do not apologize for wanting that level of relationship and access, but to get it will take a walk and life of intimacy.

Endnotes
- Graham Cooke, Facebook status update, 1 February 2013

A Life Of Intimacy

"Noah walked with God."
(Genesis 6:9)

There is a model of intimacy in the early generations that would be good for us to understand and pursue, because they had frequent encounters with the Godhead that many of us dream of having today. There are people across the world who the Lord is calling into such a walk, as a lifestyle, and who are starting to carry the glory of God through encounters with heaven.

Adam

Adam was made in God's image and lived for nine hundred and thirty years. Every generation from Adam up to and including Lamech, Noah's father, lived with the man who was the very image of God in flesh.

Recently, the Lord began to explain Genesis 2 in more detail, though I suspect I am still very much in school on the topic. The Bible tells us that God as Father, Son and Spirit decided to make a man in their image. The Hebrew word used for "image" means "an exact replica or facsimile", so when they had finished, Adam was the mirror image of the Trinity. In his created being Adam was the fullness of Father God, the fullness of Christ the Son, and the fullness of Holy Spirit. He had the mind of Christ, the fullness of the Gifts of the Spirit and the fullness of the Fruit of the Spirit. He would have been *love* because "God is love" (1 John 4), a spirit being (John 4:24) and was totally holy because "God is holy"(Leviticus 19:2). I am still only scratching the surface of who God created each of us to be.

When they had finished creating Adam, they breathed into him the *neshama*, the breath of God, and he came to life. Amazingly, the very first image Adam saw would have been looking into the eyes of Father God Himself. Adam's abilities and potential was limitless. He was *faith* and he was *peace*! Naming all the animals would have been effortless for someone with the same creativity as Father God.

Adam and Eve enjoyed unhindered access to the Godhead until the fall took place. It took significant deception to blind their eyes to the truth and rob them of all that they had been given and the freedom they enjoyed. The spirit of deception is same one we have to overcome in these days, in order to regain access to heaven and release the Kingdom of God on earth. Of course, the challenge with deception is that no one knows they are deceived until they see it, which is why the Laodicean church age - the last church age in (Revelation 3) - is told to buy eye salve from God that they would see their true condition.

"They heard the sound of the Lord God walking in the garden in the cool of the day." (Genesis 3:8)

When the Bible was translated into English after centuries of denying the supernatural, they used the word "cool" even though that is not the meaning of the Hebrew word. The Hebrew word is *ruwach*, which is most commonly translated as "the breath of God". However, in this context it has a very different meaning and the verse literally means, "They heard the voice of the Lord God walking in the garden, within the Spirit of God, as revealed in the Shekinah glory of God."

What an incredible sight that would have been to experience on a regular basis. From within the Shekinah glory came the audible voice of the Lord God calling Adam's name, wanting another face to face, intimate Father to son encounter. Not only had Adam and Eve lost their own glory covering, they had now lost such encounters with the Lord, Holy Spirit and the Shekinah. There is always a huge price to pay for deception and ever since the Garden in Eden millions have desired such intimate encounters with the Lord.

ENOCH

Noah's great-grandfather had some of the most significant encounters with heaven that were ever recorded. The Bible says that Enoch walked with God for three hundred years, meaning both a physical and a spiritual journey. Enoch's walk with God was so close and real that he gave his son Methuselah a prophetic name as a clear message to the world that, "when he dies it will come".

The Book of Enoch (see appendix) records the insight and understanding he was given about everything that had happened with the Watchers and what was about to happen on the earth. That level of insight and revelation is only given to those the Father can totally trust and comes through a lifestyle of intimacy with Him. He walked so close to God that he is one of only two people in the Bible that were caught up to heaven and did not die.

Some doubt it is possible, even this side of the cross and shed blood of Jesus, to have that level of relationship with the Lord, but I disagree. Deuteronomy 29:29 clearly tell us that the things once revealed belong to us and future generations. As I have already shown, Hebrews 6 tells us it is possible to taste the power of the age to come, which is a face to face intimate relationship with Jesus.

NOAH

By the time that Noah was born, Adam has been dead for a hundred and twenty six years. His father, Lamech, was the last of the family line to personally know the man who was the image of God, so Noah needed his own revelation and encounter with God. In the whole story of Noah and the flood, it is too often overlooked that Noah, like Enoch, walked with God.

Having a close and intimate relationship with the Lord is the key for the lifestyle of an Overcomer, the Sons of the Kingdom and the Bride of Christ. We are going to an intimate, passionate wedding in heaven, not to a governmental election, and we are invited to walk in that level of relationship now. In fact, to live the life of a Tsaddiyq requires us to have an ever closer relationship with the Lord and live at a deeper level of intimacy with Him. That takes time to pursue and develop, but the rewards far outweigh the cost.

To an increasing number of people Christianity is a twenty-four hour a day lifestyle, where the presence and person of the Lord is a daily experience, not a performance or a long abandoned expectation. There are true disciples with an inability to settle for the status quo or compromised truth for the sake of peace and quiet. Many today have a desire for a much deeper relationship with the Trinity and each other.

One of the hallmarks of our present generation is a settling for acquaintances and friendship amongst all the busyness of life, rather than taking the time to build relationship and covenant with people. Facebook and Twitter allow us to stay in touch with more people in an easy format, but do little to build true relationships. Ironically, we know more people but less about them!

I believe that the coming move of the God is going to have many first century Church characteristics. Not least will be an emphasis on community and that takes time to develop. The early day believers met together daily in each other's homes, which takes significant time and commitment to build. Out of those relationships came a covenant culture based on a level of unity not often seen today, and where there is unity the Lord commands the blessing (Psalm 133:1-3). From that place it was possible for them to have all things in common and to meet each other's needs as they arose. No wonder the Lord blessed and grew the early Church. Graham Cooke recently wrote that, "we cannot build a church without covenant relationship with God and man. We must drop the morality of the world and go for something deeper, better, and more powerful in our relationships."

Over the last few years I have been blessed with a growing number of relationships with people in many nations, in different denominations, and in positions of authority – as well as those in none. Although we do not talk or meet all the time, when we do, much time is invested in maintaining and growing the bond between us. Meals are shared, at times layovers or side trips are taken to keep connected, and support is given when needed. Not that I would say there is true covenant between us, but that will come.

Today believers are coming together, often away from organized church meetings, hungry to pursue a more intimate walk with the Lord and build relationship with like-minded people. Their motivation is to see the Kingdom of heaven released in and through them so that the world is changed and people saved, healed and delivered. Just as in previous moves of God throughout Church history, it is the passionate people who are seeing growth in numbers and God beginning to move in their communities.

PEOPLE OF HIS PRESENCE

There are two Bible characters who symbolize the desire for intimate encounters with the Lord and both learnt the importance of this early in their lives. As a result both were used to guide a nation for decades.

"Whenever Moses entered the tent, the pillar of cloud would descend and stand at the entrance of the tent …Thus the Lord used to speak to Moses face to face, just as a man speaks to his friend. When Moses returned to the camp, his servant Joshua, the son of Nun, a young man, would not depart from the tent." (Exodus 33:9-11)

Moses had a relationship with God like no one else in the Old Testament and second only to Jesus. God would come down or Moses would go up the mountain and they would speak face to face, lip to ear. So close was their relationship that he was allowed to see the back of God's goodness as it passed by. In Exodus 24, Moses and the seventy elders of Israel saw God and ate and drank in heaven.

From inside the Tent of Meeting and from the bottom of the mountain, Joshua witnessed that this level of relationship was possible. It is clear he wanted the same intimate relationship with God, because long after Moses had left, he would remain inside the tent where the presence of God was. In that place he was prepared for national leadership and, most importantly, he learnt that time in God's presence was life giving and critical in order to be prepared for the position he would hold. There are no short cuts to this, it is in His presence we are transformed into the mirror-image of His likeness.

The other person is Samuel. Much of the early part of 1 Samuel 3 is a prophetic picture of the state of the Church in many nations today:

"It happened at that time as Eli was lying down in his place (now his eyesight had begun to grow dim and he could not see well), and the lamp of God had not yet gone out, and Samuel was lying down in the temple of the Lord where the ark of God was, that the Lord called Samuel." (1 Samuel 3:2-4)

This was a hard and challenging time for Israel with compromise in the house of the God and we find Eli sleeping away from the presence of God, his sight fading. Yet, despite evidence to the contrary, the lamp of the Lord had not yet gone out in the land. There was still hope for the nation in the form of Samuel – a new generation and style of leader, whose heart was pure and whose way of ministering was very different. He was abiding and resting in God's presence as close as he could get to the Ark. That should have been Eli's position as the High Priest and even though Samuel was not ordained by man as a national leader, in the sight of God he already held such an office. Today there is a new breed of leadership starting to emerge. Most are still hidden away in the secret place, in the presence of God, learning sensitivity and obedience to His voice whilst being taught by the Spirit of God. They might not look like leaders in the natural, but in God's sight they are already ordained for high office.

Any list of Bible characters who had intimate walks with the Lord must include Abraham, who time after time would meet the Lord on his journey, who moved in obedience and received incredible favor on his life. Another would be King David, a man who was after God's heart, whose love and commitment to the Lord grew through years hiding in a cave from Saul, the current leader.

David was a very different character to Saul and his boldness, passion and confidence in God challenged and offended his older brothers, much like Joseph's did. At the time both of them were men of substance, but not yet of significance. Passion and zeal for the Lord, lives of righteousness, favor and anointing, will always offend those whose heart is in a different place or whose standards are lower.

In an increasingly busy world the critical need for intimacy with God is too often neglected, even for those of us in full time ministry. Most often the Lord speaks to me most clearly in bed, in the car, in the shower or on flights. It took me a while to see the common factor was me being still! King David was learning this when he wrote:

"He says, 'Be still, and know that I am God.'" (Psalm 46:10)

Graham Cooke put it this way: "We can be assured that God will always show up and talk to us. We can rely on Him, live in His rest and peace and adore His nature. We can be humbled by our weakness and captivated by His strength." So many live under a false sense of identity and value because they have been made into "human doings" and so are unable to "be" who they were created to be. Our identity and value comes from who we are in Christ and not what we do for Him or for other people or in ministry. I see people being driven by purpose and the need to perform in order to be accepted by others who are equally driven. We have too many orphans raising a new generation of orphans, rather than fathers raising sons to do greater than them. When our value system is based on what we do and not who we are, too often intimacy and relationship are the casualties. Jesus was always about His father's business, but He created time and space to spend alone with Agape. We are all to be Christlike in that respect too.

It was John G. Lake in the early part of the twentieth century who said that, "people are more enamored with the phenomena of God rather than the person of God." Thirty years later others, like William Branham, came to a similar conclusion. Both these men would spend hours each day with God and achieved a level of relationship with Him that allowed them to impact nations and release the Kingdom of heaven on earth.

In his book "Hosting the Presence" Bill Johnson shares one of his favorite stories in all of church history. It is about Smith Wigglesworth, a man who knew the presence of God:

"There were 11 leading Christians in the prayer with our Brother at a special afternoon meeting. Each had taken a part. The Evangelist then began to pray for the Dominion, and as he continued, each, according to their measure of spirituality, got out. The power of God filled the room and they could not remain in an atmosphere supercharged by the power of God.

"The author on hearing of this from one who was present registered a vow that if the opportunity came, he at any rate would remain whoever else went out. During the stay on the Sounds a special meeting was called to pray for the other towns in New Zealand yet to be visited. A like position to the other meeting now arose. Here was the opportunity, the challenge, the contest was on. A number prayed. Then the old saint began to lift up his voice, and strange as it may seem, the exodus began. A Divine influence began to fill the place. The room became holy. The power of God began to feel like a heavy weight. With set chin, and a definite decision not to budge, the only other one now left in the room hung on and hung on, until the pressure became too great, and he could stay no longer. With flood gates of his soul pouring out a stream of tears, and with uncontrollable sobbing he had to get out or die; a man who knew God as few do was left alone immersed in an atmosphere that few men could breathe in."

Everyone in the Bible who encountered either God or Jesus left a changed person, some for the better and some more offended and more religious! Over recent years, I have seen many who appear to soak in God's presence for hours, constantly get prayer and prophetic words, yet who never get victory in personal battles, whose character never changes and who never take what they receive to a needy world. It is as if they have become professional soakers or conference attendees.

The original meaning of Hebrews12:2 is, "to turn the eyes away from other things and fix them on Jesus the author and finisher of our faith." Turning, not glancing towards Jesus during a meeting; fixing permanently rather than being sidetracked by other things, however, good or important they are.

"I no longer call you servants, because a servant does not know his master's business. Instead, I have called you friends, for everything that I learned from my Father I have made known to you." (John 15:15)

Bobby Conner, an American prophet, once said that we are way too familiar with a God we barely know. There is an invitation to the friends of God to encounter Him at a level that few in the past have achieved. The heroes of the faith who achieved it were the forerunners of many in these days who will access heaven in order to release God's Kingdom on earth.

END TIME CHURCH AGE

In Revelation 3, the final letter was written to the messengers to the church at Laodicea, which represents this current Church age since the 1900 Pentecostal outpouring. As Paul Keith explained, this is a time when the powers of darkness are at their most violent, but also the time when, despite current appearances, a Revelation 4 Kingdom age emerges in glory and power.

The hallmark of this present Church age is compromise and deception and they are two of Satan's strongmen. Deception blinds the sight of people and deafens their ears to hearing. Laodicea is the age of *"I am rich, and have become wealthy, and have need of nothing"* which from an outward appearance appears to be true. How similar that sounds to Satan's heart:

"But you said in your heart … I will make myself like the Most High." (Isaiah 14:13)

Notice Revelation 3 does not mention them being, happy, healthy or at peace despite having so much! Knowledge has increased in line with the availability of resources, Christian TV, podcasts etc, yet how many change or apply what they have heard and seen? The finance generated by Christian ministries and churches is huge compared to even fifty years ago, never mind the days of John Wesley when ministers often had no food or income and very few possessions or comforts.

God does not look at the outward appearance, but at person's heart (1 Samuel 16:7). He does not look at how well we dress for a Sunday meeting, but at how we live, speak and love in private. His view of this Church age is the polar opposite to theirs: *"You do not realize you are wretched, pitiful, poor, blind and naked."* So it is to the messengers of this church age that He says this:

"Behold, I stand at the door and knock; if anyone hears My voice and opens the door, I will come in to him and will dine with him, and he with Me. He who overcomes, I will grant to him to sit down with Me on My throne, as I also overcame and sat down with My Father on His throne. He who has an ear, let him hear what the Spirit says to the churches." (Revelation 3:20)

Over the last ten years or so there has been an awakening around the world in those who want to go further than churches and conferences take them. The Lord has been standing at the door of churches and individual lives asking for permission to enter in order to take over. Make no mistake, His original model for church and successful Christian living is Him in charge and us dead to sin and dead to self!

At the heart of this is an invitation to a closer, more intimate walk with the Lord. He longs to come into our hearts to live and "dine with us". For us to get as close to Him as John did at the last supper, reclining so as to hear His still small voice, it requires a turning away from all distraction to fix our eyes solely on Him.

When we fall in love with someone they quickly become our focus and we long to be in their presence, to spend hours with them, to love and be loved. When Jacqueline and I were dating, we would push the time available to the absolute limit in order to eke out every last moment together. More and more she would occupy so much of my thoughts the closer it got to our wedding ... and afterwards! If that was not true you could rightly question how much we loved each other.

If we do that in human relationships, why not in our spiritual life too? Jacob so wanted the desire of his heart fulfilled he was never going to let go of God until he got what he wanted. In his closeness to Jesus, John was transformed through love from being a "son of thunder" (Mark 3:17) to being the only disciple willing to be at the crucifixion. So it is little wonder then that John was given the Revelation of the end times and of eternity.

Come up here

But Jesus coming into our lives is only half the promise. He wants to come in and dine with us, and us with Him. If Paul Keith "comes in and dines with us" he would come to our home for a meal and fellowship. But if we were to "come in and dine" with him and his wife, we would go to their home. True relationship is like that. Having shared meals with Paul Keith, spending hours on the road together is always a great time of fellowship and something I always look forward to and greatly value.

The same is true for the Church today. Jesus not only wants to come to us personally and corporately, but for us to visit heaven too. In the original revelation that John recorded, there are no chapter breaks, so Revelation 4 is a continuation from the Laodicean church age.

"After these things I looked, and behold, a door standing open in heaven, and the first voice which I had heard, like the sound of a trumpet speaking with me, said, 'Come up here, and I will show you what must take place after these things.' Immediately I was in the Spirit; and behold, a throne was standing in heaven, and One sitting on the throne." (Revelation 4:1)

The invitation is for you and I to go through a door in heaven (which is Jesus Christ), to have the fullness of Holy Spirit abiding in us and to encounter Father God in His awesome majesty and glory. This level of access is only by invitation of the Lord and we cannot make these encounters and visits happen, but we are encouraged to seek and expect such encounters.

BRIDE OF CHRIST

The promised reward for those who pay the price to overcome the spirit of this age is *"to sit down with Me on My throne, as I also overcame and sat down with My Father on His throne"* (Revelation 3:21). That is the place of intimacy and authority and the two are very much linked. This is an eternal reward and is only offered to those who overcome in this final Church age, as no prior generation has been offered a similar reward.

Unlike the United States and other nations, the United Kingdom has a monarchy, so I grew up understanding kings and monarchs, princes and princesses, about having an heir to the throne, royal titles and privileges.

Some believers are going to have a shock in heaven when they find out that it is not a democracy and there is no chance of changing the leader! In April 2011, Prince William, a future British king married his bride, Catherine

Middleton, in what was a powerful and poignant wedding ceremony. As his bride, when William becomes King she will become Queen in her own right and will sit and reign with him for the rest of his life. That is the right and privilege of her new position.

To those who overcome in these days, as the Bride of Christ we have the right and privilege to sit with Jesus on His throne for eternity. Much like the Bride of Christ, before Esther was allowed to enter the presence of the king she had to go through preparation and purging. Whether you call it sanctification or washing her robes, the Bride must pay the price needed to be ready for Him.

From the moment she became betrothed to Prince William, Catherine was a bright light which could not be hid in the nations of the world. People who meet her are attracted to her character as well as her beauty. So it will be with the Bride of Christ. It will be her difference, her character and her beauty that will draw many to Jesus, as much as the power and authority she carries.

Yet not all will answer the knocking of the Lord on their hearts in these days. When it came time to leave the wilderness and enter the Promised Land, two and half tribes preferred to stay on the banks of the Jordan and not pay the price to enter into the promise. That price started at Gilgal with circumcision, where the flesh was cut off and they were forever marked as God's people. Sadly the same will happen this time as it has throughout Church history whenever God moves on.

This debate is clearly illustrated in Song of Songs 5 when the bridegroom comes knocking on the door wanting a deeper level of relationship and encounter with her.

"I was asleep but my heart was awake.

A voice! My beloved was knocking:

'Open to me, my sister, my darling,

My dove, my perfect one!'" (Song of Songs 5:2)

The bride's response says it all:

"I have taken off my dress, how can I put it on again?

I have washed my feet, how can I dirty them again?" (Song of Songs 5:3)

Like the unprepared virgins in Jesus' parable these people will get into heaven and stand before the throne in God's incredible presence and glory for eternity. But however much they knock on the door of the bridal chamber they will never gain entry, because that most intimate of places is reserved for the Bride of Christ.

The call to each of us is for a closer, more intimate relationship with the Lord, to walk with him at the same level Noah and Enoch did. For us to encounter the Kingdom of God on a daily basis and release it on the face of the earth, it is going to mean a much closer, purer and focused daily walk. By allowing ourselves to go through preparation for visitation and habitation, the light of God in us will shine ever brighter in the midst of increasing darkness.

Like with Noah, this will be our finest hour and allow us to be obedient and faithful in the face of opposition.

Endnotes
- Graham Cooke Facebook status update, 3 February 2013
- Graham Cooke Facebook status update, 11 February 2013
- Bill Johnson, *Hosting the Presence"* Destiny Image, Page 179

Obedient At All Cost

"Thus Noah did; according to all that God commanded him, so he did."
(Genesis 6:22)

One characteristic of a Tsaddiyq is their obedience to everything the Lord has commanded them to do. Noah built an ark when no one knew what rain was; Zacharias named his son John and broke a generational tradition in the process; Joseph kept Mary as his wife and raised Jesus as his own son. Irrespective of other people's opinion or the personal cost, they never compromised and did exactly what God had told them.

Bill Johnson recently wrote that, "compromise is the door through which deception enters." When the Lord told Noah his plan, he never doubted the word of the Lord; he did not question what he had been told.

In the early seventeenth century, Sir Isaac Newton is quoted as saying, "About the Time of the End, a body of men will be raised up who will turn their attention to the Prophecies and insist upon their literal interpretation in the midst of much clamor and opposition."

Welcome to War

"Proclaim this among the nations: 'Prepare for war! Wake up the mighty men, let all the men of war draw near, let them come up. Beat your

plowshares into swords and your pruning hooks into spears; Let the weak say, 'I am strong.'" (Joel 3:9-10)

Let me apologize if no one told you that we are at war! When most of us are born again and become followers of Christ this key detail is often left out during the salvation call, but it does not change the reality that we are at war.

"For we do not wrestle against flesh and blood, but against principalities, against powers, against the rulers of the darkness of this age, against spiritual hosts of wickedness in the heavenly places." (Ephesians 6:12)

There have been a number of titles given to this radical end time generation that is rising up. The one I struggled with was the "nameless and faceless generation." I understand what is trying to be portrayed, but the title is wrong. There is a transitioning of ministry away from the priest/pastor being the only one who can minister, towards a movement where the laity are being anointed with power to minister inside and outside the Church. This means the majority of us will not have large ministries, international recognition, be on TV or Radio, or speak to thousands at conferences. This is why the "no name" and "no face" title has been suggested.

If the current model had worked churches across the western world would be full today! As you will see later, there will be people the Lord raises up to many different levels and some will have higher profiles than others, but the focus is on the many going and doing and that includes both you and me!

THE COMMANDER IN CHIEF

Recently I was driving home from a conference on the freeway when Holy Spirit said to me, "It is not a no-name army that is emerging, it is the Army of the Obedient." It took time with the Lord to get more revelation on this, since no one else I knew had ever used the same phrase.

In Joshua 3:16 we read that the Children of Israel crossed the Jordan in front of Jericho – the very thing that had disqualified the prior generation. First they camped at Gilgal, the place of circumcision and consecration, as well as the place of encounter. Today the same model applies, first comes consecration and spiritual circumcision, before personal encounters at the level and significance of Joshua's.

"And it came to pass, when Joshua was by Jericho, that he lifted his eyes and looked, and behold, a Man stood opposite him with His sword drawn in His hand. And Joshua went to Him and said to Him, 'Are You for us or for our adversaries?' So He said, 'No, but as Commander of the army of the Lord I have now come.' And Joshua fell on his face to the earth and worshiped, and said to Him, 'What does my Lord say to His servant?' Then the Commander of the Lord's army said to Joshua, 'Take your sandal off your foot, for the place where you stand is holy.' And Joshua did so." (Joshua 5:13-15)

Moses heard God speaking from within a burning bush and now Joshua had a terrifying encounter with the Lord as "Commander of the Lord's army". He appeared so powerfully that Joshua wanted to be on the same side! The moment Joshua heard the command to remove his shoes because he was on holy ground, he knew it was the Lord. In a new day and to a new generation the Lord appears in a different form and different way. If we are looking for Him to come this time as He has done before, we will most likely miss the day of His appearing. Church history is full of examples where this happened.

The Lord Himself is assuming His rightful place as the Commander-in-Chief. It is no longer optional who leads, the stakes are simply too high and the time too short. We do not have another generational timeframe to waste walking around the wilderness; we need to have Him come and take over. My prayer these days is to have an encounter like Joshua. One such encounter was promised to me on July 1, 2008 and I am constantly asking for it to happen, because every other part of the same prophecy has come to pass.

His Kingdom

The time of building an old model church or ministry has ended. Let me be clear, we will still have ministries and we will still have regular gatherings of believers. But the anointed ones are not motivated by building a ministry or a large church, rather by a consuming personal relationship with the Lord like Enoch and Noah had. The Father is making it a condition that we build His kingdom and there can be no place for the empire spirit in the Army of the Obedient. Our motivation must be for His glory and not for man's praise and recognition. We are being required to have lives totally submitted and yielded to His agenda and His will, just like any soldier has to with their commanding officer.

This move of God is not about self-sufficiency but about a deep heart-to-heart relationship with God and with each other. It saddens me to see ministries that are trying to reach the world themselves, all internally controlled, without building relationship with those who could help change lives and nations faster. There is no soldier in any army that can do it all, whether by themselves, with their company (church/ministry) or their battalion (denomination/stream). God designed us to need each other and to be in relationship and that takes time and commitment. Ask any soldier and they will tell you that being in an army is an all-consuming way of life.

ARMY RANKS

In the coming days there will be many in every state and nation that move in great anointing, who see the Kingdom of God come as they minister, irrespective of how many attend their meetings. Wade Taylor, who recently went home to heaven, is quoted as saying that, "the day is coming when the success of the meeting will not be measured by the numbers of people or the eloquence of the preacher, but by the measure of His presence."

Every army has different ranks from five-star generals all the way down to private first class, yet all are ultimately under a Commander-in-Chief. Some in this army will be appointed straight to a senior rank over those who seem to have more experience or have been a Christian longer. This in itself will expose roots that need to be dealt with, so that the enemy has nothing which could cause us to become casualties of war.

"For promotion cometh neither from the east, nor from the west, nor from the south. But God is the judge: he putteth down one, and setteth up another." (Psalm 75:6-7 KJV)

Promotion through the ranks of His army will come from the Lord Himself and it will mean passing tests and fulfilling orders. It will mean meeting the qualifications for service at a new level and proving ourselves faithful. There can be no place for offense if others are promoted ahead of us or given assignments we wanted. The fastest way for promotion is obedience and dealing with areas that would rob us of obtaining it.

"Now these were the men who came to David ... and they were among the mighty men, helpers in the war, armed with bows, using both the right hand and the left in hurling stones and shooting arrows with the bow. They were of Benjamin, Saul's brethren." (1 Chronicles 12:1-2)

This is the day of double anointing and multiple talents being released. Elisha obtained the double portion from Elijah because he stayed focused and did not compromise. Many will carry this same level of ability and authority from heaven in these coming days. But it will only be given to those who are willing to pay the price and be totally sold out for the Kingdom of Heaven. The double portion will not be given lightly by the Lord.

Just as Saul's relatives transferred to King David over time, there will be many who will transfer from a religious, legalistic structure. They will already be equipped and trained and carrying a greater anointing than others. I believe this passage also shows that some joining the army in these days will carry a double anointing – the ability to use both the right hand and the left, and to move in two or more different ministry areas at an advanced level.

OPERATING UNDER AUTHORITY

I was enjoying a foundational course for dreams and vision training until the final afternoon. The tutor then introduced a topic on the need for us all to live under authority and it was as if a short fuse had been lit under some of my fellow students, who suddenly became very vocal and animated. Many of their comments were about politics and governments of the wrong persuasion and having to obey them. The tutor lovingly made the point that to move *in* authority we have to live *under* authority. "Amen," I said, because my desire is to move in greater authority; to be one of the many in these days who are trusted and anointed enough to constantly taste the power of the age to come. So you can imagine my shock when I heard the tutor start to talk about obeying the speed limit!

I admit that staying under the speed limit had always been a problem for me and it is nothing short of a miracle that I was never caught speeding, having owned some fast cars over the years. I love speed, whether in a car, a plane or on a theme park ride! But the Lord challenged me on how much I wanted to move in more authority. It took a while before I could automatically stay under the limit, even when no one was looking. But then the anointing began to increase, more lives were healed and released, greater prophetic revelation came and more insight into Scripture was given. What a small price to pay, in a small area of life, and not everything will take great leaps of faith, sometimes we simply need to return to the foundations of the faith.

It was Jesus' free will to lay aside His majesty and be born on earth. In the Garden of Gethsemane He reaffirms this, knowing it will cost Him His life.

"O My Father, if it is possible, let this cup pass from Me; nevertheless, not as I will, but as You will." (Matthew 26:39)

It was obvious to others that Jesus was a man under authority and we must live the same way.

"But say the word, and my servant will be healed. For I also am a man placed under authority, having soldiers under me." (Luke 7:7-8)

John Paul Jackson put it this way in one of his recent eLetter's:

"Many of us talk about wanting to be like Jesus. If we really do want that, obedience is the place to start – because it is the place where Jesus started. We will never be closer to God than the degree of our obedience:

"And being found in appearance as a man, He humbled Himself and became obedient to the point of death, even death of the cross (Philippians 2:8)

"As we spend time with God and truly begin to know Him, the enemy loses the "space" that allowed him to attack us before. Every time we say, "Yes" to God, we come much closer to Him. He molds us into His image. He purifies us. We feel His hope even in the deep, hidden parts of our souls. His light increases in our lives, and the shame and desperation of the world are driven away."

Larry Randolph writes in *The Coming Shift*:

"It is impossible to reach our God-given destiny without learning the value of radical obedience ... extreme purpose in God requires extreme obedience to God. Also critical to our journey is an understanding that self-sacrifice and performance cannot replace obedience to the Lord. In every area of life, we must come into compliance with the voice of the Holy Spirit before we can fulfill the will of God in our lives."

THE KING'S SHILLING

In the eighteenth and nineteenth centuries recruits in the British army and navy were given "the King's shilling" which was about one week's pay and worth around 8 cents today. By "taking the shilling" the conscript was no longer his own since he had been bought with a price!

"And you are not your own for you were bought at a price; therefore glorify God in your body and in your spirit, which are God's." (1 Corinthians 6:19-20)

Today those serving in our military are all under authority, right up the chain of command to the president or prime minister. In boot-camp new recruits very quickly find out that their free will no longer exists and each serviceman and woman knows that they are not allowed to do what they want, when they want, or how they want, because that is rebellion. They have signed up for service with all its responsibilities and privileges, standards and expectations. Like true disciples, life in the army is a twenty-four-hour-a-day commitment to go anywhere at any time. They wear the uniform and some pay the price with their lives. Somehow these simple truths seem to have been forgotten over the years in the western Church.

As the Army of the Obedient arises in every nation across the world many are coming back to these truths. They are the foundations which we will live by, love by and some may even die by.

"I have been crucified with Christ; it is no longer I who live, but Christ lives in me; and the life which I now live in the flesh I live by faith in the Son of God, who loved me and gave Himself for me." (Galatians 2:20)

Assignments

We need to be able and willing to accept change whenever it comes. For Noah change was coming as soon as Methuselah died, whether he was ready or not. We either embrace change and transition or we resist it and stay where we are now. When I was doing my management studies at college, we spent many weeks in one class looking at the area of change management and, more interestingly, resistance to change.

Some of us are wired to love change and adventure – and my wife will tell you I am definitely one of them! Even after doing three round the world trips and over one hundred and fifty thousand miles one year, I still liked security lines in airports because it meant I was on an assignment and they are always adventures. We are all champions of change because we are commissioned to bring heaven on earth.

For the forty plus years of my Christian life I have watched people find an area of ministry in a church and then serve in that area for years if not decades, their willingness to faithfully serve masking their dreams and other gifts. I have also seen churches keep doing the same program for decades with little or no fruit. Maybe it is because we fear change or other things hold us back – such as not wanting to let people down, when in reality we are not moving when God wants us to. The pillar of cloud keeps moving on because God keeps moving and He expects us to keep up.

There is also a lie that people can only be good at one or maybe two things or in one or two areas. Each of us are made in the image of a multifaceted God, not a one dimensional Father. He is multitalented and excels in every area and we were made in His image. I have met a growing number of young people who could do any one of five or six different things, excelling in them all; talents placed in them for different seasons of life and for different assignments. The Bride of Christ will emerge with the hallmark of creative excellence and will draw people to the Person who enables and equips them to live such lives.

So much of what this emerging army does is going to be appear "out of the box" compared to where we have been. There are going to be new strategies released and new levels of authority assigned to the obedient.

In being obedient we may well be misunderstood by family and friends, as well as fellow believers. I once wrote in a letter that I could understand why our lives made no sense to the reader, because at times it made no sense to us!

In much of our full time ministry there have been seasons where we were given an assignment for a time and when it was completed God moved us on to another assignment – sometimes involving a house move and, for a while, having no home at all. The first two and a half years of our ministry was spent hosting conferences and seminars for other speakers to come and speak at. It helped break something open over regions and we saw churches and people changed. Then that assignment ended as the door opened to international travel. For the next season I ministered on four continents of the world, sometimes away from home for thirty to forty days at a time. Then the season changed and there were no more invitations. We had entered a "Selah" season, a pause, and you can guess how challenging doing nothing was. But it was in learning to be still that we were taken to new levels of faith, trust, peace and healing, and a deeper passion for the Lord. Soldiers have to return to their barracks and Jesus would go up the mountain alone at night to spend time with the Father before returning to the crowds. If your identity is in performing then being still will kill you! But then that is the Father's plan so that you can live in freedom.

As we went through the challenges of transitioning the Lord showed me a key lesson in the end-time parable of the talents (Matthew 25:14-30). Each servant was given talents and a season in which to use them. When their time was up, each came to give a report of what they had achieved and show the growth that had come. What I was shown is that when we complete an assignment, for example a ministry trip, it is like going before the King in the parable and giving an account of what we have accomplished: this is what you gave me to start with and here is the fruit from the assignment. Just as in the parable we must hand it all back to Him and, like the servants at that point, we are left with nothing. As in the parable it is when the King is ready that we get another assignment or commission and the ability to fulfill it. God has proven to me that it does not matter how full our ministry schedule is, He can still stay "stop" at any time and how we cope with that affects how soon we are released again on assignment.

Some will likely be given things that had been offered to others who hesitated or refused them. Anyone not following heaven's orders will see someone else suddenly raised up to fulfill that need. Anyone stepping back from the battle line in these days will be replaced because the time is too short.

Obedience is needed even when we do not see the assignment's purpose or understand the significance of the part we have to play in the overall strategy of heaven. Most often we only ever see in part. To live like this needs us to trust where we cannot see. The Lord is going to have this revival and is looking for obedient sons and daughters who, like Noah, will carry out His orders without question. To those who follow His direction and assignments, there will be a reward both here on earth or in heaven.

THE ONE

Another characteristic that will challenge the hearts of many, especially those seeking big numbers at meetings or fame, is our continued willingness to go for the one. When reading the life stories of people like William Branham, I am struck by their obedience when the Lord told them to go to "x", wait there until "y" happened and then to do "z". Sometimes it meant waiting for days for something to happen as the Lord said it would. I read about those who would draw thousands to a meeting any night of the week, yet who were also equally committed to spending time with one person in need. I suspect that the Lord trusted them with the many because He could trust them with the one.

I started speaking in meetings at the age of eighteen and once over the shock of standing up and speaking in front of people I would struggle with small meetings. Then I found myself on the platform at a conference with fourteen hundred people and decided somewhere in between was fine with me! Then one day the Lord asked me if I was willing to go for the one. We are coming to a place where we will pray over people corporately and healings, miracles, signs and wonders will break out all over for building. I have started to see the first signs of this happening in our meetings, because corporate healing will be the only way we see millions ministered to. But we will always have those who need a little more individual time and prayer.

HIDDEN TALENTS

John Joseph Pershing was born in 1860. Although not an especially outstanding student he was noted early on by US army officers for his leadership qualities. His career saw many promoted ahead of him and he was forty one years old when he finally made it to the rank of Captain. Like many of us life and ministry might seem to have passed us by and destiny might appear to have been lost along the way.

A little over two years later, the President mentioned Pershing's name before the US Congress and three years after that he was promoted over eight hundred and sixty two other officers to the rank of Brigadier General. His time was about to come. In 1917 America entered World War One and General Pershing was appointed to lead the still forming American Army into battle. In spite of great pressure, diplomatic, official, and otherwise, Pershing assembled an American Army of half a million men.

In September 1919, as recognition of his achievement in creating, almost from nothing, the vast structure of the national Army, Congress created the rank of General of the Armies. As such John J. Pershing was the highest ranking military officer in American history, outranking even Generals of the Army. Two years later he was appointed Chief of Staff and during his tenure of office he designed the new permanent framework of the US Army.

Many of us may never have been to war before, which means the enemy has not seen what this Army of the Obedient is capable of achieving when it moves in unity with the Father, the armies of heaven, and each other! For the most part we have been confined to barracks (inside the Church), being trained by Holy Spirit in secret. But change is coming!

In Mark 11:2-3 (NIV), the Lord sends His disciples ahead of him into the city:

"Go to the village ahead of you, and just as you enter it, you will find a colt tied there, which no one has ever ridden. Untie it and bring it here. If

anyone asks you, 'Why are you doing this?' tell him, 'The Lord needs it and will send it back here shortly.'"

This is a beautiful picture of the many the Lord is starting to use who have never done any ministry before. Like the donkey they may currently be bound and need to be set free, but they are the very people who get to carry the Lord into the city in His glory, majesty and triumph

ASSISTANCE

No army goes to war without weaponry to fight with and the same goes for us.

"For though we walk in the flesh, we do not war according to the flesh. For the weapons of our warfare are not carnal but mighty in God for pulling down strongholds." (2 Corinthians 10:3)

"The Lord has opened His armory, and has brought out the weapons of His indignation." (Jeremiah 50:25)

A breaker anointing has been released accompanied by angels of breakthrough. We need much more understanding about how to receive, interact and release the angelic and heavenly realm. The Lord has begun to release the ability to have eyes to see, ears to hear and a heart to understand, not just about heaven and the angelic realm, but with insight and revelation that previous generations longed for. This will be released to many and not just a few.

The door of heaven John saw in Revelation 4:1 is open for all of us to seek the Lord to enter through. One of the first things that John sees is a lampstand which are the seven spirits of God. Isaiah 11 tells us that these are the Spirits of Wisdom and Revelation, Council and Might, Knowledge and Awe, and the Spirit of God Himself. These descended and indwelt Jesus as He was coming out of the Jordan River and is what equipped the disciples in that upper room on the day of Pentecost. They are the power to do the same works as Jesus and the greater works, but they are only given to the mature sons of the God because, much like in any army, the heavy weaponry is not automatically given to someone fresh out of boot-camp.

Jesus spent thirty years proving Himself faithful before starting a ministry of total obedience to what the Father had for Him to do. The disciples spent over three years in training camp before being given the same level of power and authority. Noah was obedient even when he was the odd one out, when no one else understood him, and with a huge assignment from God. He was obedient in carrying it out just as the Lord commanded, without his own views and opinions getting in the way.

"For the coming of the Son of Man will be just like the days of Noah."

Endnotes
- Bill Johnson, Facebook status update, 28 December 2011.
- Pershing data source: www.firstworldwar.com
- Larry Randolph, *The Coming Shift*, MorningStar Publications, p167
- John Paul Jackdon, eLetter February 2013

FAITHFUL, NOT FEARFUL IN OPPOSITION

"And Noah did according to all that the Lord commanded him."
(Genesis 7:5)

In Noah's day the whole earth was in chaos. Reading both the Bible and Book of Enoch it is hard to underestimate how bad things were. The giants born in those days "devoured all which the lab or of men produced until it became impossible to feed them, when they turned themselves against men, in order to devour them, and began to injure birds, beasts, reptiles, and fishes, to eat their flesh one after another, and to drink their blood. Impiety increased; fornication multiplied; and they transgressed and corrupted all their ways."

"The Lord saw that the wickedness of man was great on the earth, and that every intent of the thoughts of his heart was only evil continually. The Lord was sorry that He had made man on the earth, and He was grieved in His heart. The Lord said, 'I will blot out man whom I have created from the face of the land, from man to animals to creeping things and to birds of the sky; for I am sorry that I have made them.'" (Genesis 6:5-7)

Never before or since has the evil done on the earth so grieved God, yet Enoch and Noah remained faithful in the face of such overwhelming depravity. As dark as it is now, or will get in the future, as we see Scripture fulfilled and gross darkness on people, these men demonstrate that it is possible for us to live bold and courageous lives. The book of Revelation reveals the two faithful witnesses who will live in Jerusalem when Anti-Christ opposes the Church and defies God. They will have the same spirit of boldness and courage that I believe was on Noah and Enoch.

2 Samuel 23:8-12 tells us of the boldness and courage of David's Mighty Men. Their leader was Josheb-basshebeth who, in a single battle, killed eight hundred well trained and equipped soldiers whose sole intent was to kill him. The strength and stamina needed was supernatural. The second was called Eleazar, whose boldness, confidence and courage was so great he chose to pick a fight with the Philistines. Standing his ground and fighting them until his hand froze to his sword, he prevailed! The last of the three was called Shammah who took his stand to defend a field full of lentil beans when everyone else ran away, killing all the Philistines who attacked him. Whether they were being reactive or proactive, each time it is recorded that their courage and boldness enabled the Lord to bring about a great victory. So shall it be at the coming of the Son of Man as you and I pursue heaven for the Spirit of Council and Might.

OVERCOMING FEAR

For us to operate at the same level against spiritual giants and demonic principalities we must face and overcome every aspect of Fear, Insecurity, Inferiority and Intimidation in us. There is no doubt that these four spirits are offspring of the Nephilim and dealing with them is high on heaven's priority list. Put simply, fear and faith can not co-exist. One of them will always govern an area of our life and most of us have lived with faith in one area and fear in another area, until we overcome the fear and enter into peace and rest.

This has been perfectly illustrated since the global economic shaking started in mid-2008. The number one issue that many Christians and non-Christians have had to face is their fears and insecurities. When the turmoil broke around the world the Lord showed me that this shaking was to benefit the Church, not the world. Fears arose in many lives which the

Lord wanted to deal with in order that we are anchored in faith when more serious shakings and collapses happen in the future.

There are many similarities between the days of Gideon, the days of Noah, and what we are increasingly facing as we deal with principalities and powers in the heavenly realm. In Judges 6, the Church is hiding away whilst the nation appears to be overrun by calamity.

"Because of Midian the sons of Israel made for themselves the dens which were in the mountains and the caves and the strongholds. For it was when Israel had sown, that the Midianites would come up with the Amalekites and the sons of the east and go against them. So they would camp against them and destroy the produce of the earth as far as Gaza, and leave no sustenance in Israel as well as no sheep, ox, or donkey. For they would come up with their livestock and their tents, they would come in like locusts for number, both they and their camels were innumerable; and they came into the land to devastate it." (Judges 6:2-5)

Much like we all do when calamity strikes, they cried out to the Lord for help and we do not always appreciate the reply from heaven:

"I said to you, 'I am the Lord your God; you shall not fear the gods of the Amorites in whose land you live. But you have not obeyed Me.'" (Judges 6:10)

There is so much fear about the kingdom of darkness and the demonic realm that it has weakened people to the point of hiding away and living in fear of Satan and his followers. Those who believe the negative will happen empower it by faith! As we saw in an earlier chapter we are already seated with Christ far above all principalities and powers and need to enforce the victory of the cross and blood of Jesus. How are we to let light shine in the darkness unless we are in the darkness shining brightly assured that it cannot overcome us or the light inside us?

"Gideon was beating out wheat in the wine press in order to save it from the Midianites." (Judges 6:11)

Gideon was a man with a national leadership anointing – another man of substance but not yet of standing in the nation. He was trying to get a harvest inside the winepress (a picture of the Church) rather than outside, in public view. It always takes more effort for little reward to do it that way, but the amazing thing is that he saw any harvest at all. The winepress (Church) is dry, though it would once have been full of wine (Holy Spirit). It grieves me to see how churches and denominations that started out with a move of God, have ended up with few if any of the signs that marked their birth – and no expectation for them either.

Like Joshua and Samuel, God sees the potential, calling, and anointing bestowed on us even if we cannot see it. So He speaks to Gideon of things that are not as though they are. Like many of us, Gideon tried to correct God's view of him by denying his abilities and disqualifying himself.

"The angel of the Lord appeared to him and said to him, 'The Lord is with you, O valiant warrior.' Then Gideon said to him, 'O my lord, if the Lord is with us, why then has all this happened to us? And where are all His miracles which our fathers told us about ... But now the Lord has abandoned us and given us into the hand of Midian.'

The Lord looked at him and said, 'Go in this your strength and deliver Israel from the hand of Midian. Have I not sent you?' He said to Him, 'O Lord, how shall I deliver Israel? Behold, my family is the least in Manasseh, and I am the youngest in my father's house.'" (Judges 6:12-15)

He overcomes his own fear, insecurity, inferiority and intimidation, and we desperately need leaders in the Church who have done the same in order to save nations from destruction. As soon as Gideon embraces his identity and takes up his true position, then authority begins to operate in his life.

"Now therefore come, proclaim in the hearing of the people, saying, 'Whoever is afraid and trembling, let him return and depart from Mount Gilead.' So 22,000 people returned, but 10,000 remained." (Judges 7:3)

Many were willing to fight, but few were chosen because of a stronghold of fear in their lives. Whether it came from their own experiences or generationally, fears disqualify them.

"But that no one is justified by the law in the sight of God is evident, for 'the just [Tsaddiyq] *shall live by faith.'"* (Galatians 3:11)

SPIRIT OF COMPROMISE

A key strongman we have to overcome is the spirit of compromise. We compromise the truth when watering down the gospel – by failing to release people to run faster and go further than us; when we do not take a stand against injustice and moral decay; and when we allow weaknesses and issues to remain in our lives that rob us of a victorious destiny and the power to succeed.

Yet success can also lead to compromise. I have seen ministries with a specific call and mission distracted from it by responding to the need they see rather than to Holy Spirit. They may succeed in those other areas, but in the process get sidetracked and miss their original mandate. King Solomon ended up being led astray, despite all the favor and wealth and success he had, because His eyes got diverted. Compromise will always end a revival and stop national transformation.

In the midst of the all the strongmen of his day and all the pressure to conform to how others were living their lives, Noah was faithful, despite the price of taking a stand when no one else would. He was uncompromising to the command of the Lord. We all have prophecies and promises from the Lord, but most are conditional, if only on us believing they will happen and pursing their fulfillment. When doubts creep in or we simply neglect them over time, compromise can take root and the promise is lost.

Within days of the birth of our ministry there was an attack so painful and traumatic that it would have been very easy to compromise and give up. Fortunately we knew someone with more experience and insight who was able to help us understand what was happening and show us how to deal with it. Since then there have been three other times when it would have been easy to compromise and receive position, status and financial benefits, not to mention a quiet life! Each time there was a price to pay running into hundreds of thousands of dollars. Noah kept focused on his calling and kept a pure heart and lifestyle. He did ALL that the Lord commanded him, despite the personal cost. Most often we see the big temptations and battles coming, but are not so aware or sensitive to the little ones.

"Catch the foxes for us, the little foxes that are ruining the vineyards, While our vineyards are in blossom." (Songs 2:15)

History shows us that at the height of anointing and revival, ministers and ministries can fall to the "little foxes". Under an open heaven both the good seed and the weeds in our lives accelerate in growth and fruitfulness. In 1707, Isaac Watts wrote his famous hymn, *When I Survey the Wondrous Cross*. The second verse says:

Forbid it, Lord, that I should boast,
Save in the death of Christ my God!
All the vain things that charm me most,
I sacrifice them to His blood.

BLACKSMITH'S FIRE

"'No weapon formed against you shall prosper, and every tongue which rises against you in judgment you shall condemn. This is the heritage of the servants of the Lord, and their righteousness is from Me,' says the Lord." (Isaiah 54:17)

Many have claimed this verse and even tried living in the truth of it. Most of us have experienced a measure of it or fleeting experiences of something more than we normally see. Few today constantly live in the fullness of this verse, but it is our promised heritage. Righteousness gives us our position and potential, but does not guarantee that we will see the first part of the verse happen.

On December 13, 2006, we were enjoying the start of a vacation in New Zealand when I got an email that changed our entire world and started us on a journey through the blacksmith's fire. For me that journey took until May 27, 2011, and cost us almost everything we had, both personally and as a ministry – our home, finances, ministry base, broken relationships, and much more. Now it seems worth it, but at the time it was incredibly hard.

At the center of the Father Heart message is the truth that we live in the fullness of His unconditional love for us. That position allows us to become the person He created us to be. From a place of sonship we are able to fulfill the calling on our lives. Church history is full of examples of those who started their race well, then stumbled or never ended their race well. In these end-time days the model is going to be very different. In order to become weapons against which no weapon shall prosper and to have the authority to silence judgmental voices raised against us, we have to visit the blacksmith's fire!

"Behold, I have created the blacksmith who blows the coals in the fire, who brings forth an instrument for his work..." (Isaiah 54:16)

Our loving Father, Abba, created a blacksmith's fire just for us! The heat of the fire brings to the surface the imperfections and impurities inside us, much like dross rises when gold or silver is heated up. Long buried character issues, pain and attitudes begin to come to the surface. Then we are placed on the anvil, caught between our passion for the Lord and a longing for His Kingdom to be seen on the earth, yet at the same time wanting the tempering blows to end. It is this tempering that builds strength into the core of our being. Finally, we are plunged into refreshing water and the changes are allowed to set before we head back to the fire again!

From my own experience, and of those who have gone through the same process, sometimes we went from the fire to the anvil to the fire to anvil again! The process is extremely challenging and often very discomforting, but we need to embrace it, because as Isaac Watts wrote at the end his hymn:

Love so amazing, so divine,

Demands my soul, my life, my all.

At first I thought that Isaiah 54 was the main passage that speaks about the preparation needed to be used by God, but as time has gone on I have found more of them. I mentioned earlier Joshua 5 and circumcision being the gateway into the Promised Land. Zechariah 3 is the prophetic story of Joshua the High Priest being prepared for office by having his filthy robes removed and replaced by rich robes and a new turban, so he could govern God's house. Esther spent nine months preparing for a single encounter with a king. When Pharaoh summoned Joseph to interpret his dream, he first had to be washed, shaved and a new robe given to him before he was able to move into creating a legacy for Israel. Do you see a trend here?

Malachi 3:1-3 describes the starting point for revival:

"'Behold, I send My messenger, and he will prepare the way before Me. And the Lord, whom you seek, will suddenly come to His temple, even the Messenger of the covenant, in whom you delight. Behold, He is coming,' says the Lord of hosts. 'But who can endure the day of His coming? And who can stand when He appears? For He is like a refiner's fire and like launderers' soap. He will sit as a refiner and a purifier of silver; He will purify the sons of Levi, and purge them as gold and silver, that they may offer to the Lord an offering in righteousness.'"

In his book, *The Coming Shift*, Larry Randolph writes:

"Tomorrow's success is shaped by our willingness to prepare today. This means that the depth of our anointing will be in direct proportion to our depth of preparation. The question is not whether there will be a great outpouring, but whether or not our spiritual well is deep enough to accommodate the coming rain. Like Noah, we must give ourselves to the issue of preparation long before the flood begins."

Darkness

In the end times, the prophet Isaiah tells us in Isaiah 60:2:

"For behold, the darkness shall cover the earth, and deep darkness the people; but the Lord will arise over you, and His glory will be seen upon you."

The Hebrew word for "glory" here is *kabowd* which also means "honor, abundance, splendor, riches". All these will be on a company of people in order to be a light in the escalating darkness. As challenging as the days ahead will be, this is going to be the finest hour for the Bride of Christ as she appears across the world.

To be bright lights in the darkness and to deal with the spiritual giants behind the deep darkness covering the people, we need to be ready to be brighter lights and greater glory carriers.

"The light shines in the darkness, and the darkness has not overcome it." (John 1:5)

"The people who were sitting in darkness saw a great light, and those

who were sitting in the land and shadow of death, upon them a light dawned." (Matthew 4:16)

Those two verses were written about Jesus and we are commissioned to be Christlike:

"Let your light shine before men in such a way that they may see your good works, and glorify your Father who is in heaven." (Matthew 5:16)

"But you, brethren, are not in darkness, that the day would overtake you like a thief; for you are all sons of light and sons of day." (1 Thessalonians 5:4-5)

The early Church believers understood and, more importantly, embraced this commissioning and calling. By Acts 11, they were "little Christs" and were the light of the world and the darkness could not overcome them. So long as they gave the glory to God everything went well, but when they tried to keep some of it for themselves, they were in trouble.

Compared to what is coming and how we are going to live, things are not very bright in the Church. But day by day that is changing, as a company of people complete their preparation in the blacksmith's fire and with the launderer's soap. Then we will see many who will truly be able to say the same as Jesus:

"For the ruler of this world is coming, and he has nothing in Me." (John 14:30)

For Gideon being faithful in the face of opposition meant a nation changed and at peace for the rest of his life.

"So Midian was subdued before the sons of Israel, and they did not lift up their heads anymore. And the land was undisturbed for forty years in the days of Gideon." (Judges 8:28)

For Noah it meant being chosen by God to save humanity from destruction. Now it is our turn to answer the call. It is time for this amazing company of people known as the Bride of Christ, the Sons of the Kingdom, the Overcomers, to arise!

Endnotes

Larry Randolph – *The Coming Shift*, MorningStar Publications, p167.

ANSWERING THE CALL

The invitation has been given to every believer to become part of this new move of God. My desire is that it will never be said of this generation that, *"He came to His own and those who were His own did not receive him"* (John 1: 11). Over two thousand years ago the Jews did not expect Jesus to come the way He did and many missed His appearing. I suspect this new move will use people that we do not expect.

The days ahead are like no generation has ever seen before and will require a stretching of our expectations and mindsets. Each year as we have travelled to different nations there is an increasing group of hungry and desperate disciples who are so on fire with love for the Lord that it marks them out. We have never seen what we are about to see.

"I proclaim to you new things from this time, even hidden things which you have not known. They are created now and not long ago; and before today you have not heard them, so that you will not say, 'Behold, I knew them.'" (Isaiah 48:6-7)

So much of the Lord's plan in these days is hidden, but little by little it is being released and year by year the picture becomes clearer. I believe God is doing it this way so that no one can put their hands on it and mess it up. Everyone I know who carries a prophetic anointing is saying the same thing in different ways – no one knows what it will look like when it comes.

If you love adventure, if you have had a stirring in your spirit over these last few years, then this is THE generation to be a part of. Days of surprises are upon us and the invitation is for all believers to be a part of what the Lord is about to unleash across the world.

These are days when we will recover what prior generations experienced or the anointing they moved in. Just as Isaac re-opened Abraham's wells in Genesis 16, the recovery of things lost is one step towards the fullness promised, but is still only what was lost. There is more to be released in these days than has ever been seen. Isaac's destination was Beersheba, and though there was contention (*esek*) and strife (*sitnah*) along on the way, he had to pass through Rehoboth (a wide place) in order to arrive at Beersheba, the well of the sevenfold oath, and a personal meeting with the Lord (Genesis 26:17-25).

Those who answer the call are being prepared to receive two such blessings: the release of the sevenfold spirit of God and strategic and significant encounters with the Lord. At the end of this life, Daniel is given a scroll that details all that would happen at the end of time and he saw a company of people in these days who be "illuminated ones":

"Those who have insight will shine brightly like the brightness of the expanse of heaven, and those who lead the many to righteousness, like the stars forever and ever. But as for you, Daniel, conceal these words and seal up the book until the end of time; many will go back and forth, and knowledge will increase." (Daniel 12:3)

Then he is granted a view of these days and the process of preparation and refining I have written about:

"Many will be purged, purified and refined, but the wicked will act wickedly; and none of the wicked will understand, but those who have insight will understand." (Daniel 12:10)

TRUMPET CALL

In the US Army, trumpets and bugles are used at important times of the day or to mark important events. At 6.00am the bugler sounds Reveille. Upon the last note of this call the flag is raised, the morning gun fired and the men all have to assemble for morning roll call.

The trumpet has been sounded, His banner has been raised and an assembling is taking place. The Bible tells us of this end time trumpet call that will go out around the world.

"And He will send His angels with a great sound of a trumpet, and they will gather together His elect from the four winds, from one end of heaven to the other." (Matthew 24:31)

Not only do we need eyes to see the transition that has taken place, but also ears to hear the trumpet call of heaven in these days. There is a gathering taking place and an army assembling.

Like Noah, will you answer the call?

Part Three

Appendices

THE BOOK OF ENOCH

CHAPTER 1

1 The word of the blessing of Enoch, how he blessed the elect and the righteous, who were to exist in the time of trouble; rejecting all the wicked and ungodly. Enoch, a righteous man, who was with God, answered and spoke, while his eyes were open, and while he saw a holy vision in the heavens. This the angels showed me.

2 From them I heard all things, and understood what I saw; that which will not take place in this generation, but in a generation which is to succeed at a distant period, on account of the elect.

3 Upon their account I spoke and conversed with him, who will go forth from his habitation, the Holy and Mighty One, the God of the world:

4 Who will hereafter tread upon Mount Sinai; appear with his hosts; and be manifested in the strength of his power from heaven.

5 All shall be afraid, and the Watchers be terrified.

6 Great fear and trembling shall seize them, even to the ends of the earth. The lofty mountains shall be troubled, and the exalted hills depressed, melting like a honeycomb in the flame. The earth shall be immerged, and all things which are in it perish; while judgment shall come upon all, even upon all the righteous:

7 But to them shall he give peace: he shall preserve the elect, and towards them exercise clemency.

8 Then shall all belong to God; be happy and blessed; and the splendor of the Godhead shall illuminate them.

CHAPTER 2

1 Behold, he comes with ten thousands of his saints, to execute judgment upon them, and destroy the wicked, and reprove all the carnal for everything which the sinful and ungodly have done, and committed against him.

Quoted by Jude:14-15.

CHAPTER 3

1 All who are in the heavens know what is transacted there.

2 They know that the heavenly luminaries change not their paths; that each rises and sets regularly, everyone at its proper period, without transgressing the commands, which they have received. The behold the earth, and understand what is there transacted, from the beginning to the end of it.

3 They see that every work of God is invariable in the period of its appearance. They behold summer and winter: perceiving that the whole earth is full of water; and that the cloud, the dew, and the rain refresh it.

CHAPTER 4

1 They consider and behold every tree, how it appears to wither, and every leaf to fall off, except of fourteen trees, which are not deciduous; which wait from the old, to the appearance of the new leaf, for two or three winters.

CHAPTER 5

1 Again they consider the days of summer, that the sun is upon it at its very beginning; while you seek for a covered and shady spot on account of the burning sun; while the earth is scorched up with fervid heat, and you become incapable of walking either upon the ground or upon the rocks in consequence of that heat.

CHAPTER 6

1 They consider how the trees, when they put forth their green leaves, become covered, and produce fruit; understanding everything, and knowing that He who lives forever does all these things for you:

2 That the works at the beginning of every existing year, that all his works, are subservient to him, and invariable; yet as God has appointed, so are all things brought to pass.

3 They see, too, how the seas and the rivers together complete their respective

operations:

4 But you endure not patiently, nor fulfill the commandments of the Lord; but you transgress and calumniate his greatness; and malignant are the words in your polluted mouths against his Majesty.

5 You withered in heart, no peace shall be to you!

6 Therefore your days shall you curse, and the years of your lives shall perish; perpetual execration shall be multiplied, and you shall not obtain mercy.

7 In those days shall you resign your peace with the eternal maledictions of all the righteous, and sinners shall perpetually execrate you;

8 Shall execrate you with the ungodly.

9 The elect shall possess light, joy, and peace; and they shall inherit the earth.

10 But you, you unholy, shall be accursed.

11 Then shall wisdom be given to the elect, all of whom shall live, and not again transgress by impiety or pride; but shall humble themselves, possessing prudence, and shall not repeat transgression.

12 They shall not be condemned the whole period of their lives, not die in torment and indignation; but the sum of their days shall be completed, and they shall grow old in peace; while the years of their happiness shall be multiplied with joy, and with peace, forever, the whole duration of their existence.

CHAPTER 7

1 It happened after the sons of men had multiplied in those days, that daughters were born to them, elegant and beautiful.

2 And when the angels,(3) the sons of heaven, beheld them, they became enamored of them, saying to each other, Come, let us select for ourselves wives from the progeny of men, and let us beget children.

3 Then their leader Samyaza said to them; I fear that you may perhaps be indisposed to the performance of this enterprise;

4 And that I alone shall suffer for so grievous a crime.

5 But they answered him and said; We all swear;

6 And bind ourselves by mutual execrations, that we will not change our intention, but execute our projected undertaking.

7 Then they swore all together, and all bound themselves by mutual execrations. Their whole number was two hundred, who descended upon Ardis,(4) which is the top of mount Armon.

8 That mountain therefore was called Armon, because they had sworn upon it,(5) and bound themselves by mutual execrations.

9 These are the names of their chiefs: Samyaza, who was their leader, Urakabarameel, Akibeel, Tamiel, Ramuel, Danel, Azkeel, Saraknyal, Asael, Armers, Batraal, Anane, Zavebe, Samsaveel, Ertael, Turel, Yomyael, Arazyal. These were the prefects of the two hundred angels, and the remainder were all with them.(6)

10 Then they took wives, each choosing for himself; whom they began to approach, and with whom they cohabited; teaching them sorcery, incantations, and the dividing of roots and trees.

11 And the women conceiving brought forth giants,(7)

12 Whose stature was each three hundred cubits. These devoured all which the labor of men produced; until it became impossible to feed them;

13 When they turned themselves against men, in order to devour them;

14 And began to injure birds, beasts, reptiles, and fishes, to eat their flesh one after another, (8) and to drink their blood.

15 Then the earth reproved the unrighteous.

(3) An Aramaic text reads "Watchers" here (J.T. Milik, Aramaic Fragments of Qumran Cave 4 [Oxford: Clarendon Press, 1976], p. 167).

(4) Upon Ardis. Or, "in the days of Jared" (R.H. Charles, ed. and trans., The Book of Enoch [Oxford: Clarendon Press, 1893], p. 63).

(5) Mt. Armon, or Mt. Hermon, derives its name from the Hebrew word herem, a curse (Charles, p. 63).

(6) The Aramaic texts preserve an earlier list of names of these Watchers: Semihazah; Artqoph; Ramtel; Kokabel; Ramel; Danieal; Zeqiel; Baraqel; Asael; Hermoni; Matarel; Ananel; Stawel; Samsiel; Sahriel; Tummiel; Turiel; Yomiel; Yhaddiel (Milik, p. 151).

(7) The Greek texts vary considerably from the Ethiopic text here. One Greek manuscript adds to this section, "And they [the women] bore to them [the Watchers] three races— first, the great giants. The giants brought forth [some say "slew"] the Naphelim, and the Naphelim brought forth [or "slew"] the Elioud. And they existed, increasing in power according to their greatness." See the account in the Book of Jubilees

(8) Their flesh one after another. Or, "one another's flesh." R.H. Charles notes that this phrase may refer to the destruction of one class of giants by another (Charles, p. 65).

CHAPTER 8

1 Moreover Azazyel taught men to make swords, knives, shields, breastplates, the fabrication of mirrors, and the workmanship of bracelets and ornaments, the use of paint, the beautifying of the eyebrows, the use of stones of every valuable and select kind, and all sorts of dyes, so that the world became altered.

2 Impiety increased; fornication multiplied; and they transgressed and corrupted all their ways.

3 Amazarak taught all the sorcerers, and dividers of roots:

4 Armers taught the solution of sorcery;

5 Barkayal taught the observers of the stars,(9)

6 Akibeel taught signs;

7 Tamiel taught astronomy;

8 And Asaradel taught the motion of the moon,

9 And men, being destroyed, cried out; and their voice reached to heaven.

(9) Observers of the stars. Astrologers (Charles, p. 67).

CHAPTER 9

1 Then Michael and Gabriel, Raphael, Suryal, and Uriel, looked down from heaven, and saw the quantity of blood which was shed on earth, and all the iniquity which was done upon it, and said one to another, It is the voice of their cries;

2 The earth deprived of her children has cried even to the gate of heaven.

3 And now to you, O you holy one of heaven, the souls of men complain, saying, Obtain Justice for us with(10) the Most High. Then they said to their Lord, the King, You are Lord of lords, God of gods, King of kings. The throne of your glory is forever and ever, and forever and ever is your name sanctified and glorified. You are blessed and glorified.

4 You have made all things; you possess power over all things; and all things are open and manifest before you. You behold all things, and nothing can be concealed from you.

5 You have seen what Azazyel has done, how he has taught every species of iniquity upon earth, and has disclosed to the world all the secret things which are done in the heavens.

6 Samyaza also has taught sorcery, to whom you have given authority over those who are associated with him. They have gone together to the daughters of men; have lain with them; have become polluted;

7 And have discovered crimes(11) to them.

8 The women likewise have brought forth giants.

9 Thus has the whole earth been filled with blood and with iniquity.

10 And now behold the souls of those who are dead, cry out.

11 And complain even to the gate of heaven.

12 Their groaning ascends; nor can they escape from the unrighteousness which is committed on earth. You know all things, before they exist.

13 You know these things, and what has been done by them; yet you do not speak to us.

14 What on account of these things ought we to do to them?

(10) Obtain justice for us with. Literally, "Bring judgment to us from." (Richard Laurence, ed. and trans., The Book of Enoch the Prophet [London: Kegan Paul, Trench & Co., 1883], p. 9).

(11) Discovered crimes. Or, "revealed these sins" (Charles, p. 70).

CHAPTER 10

1 Then the Most High, the Great and Holy One spoke,

2 And sent Arsayalalyur(12) to the son of Lamech,

3 Saying, Say to him in my name, Conceal yourself.

4 Then explain to him the consummation which is about to take place; for all the earth shall perish; the waters of a deluge shall come over the whole earth, and all things which are in it shall be destroyed.

5 And now teach him how he may escape, and how his seed may remain in all the earth.

6 Again the Lord said to Raphael, Bind Azazyel hand and foot; cast him into darkness; and opening the desert which is in Dudael, cast him in there.

7 Throw upon him hurled and pointed stones, covering him with darkness;

8 There shall he remain forever; cover his face, that he may not see the light.

9 And in the great day of judgment let him be cast into the fire.

10 Restore the earth, which the angels have corrupted; and announce life to it, that I may revive it.

11 All the sons of men shall not perish in consequence of every secret, by which the Watchers have destroyed, and which they have taught, their offspring.

12 All the earth has been corrupted by the effects of the teaching of Azazyel. To him therefore ascribe the whole crime.

13 To Gabriel also the Lord said, Go to the biters,(13) to the reprobates, to the children of fornication; and destroy the children of fornication, the offspring of the Watchers, from among men; bring them forth, and excite them one against another. Let them perish by mutual slaughter; for length of days shall not be theirs.

14 They shall all entreat you, but their fathers shall not obtain their wishes respecting them; for they shall hope for eternal life, and that they may live, each of them, five hundred years.

15 To Michael likewise the Lord said, Go and announce his crime to Samyaza, and to the others who are with him, who have been associated with women, that they might be polluted with all their impurity. And when all their sons shall be slain, when they shall see the perdition of their beloved, bind them for seventy generations underneath the earth, even to the day of judgment, and of consummation, until the judgment, the effect of which will last forever, be completed.

16 Then shall they be taken away into the lowest depths of the fire in torments; and in confinement shall they be shut up forever.

17 Immediately after this shall he,(14) together with them, burn and perish; they shall be bound until the consummation of many generations.

18 Destroy all the souls addicted to dalliance,(15) and the offspring of the Watchers, for they have tyrannized over mankind.

19 Let every oppressor perish from the face of the earth;

20 Let every evil work be destroyed;

21 The plant of righteousness and of rectitude appear, and its produce become a blessing.

22 Righteousness and rectitude shall be forever planted with delight.

23 And then shall all the saints give thanks, and live until they have begotten a thousand children, while the whole period of their youth, and their sabbaths shall be completed in peace. In those days all the earth shall be cultivated in righteousness; it shall be wholly planted with trees, and filled with benediction; every tree of delight shall be planted in it.

24 In it shall vines be planted; and the vine which shall be planted in it shall yield fruit to satiety; every seed, which shall be sown in it, shall produce for one measure a thousand; and one measure of olives shall produce ten presses of oil.

25 Purify the earth from all oppression, from all injustice, from all crime, from all impiety, and from all the pollution which is committed upon it. Exterminate them from the earth.

26 Then shall all the children of men be righteous, and all nations shall pay me divine honors, and bless me; and all shall adore me.

27 The earth shall be cleansed from all corruption, from every crime, from all punishment, and from all suffering; neither will I again send a deluge upon it from generation to generation forever.

28 In those days I will open the treasures of blessing which are in heaven, that I may cause them to descend upon earth, and upon all the works and labor of man.

29 Peace and equity shall associate with the sons of men all the days of the world, in every generation of it.

(12) Arsayalalyur. Here one Greek text reads "Uriel."
(13) Biters. More accurately, "bastards" (Charles, p. 73; Michael A. Knibb, ed. and trans., The Ethiopic Book of Enoch [Oxford: Clarendon Press, 1978], p. 88).
(14) He. I.e., Samyaza.
(15) Dalliance. Or, "lust" (Knibb, p. 90; cp. Charles, p. 76).

No Chapter 11

Chapter 12

1 Before all these things Enoch was concealed; nor did any one of the sons of men know where he was concealed, where he had been, and what had happened.

2 He was wholly engaged with the holy ones, and with the Watchers in his days.

3 I, Enoch, was blessing the great Lord and King of peace.

4 And behold the Watchers called me Enoch the scribe.

5 Then the Lord said to me: Enoch, scribe of righteousness, go tell the Watchers of heaven, who have deserted the lofty sky, and their holy everlasting station, who have been polluted with women.

6 And have done as the sons of men do, by taking to themselves wives, and who have been greatly corrupted on the earth;

7 That on the earth they shall never obtain peace and remission of sin. For they shall not rejoice in their offspring; they shall behold the slaughter of their beloved; shall lament for the destruction of their sons; and shall petition for ever; but shall not obtain mercy and peace.

Chapter 13

1 Then Enoch, passing on, said to Azazyel: You shalt not obtain peace. A great sentence is gone forth against you. He shall bind you;

2 Neither shall relief, mercy, and supplication be yours, on account of the oppression which you have taught;

3 And on account of every act of blasphemy, tyranny, and sin, which you have discovered to the children of men.

4 Then departing from him I spoke to them all together;

5 And they all became terrified, and trembled;

6 Beseeching me to write for them a memorial of supplication, that they

might obtain forgiveness; and that I might make the memorial of their prayer ascend up before the God of heaven; because they could not themselves thenceforwards address him, nor raise up their eyes to heaven on account of the disgraceful offence for which they were judged.

7 Then I wrote a memorial of their prayer and supplications, for their spirits, for everything which they had done, and for the subject of their entreaty, that they might obtain remission and rest.

8 Proceeding on, I continued over the waters of Danbadan(16) which is on the right to the west of Armon, reading the memorial of their prayer, until I fell asleep.

9 And behold a dream came to me, and visions appeared above me. I fell down and saw a vision of punishment, that I might relate it to the sons of heaven, and reprove them. When I awoke I went to them. All being collected together stood weeping in Oubelseyael, which is situated between Libanos and Seneser,(17) with their faces veiled.

10 I related in their presence all the visions which I had seen, and my dream;

11 And began to utter these words of righteousness, reproving the Watchers of heaven.

(16) Danbadan. Dan in Dan (Knibb, p. 94).

(17) Libanos and Seneser. Lebanon and Senir (near Damascus).

CHAPTER 14

1 This is the book of the words of righteousness, and of the reproof of the Watchers, who belong to the world,(18) according to that which He, who is holy and great, commanded in the vision. I perceived in my dream, that I was now speaking with a tongue of flesh, and with my breath, which the Mighty One has put into the mouth of men, that they might converse with it.

2 And understand with the heart. As he has created and given to men the power of comprehending the word of understanding, so has he created and given to me the power of reproving the Watchers, the offspring of heaven. I have written your petition; and in my vision it has been shown me, that what you request will not be granted you as long as the world endures.

3 Judgment has been passed upon you: your request will not be granted you.

4 From this time forward, never shall you ascend into heaven; He has said, that on the earth He will bind you, as long as the world endures.

5 But before these things you shall behold the destruction of your beloved

sons; you shall not possess them, but they shall fall before you by the sword.

6 Neither shall you entreat for them, not for yourselves;

7 But you shall weep and supplicate in silence. The words of the book which I wrote.(19)

8 A vision thus appeared to me.

9 Behold, in that vision clouds and a mist invited me; agitated stars and flashes of lightning impelled and pressed me forwards, while winds in the vision assisted my flight, accelerating my progress.

10 They elevated me aloft to heaven. I proceeded, until I arrived at a wall built with stones of crystal. A vibrating flame(20) surrounded it, which began to strike me with terror.

11 Into this vibrating flame I entered;

12 And drew nigh to a spacious habitation built also with stones of crystal. Its walls too, as well as pavement, were formed with stones of crystal, and crystal likewise was the ground. Its roof had the appearance of agitated stars and flashes of lightning; and among them were cherubim of fire in a stormy sky.(21) A flame burned around its walls; and its portal blazed with fire. When I entered into this dwelling, it was hot as fire and cold as ice. No trace of delight or of life was there. Terror overwhelmed me, and a fearful shaking seized me.

13 Violently agitated and trembling, I fell upon my face. In the vision I looked.

14 And behold there was another habitation more spacious than the former, every entrance to which was open before me, erected in the midst of a vibrating flame.

15 So greatly did it excel in all points, in glory, in magnificence, and in magnitude, that it is impossible to describe to you either the splendour or the extent of it.

16 Its floor was on fire; above were lightnings and agitated stars, while its roof exhibited a blazing fire.

17 Attentively I surveyed it, and saw that it contained an exalted throne;

18 The appearance of which was like that of frost; while its circumference resembled the orb of the brilliant sun; and there was the voice of the cherubim.

19 From underneath this mighty throne rivers of flaming fire issued.

20 To look upon it was impossible.

21 One great in glory sat upon it:

22 Whose robe was brighter than the sun, and whiter than snow.

23 No angel was capable of penetrating to view the face of Him, the Glorious and the Effulgent; nor could any mortal behold Him. A fire was flaming around Him.

24 A fire also of great extent continued to rise up before Him; so that not one

of those who surrounded Him was capable of approaching Him, among the myriads of myriads(22) who were before Him. To Him holy consultation was needless. Yet did not the sanctified, who were near Him, depart far from Him either by night or by day; nor were they removed from Him. I also was so far advanced, with a veil on my face, and trembling. Then the Lord with his own mouth called me, saying, Approach hither, Enoch, at my holy word.

25 And He raised me up, making me draw near even to the entrance. My eye was directed to the ground.

(18) Who belong to the world. Or, "who (are) from eternity" (Knibb, p. 95).

(19) But you shall weep…I wrote. Or, "Likewise despite your tears and prayers you will receive nothing whatever contained in the writing which I have written" (Charles, p. 80).

(20) Vibrating flame. Literally, "a tongue of fire"

(21)In a stormy sky. Literally, "and their heaven was water" (Charles, p. 81).

(22) Myriads of myriads. Ten thousand times ten thousands (Knibb, p. 99).

CHAPTER 15

1 Then addressing me, He spoke and said, Hear, neither be afraid, O righteous Enoch, you scribe of righteousness: approach hither, and hear my voice. Go, say to the Watchers of heaven, who have sent you to pray for them, You ought to pray for men, and not men for you.

2 Wherefore have you forsaken the lofty and holy heaven, which endures forever, and have lain with women; have defile yourselves with the daughters of men; have taken to yourselves wives; have acted like the sons of the earth, and have begotten an impious offspring?(23)

3 You being spiritual, holy, and possessing a life which is eternal, have polluted yourselves with women; have begotten in carnal blood; have lusted in the blood of men; and have done as those who are flesh and blood do.

4 These however die and perish.

5 Therefore have I given to them wives, that they might cohabit with them; that sons might be born of them; and that this might be transacted upon earth.

6 But you from the beginning were made spiritual, possessing a life which is eternal, and not subject to death for ever.

7 Therefore I made not wives for you, because, being spiritual, your dwelling is in heaven.

8 Now the giants, who have been born of spirit and of flesh, shall be called upon earth evil spirits, and on earth shall be their habitation. Evil spirits shall proceed from their flesh, because they were created from above; from the holy

Watchers was their beginning and primary foundation. Evil spirits shall they be upon earth, and the spirits of the wicked shall they be called. The habitation of the spirits of heaven shall be in heaven; but upon earth shall be the habitation of terrestrial spirits, who are born on earth.(24)

9 The spirits of the giants shall be like clouds,(25) which shall oppress, corrupt, fall, content, and bruise upon earth.

10 They shall cause lamentation. No food shall they eat; and they shall be thirsty; they shall be concealed, (26) rise up against the sons of men, and against women; for they come forth during the days of slaughter and destruction.

(23) An impious offspring. Literally, "giants" (Charles, p. 82; Knibb, p. 101).
Book of Enoch http://www.johnpratt.com/items/docs/enoch.html
(24) Note the many implications of vss. 3-8 regarding the progeny of evil spirits.
(25) The Greek word for "clouds" here, nephelas, may disguise a more ancient reading, Napheleim (Nephilim).
(26) Shall not. Nearly all manuscripts contain this negative, but Charles, Knibb, and others believe the "not" should be deleted so the phrase reads "shall rise up."

CHAPTER 16

1 And as to the death of the giants, wheresoever their spirits depart from their bodies, let their flesh, that which is perishable, be without judgment. (27) Thus shall they perish, until the day of the great consummation of the great world. A destruction shall take place of the Watchers and the impious.

2 And now to the Watchers, who have sent you to pray for them, who in the beginning were in heaven,

3 Say, In heaven have you been; secret things, however, have not been manifested to you; yet have you known a reprobated mystery.

4 And this you have related to women in the hardness of your heart, and by that mystery have women and mankind multiplied evils upon the earth.

5 Say to them, Never therefore shall you obtain peace.

(27) Let their flesh...be without judgment. Or, "their flesh shall be destroyed before the judgment" (Knibb, p. 102).

CHAPTER 17

1 They raised me up into a certain place, where there was(28) the appearance of a burning fire; and when they pleased they assumed the likeness of men.

2 They carried me to a lofty spot, to a mountain, the top of which reach to heaven.

3 And I beheld the receptacles of light and of thunder at the extremities of the place, where it was deepest. There was a bow of fire, and arrows in their quiver, a sword of fire, and every species of lightning.

4 Then they elevated me to a babbling stream,(29) and to a fire in the west, which received all the setting of the sun. I came to a river of fire, which flowed like water, and emptied itself into the great sea westwards.

5 I saw every large river, until I arrived at the great darkness. I went to where all of flesh migrate; and I beheld the mountains of the gloom which constitutes winter, and the place from which issues the later in every abyss.

6 I saw also the mouths of all the rivers in the world, and the mouths of the deep.

(28) Where there was. Or, "where they [the angels] were like" (Knibb, p. 103).

(29) To a babbling stream. Literally, "to water of life, which spoke" (Laurence, p. 23).

CHAPTER 18

1 I then surveyed the receptacles of all the winds, perceiving that they contributed to adorn the whole creation, and to preserve the foundation of the earth.

2 I surveyed the stone which supports the corners of the earth.

3 I also beheld the four winds, which bear up the earth, and the firmament of heaven.

4 And I beheld the winds occupying the exalted sky.

5 Arising in the midst of heaven and of earth, and constituting the pillars of heaven.

6 I saw the winds which turn the sky, which cause the orb of the sun and of all the stars to set; and over the earth I saw the winds which support the clouds.

7 I saw the path of the angels.

8 I perceived at the extremity of the earth the firmament of heaven above it. Then I passed on towards the south;

9 Where burnt, both by day and night, six mountains formed of glorious stones; three towards the east, and three towards the south.

10 Those which were towards the east were of a variegated stone; one of which was of margarite, and another of antimony. Those towards the south were of a red stone. The middle one reached to heaven like the throne of God; a throne composed of alabaster, the top of which was of sapphire. I saw, too, a blazing fire hanging over all the mountains.

11 And there I saw a place on the other side of an extended territory, where waters were collected.

12 I likewise beheld terrestrial fountains, deep in the fiery columns of heaven.

13 And in the columns of heaven I beheld fires, which descended without number, but neither on high, nor into the deep. Over these fountains also I perceived a place which had neither the firmament of heaven above it, nor the solid ground underneath it; neither was there water above it; nor anything on wing; but the spot was desolate.

14 And there I beheld seven stars, like great blazing mountains, and like spirits entreating me.

15 Then the angel said, This place, until the consummation of heaven and earth, will be the prison of the stars, and the host of heaven.

16 The stars which roll over fire are those which transgressed the commandment of God before their time arrived; for they came not in their proper season. Therefore was He offended with them, and bound them, until the period of the consummation of their crimes in the secret year.

CHAPTER 19

1 Then Uriel said, Here the angels, who cohabited with women, appointed their leaders;

2 And being numerous in appearance(30) made men profane, and caused them to err; so that they sacrificed to devils as to gods. For in the great day there shall be a judgment, with which they shall be judged, until they are consumed; and their wives also shall be judged, who led astray the angels of heaven that they might salute them.

3 And I, Enoch, I alone saw the likeness of the end of all things. Nor did any human being see it, as I saw it.

(30) Being numerous in appearance. Or, "assuming many forms" (Knibb, p. 106).

CHAPTER 20

1 These are the names of the angels who watch.

2 Uriel, one of the holy angels, who presides over clamor and terror.

3 Raphael, one of the holy angels, who presides over the spirits of men.

4 Raguel, one of the holy angels, who inflicts punishment on the world and the luminaries.

5 Michael, one of the holy angels, who, presiding over human virtue, commands

the nations.

6 Sarakiel, one of the holy angels, who presides over the spirits of the children of men that transgress.

7 Gabriel, one of the holy angels, who presides over Ikisat, (31) over paradise, and over the cherubim.

(31) Ikisat. The serpents (Charles, p. 92; Knibb, p. 107).

CHAPTER 21

1 Then I made a circuit to a place in which nothing was completed.

2 And there I beheld neither the tremendous workmanship of an exalted heaven, nor of an established earth, but a desolate spot, prepared, and terrific.

3 There, too, I beheld seven stars of heaven bound in it together, like great mountains, and like a blazing fire. I exclaimed, For what species of crime have they been bound, and why have they been removed to this place? Then Uriel, one of the holy angels who was with me, and who conducted me, answered: Enoch, wherefore do you ask; wherefore do you reason with yourself, and anxiously inquire? These are those of the stars which have transgressed the commandment of the most high God; and are here bound, until the infinite number of the days of their crimes be completed.

4 From there I afterwards passed on to another terrific place;

5 Where I beheld the operation of a great fire blazing and glittering, in the midst of which there was a division. Columns of fire struggled together to the end of the abyss, and deep was their descent. But neither its measurement nor magnitude was I able to discover; neither could I perceive its origin. Then I exclaimed, How terrible is this place, and how difficult to explore!

6 Uriel, one of the holy angels who was with me, answered and said: Enoch, why are you alarmed and amazed at this terrific place, at the sight of this place of suffering? This, he said, is the prison of the angels; and here they are kept forever.

CHAPTER 22

1 From there I proceeded to another spot, where I saw on the west a great and lofty mountain, a strong rock, and four delightful places.

2 Internally it was deep, capacious, and very smooth; as smooth as if it had been rolled over: it was both deep and dark to behold.

3 Then Raphael, one of the holy angels who were with me, answered and said,

These are the delightful places where the spirits, the souls of the dead, will be collected; for them were they formed; and here will be collected all the souls of the sons of men.

4 These places, in which they dwell, shall they occupy until the day of judgment, and until their appointed period.

5 Their appointed period will be long, even until the great judgment. And I saw the spirits of the sons of men who were dead; and their voices reached to heaven, while they were accusing.

6 Then I inquired of Raphael, an angel who was with me, and said, Whose spirit is that, the voice of which reaches to heaven, and accuses?

7 He answered, saying, This is the spirit of Abel who was slain by Cain his brother; and who will accuse that brother, until his seed be destroyed from the face of the earth;

8 Until his seed perish from the seed of the human race.

9 At that time therefore I inquired respecting him, and respecting the general judgment, saying, Why is one separated from another? He answered, Three separations have been made between the spirits of the dead, and thus have the spirits of the righteous been separated.

10 Namely, by a chasm, by water, and by light above it.

11 And in the same way likewise are sinners separated when they die, and are buried in the earth; judgment not overtaking them in their lifetime.

12 Here their souls are separated. Moreover, abundant is their suffering until the time of the great judgment, the castigation, and the torment of those who eternally execrate, whose souls are punished and bound there forever.

13 And thus has it been from the beginning of the world. Thus has there existed a separation between the souls of those who utter complaints, and of those who watch for their destruction, to slaughter them in the day of sinners.

14 A receptacle of this sort has been formed for the souls of unrighteous men, and of sinners; of those who have completed crime, and associated with the impious, whom they resemble. Their souls shall not be annihilated in the day of judgment, neither shall they arise from this place. Then I blessed God,

15 And said, Blessed by my Lord, the Lord of glory and of righteousness, who reigns over all forever and forever.

CHAPTER 23

1 From there I went to another place, towards the west, unto the extremities of the earth.

2 Where I beheld a fire blazing and running along without cessation, which intermitted its course neither by day nor by night; but continued always the same.

3 I inquired, saying, What is this, which never ceases?

4 Then Raguel, one of the holy angels who were with me, answered,

5 And said, This blazing fire, which you behold running towards the west, is that of all the luminaries of heaven.

CHAPTER 24

1 I went from there to another place, and saw a mountain of fire flashing both by day and night. I proceeded towards it; and perceived seven splendid mountains, which were all different from each other.

2 Their stones were brilliant and beautiful; all were brilliant and splendid to behold; and beautiful was their surface. Three mountains were towards the east, and strengthened by being placed one upon another; and three were towards the south, strengthened in a similar manner. There were likewise deep valleys, which did not approach each other. And the seventh mountain was in the midst of them. In length they all resembled the seat of a throne, and odoriferous trees surrounded them.

3 Among these there was a tree of an unceasing smell; nor of those which were in Eden was there one of all the fragrant trees which smelt like this. Its leaf, its flower, and its bark never withered, and its fruit was beautiful.

4 Its fruit resembled the cluster of the palm. I exclaimed, Behold! This tree is goodly in aspect, pleasing in its leaf, and the sight of its fruit is delightful to the eye. Then Michael, one of the holy and glorious angels who were with me, and one who presided over them, answered,

5 And said: Enoch, why do you inquire respecting the odour of this tree?

6 Why are you inquisitive to know it?

7 Then I, Enoch, replied to him, and said, Concerning everything I am desirous of instruction, but particularly concerning this tree.

8 He answered me, saying, That mountain which you behold, the extent of whose head resembles the seat of the Lord, will be the seat on which shall sit the holy and great Lord of glory, the everlasting King, when he shall come and descend to visit the earth with goodness.

9 And that tree of an agreeable smell, not one of carnal odor, there shall be no power to touch, until the period of the great judgment. When all shall be punished and consumed forever, this shall be bestowed on the righteous and

humble. The fruit of the tree shall be given to the elect. For towards the north life shall be planted in the holy place, towards the habitation of the everlasting King.

10 Then shall they greatly rejoice and exult in the Holy One. The sweet odor shall enter into their bones; and they shall live a long life on the earth as your forefathers have lived; neither in their days shall sorrow, distress, trouble, and punishment afflict them.

11 And I blessed the Lord of glory, the everlasting King, because He has prepared this tree for the saints, formed it, and declared that He would give it to them.

CHAPTER 25

1 From there I proceeded to the middle of the earth, and beheld a happy and fertile spot, which contained branches continually sprouting from the trees which were planted in it. There I saw a holy mountain, and underneath it water on the eastern side, which flowed towards the south. I saw also on the east another mountain as high as that; and between them there were deep, but not wide valleys.

2 Water ran towards the mountain to the west of this; and underneath there was likewise another mountain.

3 There was a valley, but not a wide one, below it; and in the midst of them were other deep and dry valleys towards the extremity of the three. All these valleys, which were deep, but not side, consisted of a strong rock, with a tree which was planted in them. And I wondered at the rock and at the valleys, being extremely surprised.

CHAPTER 26

1 Then I said, What means this blessed land, all these lofty trees, and the accursed valley between them?

2 Then Uriel, one of the holy angels who were with me, replied, This valley is the accursed of the accursed forever. Here shall be collected all who utter with their mouths unbecoming language against God, and speak harsh things of His glory. Here shall they be collected. Here shall be their territory.

3 In the latter days an example of judgment shall be made of them in righteousness before the saints; while those who have received mercy shall forever, all their days, bless God, the everlasting King.

4 And at the period of judgment shall they bless Him for his mercy, as He has distributed it to them. Then I blessed God, addressing myself to Him, and

making mention, as was meet, of His greatness.

CHAPTER 27
1 From there I proceeded towards the east to the middle of the mountain in the desert, the level surface only of which I perceived.
2 It was full of trees of the seed alluded to; and water leaped down upon it.
3 There appeared a cataract composed as of many cataracts both towards the west and towards the east. Upon one side were trees; upon the other water and dew.

CHAPTER 28
1 Then I went to another place from the desert; towards the east of that mountain which I had approached.
2 There I beheld choice trees,(32) particularly, those which produce the sweet-smelling opiate, frankincense and myrrh; and trees unlike to each other.
3 And over it, above them, was the elevation of the eastern mountain at no great distance.

(32) Choice trees. Literally, "trees of judgment" (Laurence, p. 35; Knibb, p. 117).

CHAPTER 29
1 I likewise saw another place with valleys of water which never wasted,
2 Where I perceived a goodly tree, which in smell resembled Zasakinon.(33)
3 And towards the sides of these valleys I perceived cinnamon of a sweet odour. Over them I advanced towards the east.

(33) Zasakinon. The mastic tree (Knibb, p. 118).

CHAPTER 30
1 Then I beheld another mountain containing trees, from which water flowed like Neketro,(34) Its name was Sarira, and Kalboneba.(35) And upon this mountain I beheld another mountain, upon which were trees of Alva. (36)
2 These trees were full, like almond trees, and strong; and when they produced fruit, it was superior to all redolence.

(34) Neketro. A nectar (Knibb, p. 119).
(35) Sarira, and Kalboneba. Styrax and galbanum (Knibb, p. 119).
(36) Alva. Aloe (Knibb, p. 119).

CHAPTER 31

1 After these things, surveying the entrances of the north, above the mountains, I perceived seven mountains replete with pure nard, odoriferous trees, cinnamon and papyrus.

2 From there I passed on above the summits of those mountains to some distance eastwards, and went over the Erythraean sea.(37) And when I was advanced far beyond it, I passed along above the angel Zateel, and arrived at the garden of righteousness. In this garden I beheld, among other trees, some which were numerous and large, and which flourished there.

3 Their fragrance was agreeable and powerful, and their appearance both varied and elegant. The tree of knowledge also was there, of which if any one eats, he becomes endowed with great wisdom.

4 It was like a species of the tamarind tree, bearing fruit which resembled grapes extremely fine; and its fragrance extended to a considerable distance. I exclaimed, How beautiful is this tree, and how delightful is its appearance!

5 Then holy Raphael, an angel who was with me, answered and said, This is the tree of knowledge, of which your ancient father and your aged mother ate, who were before you; and who, obtaining knowledge, their eyes being opened, and knowing themselves to be naked, were expelled from the garden.

(37) Erythraean sea. The Red Sea.

CHAPTER 32

1 From there I went on towards the extremities of the earth; where I saw large beasts different from each other, and birds various in their countenances and forms, as well as with notes of different sounds.

2 To the east of these beasts I perceived the extremities of the earth, where heaven ceased. The gates of heaven stood open, and I beheld the celestial stars come forth. I numbered them as they proceeded out of the gate, and wrote them all down, as they came out one by one according to their number. I wrote down their names altogether, their times and their seasons, as the angel Uriel, who was with me, pointed them out to me.

3 He showed them all to me, and wrote down an account of them.

4 He also wrote down for me their names, their regulations, and their operations.

CHAPTER 33

1 From there I advanced on towards the north, to the extremities of the earth.

2 And there I saw a great and glorious wonder at the extremities of the whole earth.

3 I saw there heavenly gates opening into heaven; three of them distinctly separated. The northern winds proceeded from them, blowing cold, hail, frost, snow, dew, and rain.

4 From one of the gates they blew mildly; but when they blew from the two other gates, it was with violence and force. They blew over the earth strongly.

CHAPTER 34

1 From there I went to the extremities of the world westwards;

2 Where I perceived three gates open, as I had seen in the north; the gates and passages through them being of equal magnitude.

CHAPTER 35

1 Then I proceeded to the extremities of the earth southwards; where I saw three gates open to the south, from which issued dew, rain, and wind.

2 From there I went to the extremities of heaven eastwards; where I saw three heavenly gates open to the east, which had smaller gates within them. Through each of these small gates the stars of heaven passed on, and proceeded towards the west by a path which was seen by them, and that at every period of their appearance.

3 When I beheld them, I blessed; every time in which they appeared, I blessed the Lord of glory, who had made those great and splendid signs, that they might display the magnificence of this works to angels and to the souls of men; and that these might glorify all his works and operations; might see the effect of his power; might glorify the great labour of his hands; and bless him forever.

NO CHAPTER 36

CHAPTER 37

1 The vision which he saw, the second vision of wisdom, which Enoch saw, the son of Jared, the son of Malaleel, the son of Canan, the son of Enos, the son of Seth, the son of Adam. This is the commencement of the word of wisdom, which I received to declare and tell to those who dwell upon earth. Hear from the beginning, and understand to the end, the holy things which I utter in the

presence of the Lord of spirits. Those who were before us thought it good to speak;

2 And let not us, who come after, obstruct the beginning of wisdom. Until the present period never has there been given before the Lord of spirits that which I have received, wisdom according the capacity of my intellect, and according to the pleasure of the Lord of spirits; that which I have received from him, a portion of life eternal.

3 And I obtained three parables, which I declared to the inhabitants of the world.

CHAPTER 38

1 Parable the first. When the congregation of the righteous shall be manifested; and sinners be judged for their crimes, and be troubled in the sight of the world;

2 When righteousness shall be manifested(38) in the presence of the righteous themselves, who will be elected for their good works duly weighed by the Lord of spirits; and when the light of the righteous and the elect, who dwell on earth, shall be manifested; where will the habitation of sinners be? And where the place of rest for those who have rejected the Lord of spirits? It would have been better for them, had they never been born.

3 When, too, the secrets of the righteous shall be revealed, then shall sinners be judged; and impious men shall be afflicted in the presence of the righteous and the elect.

4 From that period those who possess the earth shall cease to be powerful and exalted. Neither shall they be capable of beholding the countenances of the holy; for the light of the countenances of the holy, the righteous, and the elect, has been seen by the Lord of spirits.(39)

5 Yet shall not the mighty kings of that period be destroyed; but be delivered into the hands of the righteous and the holy.

6 Nor thenceforwards shall any obtain commiseration from the Lord of spirits, because their lives in this world will have been completed.

(38) When righteousness shall be manifested. Or, "when the Righteous One appears" (Knibb, p. 125; cp. Charles, p. 112).
(39) For the light...Lord of spirits. Or, "for the light of the Lord of spirits will have appeared on the face of the holy, the righteous, and the chosen" (Knibb, p. 126).

CHAPTER 39

1 In those days shall the elect and holy race descend from the upper heavens, and their seed shall then be with the sons of men. Enoch received books of indignation and wrath, and books of hurry and agitation.

2 Never shall they obtain mercy, saith the Lord of spirits.

3 A cloud then snatched me up, and the wind raised me above the surface of the earth, placing me at the extremity of the heavens.

4 There I saw another vision; I saw the habitations and resting places of the saints. There my eyes beheld their habitations with the angels, and their resting places with the holy ones. They were entreating, supplicating, and praying for the sons of men; while righteousness like water flowed before them, and mercy like dew was scattered over the earth. And thus shall it be with them forever and forever.

5 At that time my eyes beheld the dwelling of the elect, of truth, faith, and righteousness.

6 Countless shall be the number of the holy and the elect, in the presence of God for ever and forever.

7 Their residence I beheld under the wings of the Lord of spirits. All the holy and the elect sung before him, in appearance like a blaze of fire; their mouths being full of blessings, and their lips glorifying the name of the Lord of spirits. And righteousness incessantly dwelt before him.

8 There was I desirous of remaining, and my soul longed for that habitation. There was my antecedent inheritance; for thus had I prevailed before the Lord of spirits.

9 At that time I glorified and extolled the name of the Lord of spirits with blessing and with praise; for he has established it with blessing and with praise, according to his own good pleasure.

10 That place long did my eyes contemplate. I blessed and said, Blessed be he, blessed from the beginning for ever. In the beginning, before the world was created, and without end is his knowledge.

11 What is this world? Of every existing generation those shall bless you who do not spiritually sleep but stand before your glory, blessing, glorifying, exalting you, and saying, The holy, holy, Lord of spirits, fills the whole world of spirits.

12 There my eyes beheld all who, without sleeping, stand before him and bless him, saying, Blessed be you, and blessed be the name of God for ever and forever. Then my countenance became changed, until I was incapable of seeing.

Chapter 40

1 After this I beheld thousands of thousands, and myriads of myriads, and an infinite number of people, standing before the Lord of spirits.

2 On the four wings likewise of the Lord of spirits, on the four sides, I perceived others, besides those who were standing before him. Their names, too, I know; because the angel, who proceeded with me, declared them to me, discovering to me every secret thing.

3 Then I heard the voices of those upon the four sides magnifying the Lord of glory.

4 The first voice blessed the Lord of spirits forever and forever.

5 The second voice I heard blessing the Elect One, and the elect who suffer on account of the Lord of spirits.

6 The third voice I heard petitioning and praying for those who dwell upon earth, and supplicate the name of the Lord of spirits.

7 The fourth voice I heard expelling the impious angels,(40) and prohibiting them from entering into the presence of the Lord of spirits, to prefer accusations against(41) the inhabitants of the earth.

8 After this I besought the angel of peace, who proceeded with me, to explain all that was concealed. I said to him, Who are those whom I have seen on the four sides, and who words I have heard and written down? He replied, The first is the merciful, the patient, the holy Michael.

9 The second is he who presides over every suffering and every affliction of the sons of men, the holy Raphael. The third, who presides over all that is powerful, is Gabriel. And the fourth, who presides over repentance, and the hope of those who will inherit eternal life, is Phanuel. These are the four angels of the most high God, and their four voices, which at that time I heard.

(40) Impious angels. Literally, "the Satans" (Laurence, p. 45; Knibb, p. 128). Ha-satan in Hebrew ("the adversary") was originally the title of an office, not the name of an angel.
(41) Prefer accusations against. Or, "to accuse" (Charles, p. 119).

Chapter 41

1 After this I beheld the secrets of the heavens and of paradise, according to its divisions; and of human action, as they weight it there in balances. I saw the habitations of the elect, and the habitations of the holy. And there my eyes beheld all the sinners, who denied the Lord of glory, and whom they were expelling from there, and dragging away, as they stood there; no punishment

proceeding against them from the Lord of spirits.

2 There, too, my eyes beheld the secrets of the lightning and the thunder; and the secrets of the winds, how they are distributed as they blow over the earth: the secrets of the winds, of the dew, and of the clouds. There I perceived the place from which they issued forth, and became saturated with the dust of the earth.

3 There I saw the wooden receptacles out of which the winds became separated, the receptacle of hail, the receptacle of snow, the receptacle of the clouds, and the cloud itself, which continued over the earth before the creation of the world.

4 I beheld also the receptacles of the moon, whence they came, whither they proceeded, their glorious return, and how one became more splendid than another. I marked their rich progress, their unchangeable progress, their disunited and undiminished progress; their observance of a mutual fidelity by a stable oath; their proceeding forth before the sun, and their adherence to the path allotted them,(42) in obedience to the command of the Lord of spirits. Potent is his name for ever and forever.

5 After this I perceived, that the path both concealed and manifest of the moon, as well as the progress of its path, was there completed by day and by night; while each, one with another, looked towards the Lord of spirits, magnifying and praising without cessation, since praise to them is rest; for in the splendid sun there is a frequent conversion to blessing and to malediction.

6 The course of the moon's path to the righteous is light, but to sinners it is darkness; in the name of the Lord of spirits, who created a division between light and darkness, and, separating the spirits of men, strengthened the spirits of the righteous in the name of his own righteousness.

7 Nor does the angel prevent this, neither is he endowed with the power of preventing it; for the Judge beholds them all, and judges them all in his own presence.

(42) Their proceeding forth...path allotted them. Or, "the sun goes out first and completes its journey" (Knibb, p. 129; cp. Charles, p. 122).

Chapter 42

1 Wisdom found not a place on earth where she could inhabit; her dwelling therefore is in heaven.

2 Wisdom went forth to dwell among the sons of men, but she obtained not

a habitation. Wisdom returned to her place, and seated herself in the midst of the angels. But iniquity went forth after her return, who unwillingly found a habitation, and resided among them, as rain in the desert, and as a dew in a thirsty land.

Chapter 43

1 I beheld another splendour, and the stars of heaven. I observed that he called them all by their respective names, and that they heard. In a righteous balance I saw that he weighed out with their light the amplitude of their places, and the day of their appearance, and their conversion. Splendour produced splendour; and their conversion was into the number of the angels, and of the faithful.

2 Then I inquired of the angel, who proceeded with me, and explained to me secret things, What their names were. He answered. A similitude of those has the Lord of spirits shown you. They are names of the righteous who dwell upon earth, and who believe in the name of the Lord of spirits forever and forever.

Chapter 44

1 Another thing also I saw respecting splendour; that it rises out of the stars, and becomes splendour; being incapable of forsaking them.

Chapter 45

1 Parable the second, respecting these who deny the name of the habitation of the holy ones, and of the Lord of spirits.

2 Heaven they shall not ascend, nor shall they come on the earth. This shall be the portion of sinners, who deny the name of the Lord of spirits, and who are thus reserved for the day of punishment and of affliction.

3 In that day shall the Elect One sit upon a throne of glory; and shall choose their conditions and countless habitations, while their spirits within them shall be strengthened, when they behold my Elect One, for those who have fled for protection to my holy and glorious name.

4 In that day I will cause my Elect One to dwell in the midst of them; will change the face of heaven; will bless it, and illuminate it forever.

5 I will also change the face of the earth, will bless it; and cause those whom I have elected to dwell upon it. But those who have committed sin and iniquity shall not inhabit it, for I have marked their proceedings. My righteous ones will I satisfy with peace, placing them before me; but the condemnation of sinners shall draw near, that I may destroy them from the face of the earth.

CHAPTER 46

1 There I beheld the Ancient of days, whose head was like white wool, and with him another, whose countenance resembled that of man. His countenance was full of grace, like that of one of the holy angels. Then I inquired of one of the angels, who went with me, and who showed me every secret thing, concerning this Son of man; who he was; whence he was and why he accompanied the Ancient of days.

2 He answered and said to me, This is the Son of man, to whom righteousness belongs; with whom righteousness has dwelt; and who will reveal all the treasures of that which is concealed: for the Lord of spirits has chosen him; and his portion has surpassed all before the Lord of spirits in everlasting uprightness.

3 This Son of man, whom you behold, shall raise up kings and the mighty from their dwelling places, and the powerful from their thrones; shall loosen the bridles of the powerful, and break in pieces the teeth of sinners.

4 He shall hurl kings from their thrones and their dominions; because they will not exalt and praise him, nor humble themselves before him, by whom their kingdoms were granted to them. The countenance likewise of the mighty shall He cast down, filling them with confusion. Darkness shall be their habitation, and worms shall be their bed; nor from that their bed shall they hope to be again raised, because they exalted not the name of the Lord of spirits.

5 They shall condemn the stars of heaven, shall lift up their hands against the Most High, shall tread upon and inhabit the earth, exhibiting all their acts of iniquity, even their works of iniquity. Their strength shall be in their riches, and their faith in the gods whom they have formed with their own hands. They shall deny the name of the Lord of spirits, and shall expel him from the temples, in which they assemble;

6 And with him the faithful,(43) who suffer in the name of the Lord of spirits.

(43) Shall expel him...the faithful. Or, "will be driven from the houses of his congregation, and of the faithful" (Knibb, p. 132; cp. Charles, p. 131).

CHAPTER 47

1 In that day the prayer of the holy and the righteous, and the blood of the righteous, shall ascend from the earth into the presence of the Lord of spirits.

2 In that day shall the holy ones assemble, who dwell above the heavens, and with united voice petition, supplicate, praise, laud, and bless the name of the Lord of spirits, on account of the blood of the righteous which has been shed;

that the prayer of the righteous may not be intermitted before the Lord of spirits; that for them he would execute judgment; and that his patience may not endure forever.(44)

3 At that time I beheld the Ancient of days, while he sat upon the throne of his glory, while the book of the living was opened in his presence, and while all the powers which were above the heavens stood around and before him.

4 Then were the hearts of the saints full of joy, because the consummation of righteousness was arrived, the supplication of the saints heard, and the blood of the righteous appreciated by the Lord of spirits.

(44) That his patience...endure forever. Or, "(that) their patience may not have to last forever" (Knibb, p. 133).

CHAPTER 48

1 In that place I beheld a fountain of righteousness, which never failed, encircled by many springs of wisdom. Of these all the thirsty drank, and were filled with wisdom, having their habitation with the righteous, the elect, and the holy.

2 In that hour was this Son of man invoked before the Lord of spirits, and his name in the presence of the Ancient of days.

3 Before the sun and the signs were created, before the stars of heaven were formed, his name was invoked in the presence of the Lord of spirits. A support shall he be for the righteous and the holy to lean upon, without falling; and he shall be the light of nations.

4 He shall be the hope of those whose hearts are troubled. All, who dwell on earth, shall fall down and worship before him; shall bless and glorify him, and sing praises to the name of the Lord of spirits.

5 Therefore the Elect and the Concealed One existed in his presence, before the world was created, and forever.

6 In his presence he existed, and has revealed to the saints and to the righteous the wisdom of the Lord of spirits; for he has preserved the lot of the righteous, because they have hated and rejected this world of iniquity, and have detested all its works and ways, in the name of the Lord of spirits.

7 For in his name shall they be preserved; and his will shall be their life. In those days shall the kings of the earth and the mighty men, who have gained the world by their achievements, become humble in countenance.

8 For in the day of their anxiety and trouble their souls shall not be saved; and they shall be in subjection to those whom I have chosen.

9 I will cast them like hay into the fire, and like lead into the water. Thus shall they burn in the presence of the righteous, and sink in the presence of the holy; nor shall a tenth part of them be found.

10 But in the day of their trouble, the world shall obtain tranquillity.

11 In his presence shall they fall, and not be raised up again; nor shall there be any one to take them out of his hands, and to lift them up: for they have denied the Lord of spirits, and his Messiah. The name of the Lord of spirits shall be blessed.

CHAPTER 48A(45)

1 Wisdom is poured forth like water, and glory fails not before him forever and ever; for potent is he in all the secrets of righteousness.

2 But iniquity passes away like a shadow, and possesses not a fixed station: for the Elect One stands before the Lord of spirits; and his glory is forever and ever; and his power from generation to generation.

3 With him dwells the spirit of intellectual wisdom, the spirit of instruction and of power, and the spirit of those who sleep in righteousness; he shall judge secret things.

4 Nor shall any be able to utter a single word before him; for the Elect One is in the presence of the Lord of Spirits, according to his own pleasure.

(45) Two consecutive chapters are numbered "48."

CHAPTER 49

1 In those days the saints and the chosen shall undergo a change. The light of day shall rest upon them; and the splendour and glory of the saints shall be changed.

2 In the day of trouble evil shall be heaped up upon sinners; but the righteous shall triumph in the name of the Lord of spirits.

3 Others shall be made to see, that they must repent, and forsake the works of their hands; and that glory awaits them not in the presence of the Lord of spirits; yet that by his name they may be saved. The Lord of spirits will have compassion on them; for great is his mercy; and righteousness is in his judgment, and in the presence of his glory; nor in his judgment shall iniquity stand. He who repents not before him shall perish.

4 Henceforward I will not have mercy on them, saith the Lord of spirits.

Chapter 50

1 In those days shall the earth deliver up from her womb, and hell deliver up from hers, that which it has received; and destruction shall restore that which it owes.

2 He shall select the righteous and holy from among them; for the day of their salvation has approached.

3 And in those days shall the Elect One sit upon his throne, while every secret of intellectual wisdom shall proceed from his mouth, for the Lord of spirits has gifted and glorified him.

4 In those days the mountains shall skip like rams, and the hills shall leap like young sheep(46) satiated with milk; and all the righteous shall become like angels in heaven.

5 Their countenance shall be bright with joy; for in those days shall the Elect One be exalted. The earth shall rejoice; the righteous shall inhabit it, and the elect possess it.

(46) Cp. Psalm 114:4

Chapter 51

1 After that period, in the place where I had seen every secret sight, I was snatched up in a whirlwind, and carried off westwards.

2 There my eyes beheld the secrets of heaven, and all which existed on earth; a mountain of iron, a mountain of copper, a mountain of silver, a mountain of gold, a mountain of fluid metal, and a mountain of lead.

3 And I inquired of the angel who went with me, saying, What are these things, which in secret I behold?

4 He said, All these things which you behold shall be for the dominion of the Messiah, that he may command, and be powerful upon earth.

5 And that angel of peace answered me, saying, Wait but a short time, and you shalt understand, and every secret thing shall be revealed to you, which the Lord of spirits has decreed. Those mountains which you have seen, the mountain of iron, the mountain of copper, the mountain of silver, the mountain of gold, the mountain of fluid metal, and the mountain of lead, all these in the presence of the Elect One shall be like a honeycomb before the fire, and like water descending from above upon these mountains; and shall become debilitated before his feet.

6 In those days men shall not be saved by gold and by silver.

7 Nor shall they have it in their power to secure themselves, and to fly.

8 There shall be neither iron for was, nor a coat of mail for the breast.

9 Copper shall be useless; useless also that which neither rusts nor consumes away; and lead shall not be coveted.

10 All these things shall be rejected, and perish from off the earth, when the Elect One shall appear in the presence of the Lord of spirits.

CHAPTER 52

1 There my eyes beheld a deep valley; and wide was its entrance.

2 All who dwell on land, on the sea, and in islands, shall bring to it gifts, presents, and offerings; yet that deep valley shall not be full. Their hands shall commit iniquity. Whatsoever they produce by labour, the sinners shall devour with crime. But they shall perish from the face of the Lord of spirits, and from the face of his earth. They shall stand up, and shall not fail forever and ever.

3 I beheld the angels of punishment, who were dwelling there, and preparing every instrument of Satan.

4 Then I inquired of the angel of peace, who proceeded with me, for whom those instruments were preparing.

5 He said, These they are preparing for the kings and powerful ones of the earth, that thus they may perish.

6 After which the righteous and chosen house of his congregation shall appear, and thenceforward unchangeable in the name of the Lord of spirits.

7 Nor shall those mountains exist in his presence as the earth and the hills, as the fountains of water exist. And the righteous shall be relieved from the vexation of sinners.

CHAPTER 53

1 Then I looked and turned myself to another part of the earth, where I beheld a deep valley burning with fire.

2 To this valley they brought monarchs and the mighty.

3 And there my eyes beheld the instruments which they were making, fetters of iron without weight. (47)

4 Then I inquired of the angel of peace, who proceeded with me, saying, For whom are these fetters and instruments prepared?

5 He replied, These are prepared for the host of Azazeel, that they may be delivered over and adjudged to the lowest condemnation; and that their angels may be overwhelmed with hurled stones, as the Lord of spirits has commanded.

6 Michael and Gabriel, Raphael and Phanuel shall be strengthened in that day, and shall then cast them into a furnace of blazing fire, that the Lord of spirits may be avenged of them for their crimes; because they became ministers of Satan, and seduced those who dwell upon earth.

7 In those days shall punishment go forth from the Lord of spirits; and the receptacles of water which are above the heavens shall be opened, and the fountains likewise, which are under the heavens and under the earth.

8 All the waters, which are in the heavens and above them, shall be mixed together.

9 The water which is above heaven shall be the agent;(48)

10 And the water which is under the earth shall be the recipient:(49) and all shall be destroyed who dwell upon earth, and who dwell under the extremities of heaven.

11 By these means shall they understand the iniquity which they have committed on earth: and by these means shall they perish.

(47) Without weight. Or, "of immeasurable weight" (Knibb, p. 138).
(48) Agent. Literally, "male" (Laurence, p. 61).
(49) Recipient. Literally, "female" (Laurence, p. 61).

CHAPTER 54

1 Afterwards the Ancient of days repented, and said, In vain have I destroyed all the inhabitants of the earth.

2 And he sware by his great name, saying, Henceforwards I will not act thus towards all those who dwell upon earth.

3 But I will place a sign in the heavens;(50) and it shall be a faithful witness between me and them forever, as long as the days of heaven and earth last upon the earth.

4 Afterwards, according to this my decree, when I shall be disposed to seize them beforehand, by the instrumentality of angels, in the day of affliction and trouble, my wrath and my punishment shall remain upon them, my punishment and my wrath, saith God the Lord of spirits.

5 O you kings, O you mighty, who inhabit the world you shall behold my Elect One, sitting upon the throne of my glory. And he shall judge Azazeel, all his associates, and all his hosts, in the name of the Lord of spirits.

6 There likewise I beheld hosts of angels who were moving in punishment, confined in a net-work of iron and brass. Then I inquired of the angel of peace,

who proceeded with me, To whom those under confinement were going.

7 He said, To each of their elect and their beloved,(51) that they may be cast into the fountains and deep recesses of the valley.

8 And that valley shall be filled with their elect and beloved; the days of whose life shall be consumed, but the days of their error shall be innumerable.

9 Then shall princes(52) combine together, and conspire. The chiefs of the east, among the Parthians and Medes, shall remove kings, in whom a spirit of perturbation shall enter. They shall hurl them from their thrones, springing as lions from their dens, and like famished wolves into the midst of the flock.

10 They shall go up, and tread upon the land of their elect. The land of their elect shall be before them. The threshing-floor, the path, and the city of my righteous people shall impede the progress of their horses. They shall rise up to destroy each other; their right hand shall be strengthened; nor shall a man acknowledge his friend or his brother;

11 Nor the son his father and his mother; until the number of the dead bodies shall be completed, by their death and punishment. Neither shall this take place without cause.

12 In those days shall the mouth of hell be opened, into which they shall be immerged; hell shall destroy and swallow up sinners from the face of the elect.

(50) Cp. Gen. 9:13, "I do set my bow in the cloud, and it shall be for a token of a covenant between me and the earth."
(51) To each of...their beloved. Or, "Each to his own chosen ones and to his own beloved ones" (Knibb, p. 139).
(52) Princes. Or, "angels" (Charles, p. 149; Knibb, p. 140).

CHAPTER 55

1 After this I beheld another army of chariots with men riding in them.

2 And they came upon the wind from the east, from the west, and from the south.(53)

3 The sound of the noise of their chariots was heard.

4 And when that agitation took place; the saints out of heaven perceived it; the pillar of the earth shook from its foundation; and the sound was heard from the extremities of the earth unto the extremities of heaven at the same time.

5 Then they all fell down, and worshipped the Lord of spirits.

6 This is the end of the second parable.

(53) From the south. Literally, "from the midst of the day" (Laurence, p. 63).

Chapter 56

1 I now began to utter the third parable, concerning the saints and the elect.

2 Blessed are you, O saints and elect, for glorious is your lot.

3 The saints shall exist in the light of the sun, and the elect in the light of everlasting life, the days of whose life shall never terminate; nor shall the days of the saints be numbered, who seek for light, and obtain righteousness with the Lord of spirits.

4 Peace be to the saints with the Lord of the world.

5 Henceforward shall the saints be told to seek in heaven the secrets of righteousness, the portion of faith; for like the sun has it arisen upon the earth, while darkness has passed away. There shall be light interminable; nor shall they enter upon the enumeration of time; for darkness shall be previously destroyed, and light shall increase before the Lord of spirits; before the Lord of spirits shall the light of uprightness increase for ever.

Chapter 57

1 In those days my eyes beheld the secrets of the lightnings and the splendours, and the judgment belonging to them.

2 They lighten for a blessing and for a curse, according to the will of the Lord of spirits.

3 And there I saw the secrets of the thunder, when it rattles above in heaven, and its sound is heard.

4 The habitations also of the earth were shown to me. The sound of the thunder is for peace and for blessing, as well as for a curse, according to the word of the Lord of spirits.

5 Afterwards every secret of the splendours and of the lightnings was seen by me. For blessing and for fertility they lighten.

Chapter 58

1 In the five hundredth year, and in the seventh month, on the fourteenth day of the month, of the lifetime of Enoch, in that parable, I saw that the heaven of heavens shook; that it shook violently; and that the powers of the Most High, and the angels, thousands and thousands, and myriads of myriads, were agitated with great agitation. And when I looked, the Ancient of days was sitting on the throne of his glory, while the angels and saints were standing around him. A great trembling came upon me, and terror seized me. My loins were bowed down and loosened; my reins were dissolved; and I fell upon my face.

The holy Michael, another holy angel, one of the holy ones, was sent, who raised me up.

2 And when he raised me, my spirit returned; for I was incapable of enduring this vision of violence, its agitation, and the concussion of heaven.

3 Then holy Michael said to me, Why are you disturbed at this vision?

4 Hitherto has existed the day of mercy; and he has been merciful and longsuffering towards all who dwell upon the earth.

5 But when the time shall come, then shall the power, the punishment, and the judgment take place, which the Lord of spirits has prepared for those who prostrate themselves to the judgment of righteousness, for those who abjure that judgment, and for those who take his name in vain.

6 That day has been prepared for the elect as a day of covenant; and for sinners as a day of inquisition.

7 In that day shall be distributed for food(54) two monsters; a female monster, whose name is Leviathan, dwelling in the depths of the sea, above the springs of waters;

8 And a male monster, whose name is Behemoth; which possesses, moving on his breast, the invisible wilderness.

9 His name was Dendayen in the east of the garden, where the elect and the righteous will dwell; where he received it from my ancestor, who was man, from Adam the first of men,(55) whom the Lord of spirits made.

10 Then I asked of another angel to show me the power of those monsters, how they became separated, how they became separated on the same day, one being in the depths of the sea, and one in the dry desert.

11 And he said, You, son of man, are here desirous of understanding secret things.

12 And the angel of peace, who was with me, said, These two monsters are by the power of God prepared to become food, that the punishment of God may not be in vain.

13 Then shall children be slain with their mothers, and sons with their fathers.

14 And when the punishment of the Lord of spirits shall continue, upon them shall it continue, that the punishment of the Lord of spirits may not take place in vain. After that, judgment shall exist with mercy and longsuffering.

(54) Distributed for food. Or, "separated from one another" (Knibb, p. 143).
(55) He received it...first of men. Or, "my [great-] grandfather was taken up, the seventh from Adam" (Charles, p. 155). This implies that this section of the book was written by Noah, Enoch's descendant, rather than Enoch. Scholars have speculated that this

portion of the book may contain fragments of the lost Apocalypse of Noah.

CHAPTER 59

1 Then another angel, who proceeded with me, spoke to me;

2 And showed me the first and last secrets in heaven above, and in the depths of the earth:

3 In the extremities of heaven, and in the foundations of it, and in the receptacle of the winds.

4 He showed me how their spirits were divided; how they were balanced; and how both the springs and the winds were numbered according to the force of their spirit.

5 He showed me the power of the moon's light, that its power is a just one; as well as the divisions of the stars, according to their respective names;

6 That every division is divided; that the lightning flashes;

7 That its troops immediately obey; and that a cessation takes place during thunder in continuance of its sound. Nor are the thunder and the lightning separated; neither do both of them move with one spirit; yet they are not separated.

8 For when the lightning lightens, the thunder sounds, and the spirit at a proper period pauses, making an equal division between them; for the receptacle, upon which their periods depend, is loose as sand. Each of them at a proper season is restrained with a bridle; and turned by the power of the spirit, which thus propels them according to the spacious extent of the earth.

9 The spirit likewise of the sea is potent and strong; and as a strong power causes it to ebb, so is it driven forwards, and scattered against the mountains of the earth. The spirit of the frost has its angel; in the spirit of hail there is a good angel; the spirit of snow ceases in its strength, and a solitary spirit is in it, which ascends from it like vapour, and is called refrigeration.

10 The spirit also of mist dwells with them in their receptacle; but it has a receptacle to itself; for its progress is in splendour.

11 In light, and in darkness, in winter and in summer. Its receptacle is bright, and an angel is in it.

12 The spirit of dew has its abode in the extremities of heaven, in connection with the receptacle of rain; and its progress is in winter and in summer. The cloud produced by it, and the cloud of the mist, become united; one gives to the other; and when the spirit of rain is in motion from its receptacle, angels come, and opening its receptacle, bring it forth.

13 When likewise it is sprinkled over all the earth, it forms an union with every kind of water on the ground; for the waters remain on the ground, because they afford nourishment to the earth from the Most High, who is in heaven.

14 Upon this account therefore there is a regulation in the quantity of rain, which the angels receive.

15 These things I saw; all of them, even paradise.

CHAPTER 60

1 In those days I beheld long ropes given to those angels; who took to their wings, and fled, advancing towards the north.

2 And I inquired of the angel, saying, Wherefore have they taken those long ropes, and gone forth? He said, They are gone forth to measure.

3 The angel, who proceeded with me, said, These are the measures of the righteous; and cords shall the righteous bring, that they may trust in the name of the Lord of spirits forever and ever.

4 The elect shall begin to dwell with the elect.

5 And these are the measures which shall be given to faith, and which shall strengthen the words of righteousness.

6 These measures shall reveal all the secrets in the depth of the earth.

7 And it shall be, that those who have been destroyed in the desert, and who have been devoured by the fish of the sea, and by wild beasts, shall return, and trust in the day of the Elect One; for none shall perish in the presence of the Lord of spirits, nor shall any be capable of perishing.

8 Then they received the commandment, all who were in the heavens above; to whom a combined power, voice, and splendour, like fire, were given.

9 And first, with their voice, they blessed him, they exalted him, they glorified him with wisdom, and ascribed to him wisdom with the word, and with the breath of life.

10 Then the Lord of spirits seated upon the throne of his glory the Elect One;

11 Who shall judge all the works of the holy, in heaven above, and in a balance shall he weigh their actions. And when he shall lift up his countenance to judge their secret ways in the word of the name of the Lord of spirits, and their progress in the path of the righteous judgment of God most high;

12 They shall all speak with united voice; and bless, glorify, exalt, and praise, in the name of the Lord of spirits.

13 He shall call to every power of the heavens, to all the holy above, and to the power of God. The Cherubim, the Seraphim, and the Ophanin, all the angels

of power, and all the angels of the Lords, namely, of the Elect One, and of the other Power, who was upon earth over the water on that day,

14 Shall raise their united voice; shall bless, glorify, praise, and exalt with the spirit of faith, with the spirit of wisdom and patience, with the spirit of mercy, with the spirit of judgment and peace, and with the spirit of benevolence; all shall say with united voice; Blessed is He; and the name of the Lord of spirits shall be blessed forever and forever; all, who sleep not, shall bless it in heaven above.

15 All the holy in heaven shall bless it; all the elect who dwell in the garden of life; and every spirit of light, who is capable of blessing, glorifying, exalting, and praising your holy name; and every mortal man,(56) more than the powers of heaven, shall glorify and bless your name forever and ever.

16 For great is the mercy of the Lord of spirits; long-suffering is he; and all his works, all his power, great as are the things which he has done, has he revealed to the saints and to the elect, in the name of the Lord of spirits.

(56) Every mortal man. Literally, "all of flesh" (Laurence, p. 73).

CHAPTER 61

1 Thus the Lord commanded the kings, the princes, the exalted, and those who dwell on earth, saying, Open your eyes, and lift up your horns, if you are capable of comprehending the Elect One.

2 The Lord of spirits sat upon the throne of his glory.

3 And the spirit of righteousness was poured out over him.

4 The word of his mouth shall destroy all the sinners and all the ungodly, who shall perish at his presence.

5 In that day shall all the kings, the princes, the exalted, and those who possess the earth, stand up, behold, and perceive, that he is sitting on the throne of his glory; that before him the saints shall be judged in righteousness;

6 And that nothing, which shall be spoken before him, shall be spoken in vain.

7 Trouble shall come upon them, as upon a woman in travail, whose labour is severe, when her child comes to the mouth of the womb, and she finds it difficult to bring forth.

8 One portion of them shall look upon another. They shall be astonished, and shall humble their countenance;

9 And trouble shall seize them, when they shall behold this Son of woman sitting upon the throne of his glory.

10 Then shall the kings, the princes, and all who possess the earth, glorify him who has dominion over all things, him who was concealed; for from the beginning the Son of man existed in secret, whom the Most High preserved in the presence of his power, and revealed to the elect.

11 He shall sow the congregation of the saints, and of the elect; and all the elect shall stand before him in that day.

12 All the kings, the princes, the exalted, and those who rule over all the earth, shall fall down on their faces before him, and shall worship him.

13 They shall fix their hopes on this Son of man, shall pray to him, and petition him for mercy.

14 Then shall the Lord of spirits hasten to expel them from his presence. Their faces shall be full of confusion, and their faces shall darkness cover. The angels shall take them to punishment, that vengeance may be inflicted on those who have oppressed his children and his elect. And they shall become an example to the saints and to his elect. Through them shall these be made joyful; for the anger of the Lord of spirits shall rest upon them.

15 Then the sword of the Lord of spirits shall be drunk with their blood; but the saints and elect shall be safe in that day; nor the face of the sinners and the ungodly shall they thenceforwards behold.

16 The Lord of spirits shall remain over them:

17 And with this Son of man shall they dwell, eat, lie down, and rise up, forever and ever.

18 The saints and the elect have arisen from the earth, have left off to depress their countenances, and have been clothed with the garment of life. That garment of life is with the Lord of spirits, in whose presence your garment shall not wax old, nor shall your glory diminish.

CHAPTER 62

1 In those days the kings who possess the earth shall be punished by the angels of his wrath, wheresoever they shall be delivered up, that he may give rest for a short period; and that they may fall down and worship before the Lord of spirits, confessing their sins before him.

2 They shall bless and glorify the Lord of spirits, saying, Blessed is the Lord of spirits, the Lord of kings, the Lord of princes, the Lord of the rich, the Lord of glory, and the Lord of wisdom.

3 He shall enlighten every secret thing.

4 Your power is from generation to generation; and your glory forever and ever.

5 Deep are all your secrets, and numberless; and your righteousness cannot be calculated.

6 Now we know, that we should glorify and bless the Lord of kings, him who is King over all things.

7 They shall also say, Who has granted us rest to glorify, laud, bless, and confess in the presence of his glory?

8 And now small is the rest we desire; but we do not find it; we reject, and do not possess it. Light has passed away from before us; and darkness has covered our thrones forever.

9 For we have not confessed before him; we have not glorified the name of the Lord of kings; we have not glorified the Lord in all his works; but we have trusted in the sceptre of our dominion and of our glory.

10 In the day of our suffering and of our trouble he will not save us, neither shall we find rest. We confess that our Lord is faithful in all his works, in all his judgments, and in his righteousness.

11 In his judgments he pays no respect to persons; and we must depart from his presence, on account of our evil deeds.

12 All our sins are truly without number.

13 Then shall they say to themselves, Our souls are satiated with the instruments of crime;

14 But that prevents us not from descending to the flaming womb of hell.

15 Afterwards, their countenances shall be filled with darkness and confusion before the Son of man; from whose presence they shall be expelled, and before whom the sword shall remain to expel them.

16 Thus saith the Lord of spirits, This is the decree and the judgment against the princes, the kings, the exalted, and those who possess the earth, in the presence of the Lord of spirits.

CHAPTER 63

1 I saw also other countenances in that secret place. I heard the voice of an angel, saying, These are the angels who have descended from heaven to earth, and have revealed secrets to the sons of men, and have seduced the sons of men to the commission of sin.

(Chapters 64, 65, 66 and the first verse of 67 evidently contain a vision of Noah and not of Enoch (Laurence, p. 78).

CHAPTER 64

1 In those days Noah saw that the earth became inclined, and that destruction approached.

2 Then he lifted up his feet, and went to the ends of the earth, to the dwelling of his great-grandfather Enoch.

3 And Noah cried with a bitter voice, Hear me; hear me; hear me: three times. And he said, Tell me what is transacting upon the earth; for the earth labours, and is violently shaken. Surely I shall perish with it.

4 After this there was a great perturbation on earth, and a voice was heard from heaven. I fell down on my face, when my great-grandfather Enoch came and stood by me.

5 He said to me, Why have you cried out to me with a bitter cry and lamentation?

6 A commandment has gone forth from the Lord against those who dwell on the earth, that they may be destroyed; for they know every secret of the angels, every oppressive and secret power of the devils,(58) and every power of those who commit sorcery, as well as of those who make molten images in the whole earth.

7 They know how silver is produced from the dust of the earth, and how on the earth the metallic drop exists; for lead and tin are not produced from earth, as the primary fountain of their production.

8 There is an angel standing upon it, and that angel struggles to prevail.

9 Afterwards my great-grandfather Enoch seized me with his hand, raising me up, and saying to me, Go, for I have asked the Lord of spirits respecting this perturbation of the earth; who replied, On account of their impiety have their innumerable judgments been consummated before me. Respecting the moons have they inquired, and they have known that the earth will perish with those who dwell upon it,(59) and that to these there will be no place of refuge for ever.

10 They have discovered secrets, and they are those who have been judged; but not you my son. The Lord of spirits knows that you are pure and good, free from the reproach of discovering secrets.

11 He, the holy One, will establish your name in the midst of the saints, and will preserve you from those who dwell upon the earth. He will establish your seed in righteousness, with dominion and great glory;(60) and from your seed shall spring forth righteousness and holy men without number forever.

(58) The devils. Literally, "the Satans" (Laurence, p. 78).

(59) Respecting the moons...dwell upon it. Or, "Because of the sorceries which they have searched out and learnt, the earth and those who dwell upon it will be destroyed" (Knibb, p. 155).

(60) With dominion...glory. Literally, "for kings, and for great glory" (Laurence, p. 79).

CHAPTER 65

1 After this he showed me the angels of punishment, who were prepared to come, and to open all the mighty waters under the earth:

2 That they may be for judgment, and for the destruction of all those who remain and dwell upon the earth.

3 And the Lord of spirits commanded the angels who went forth, not to take up the men and preserve them.

4 For those angels presiding over all the mighty waters. Then I went out from the presence of Enoch.

CHAPTER 66

1 In those days the word of God came to me, and said, Noah, behold, your lot has ascended up to me, a lot void of crime, a lot beloved and upright.

2 Now then shall the angels labour at the trees;(61) but when they proceed to this, I will put my hand upon it, and preserve it.

3 The seed of life shall arise from it, and a change shall take place, that the dry land shall not be left empty. I will establish your seed before me forever and ever, and the seed of those who dwell with you on the surface of the earth. It shall be blessed and multiplied in the presence of the earth, in the name of the Lord.

4 And they shall confine those angels who disclosed impiety. In that burning valley it is, that they shall be confined, which at first my great-grandfather Enoch showed me in the west, where there were mountains of gold and silver, of iron, of fluid metal, and of tin.

5 I beheld that valley in which there was great perturbation, and where the waters were troubled.

6 And when all this was effected, from the fluid mass of fire, and the perturbation which prevailed(62) in that place, there arose a strong smell of sulphur, which became mixed with the waters; and the valley of the angels, who had been guilty of seduction, burned underneath its soil.

7 Through that valley also rivers of fire were flowing, to which those angels shall be condemned, who seduced the inhabitants of the earth.

8 And in those days shall these waters be to kings, to princes, to the exalted, and to the inhabitants of the earth, for the healing of the soul and body, and for the judgment of the spirit.

9 Their spirits shall be full of revelry,(63) that they may be judged in their bodies; because they have denied the Lord of spirits, and although they perceive their condemnation day by day, they believe not in his name.

10 And as the inflammation of their bodies shall be great, so shall their spirits undergo a change forever.

11 For no word which is uttered before the Lord of spirits shall be in vain.

12 Judgment has come upon them, because they trusted in their carnal revelry, and denied the Lord of spirits.

13 In those days shall the waters of that valley be changed; for when the angels shall be judged, then shall the heat of those springs of water experience an alteration.

14 And when the angels shall ascend, the water of the springs shall again undergo a change, and be frozen. Then I heard holy Michael answering and saying, This judgment, with which the angels shall be judged, shall bear testimony against the kings, the princes, and those who possess the earth.

15 For these waters of judgment shall be for their healing, and for the death(64) of their bodies. But they shall not perceive and believe that the waters will be changed, and become a fire, which shall blaze forever.

(61) Shall...labour at the trees. Or, "are making a wooden (structure)" (Knibb, p. 156).
(62) The perturbation which prevailed. Literally, "troubled them" (Laurence, p. 81).
(63) Revelry. Or, "lust" (Knibb, p. 157).
(64) Death. Or, "lust" (Charles, p. 176; Knibb, p. 158).

CHAPTER 67

1 After this he gave me the characteristical marks(65) of all the secret things in the book of my great-grandfather Enoch, and in the parables which had been given to him; inserting them for me among the words of the book of parables.

2 At that that time holy Michael answered and said to Raphael, The power of the spirit hurries me away, and impels me on. The severity of the judgment, of the secret judgment of the angels, who is capable of beholding–the endurance of that severe judgment which has taken place and been made permanent– without being melted at the site of it? Again holy Michael answered and said to holy Raphael, Who is there whose heart is not softened by it, and whose reins are not troubled at this thing?

3 Judgment has gone forth against them by those who have thus dragged them away; and that was, when they stood in the presence of the Lord of spirits.

4 In like manner also holy Rakael said to Raphael, They shall not be before the eye of the Lord;(66) since the Lord of spirits has been offended with them; for like Lords(67) have they conducted themselves. Therefore will he bring upon them a secret judgment forever and ever.

5 For neither shall angel nor man receive a portion of it; but they alone shall receive their own judgment for ever end ever.

(65) Characteristical marks. Literally, "the signs" (Laurence, p. 83).

(66) They shall not...eye of the Lord. Or, "I will not take their part under the eye of the Lord" (Knibb, p. 159).

(67) For like Lords. Or, "for they act as if they were Lord" (Knibb, p. 159).

CHAPTER 68

1 After this judgment they shall be astonished and irritated; for it shall be exhibited to the inhabitants of the earth.

2 Behold the names of those angels. These are their names. The first of them is Samyaza; the second, Arstikapha; the third, Armen; the fourth, Kakabael; the fifth, Turel; the sixth, Rumyel; the seventh, Danyal; the eighth, Kael; the ninth, Barakel; the tenth, Azazel; the eleventh, Armers; the twelfth, Bataryal; the thirteenth, Basasael; the fourteenth, Ananel; the fifteenth, Turyal; the sixteenth, Simapiseel; the seventeenth, Yetarel; the eighteenth, Tumael; the nineteenth, Tarel; the twentieth, Rumel; the twenty-first, Azazyel.

3 These are the chiefs of their angels, and the names of the leaders of their hundreds, and the leaders of their fifties, and the leaders of their tens.

4 The name of the first is Yekun:(68) he it was who seduced all the sons of the holy angels; and causing them to descend on earth, led astray the offspring of men.

5 The name of the second is Kesabel, who pointed out evil counsel to the sons of the holy angels, and induced them to corrupt their bodies by generating mankind.

6 The name of the third is Gadrel: he discovered every stroke of death to the children of men.

7 He seduced Eve; and discovered to the children of men the instruments of death, the coat of mail, the shield, and the sword for slaughter; every instrument of death to the children of men.

8 From his hand were these things derived to them who dwell upon earth, from that period for ever.

9 The name of the fourth is Penemue: he discovered to the children of men bitterness and sweetness;

10 And pointed out to them every secret of their wisdom.

11 He taught men to understand writing, and the use of ink and paper.

12 Therefore numerous have been those who have gone astray from every period of the world, even to this day.

13 For men were not born for this, thus with pen and with ink to confirm their faith;

14 Since they were not created, except that, like the angels, they might remain righteous and pure.

15 Nor would death, which destroys everything, have effected them;

16 But by this their knowledge they perish, and by this also its power consumes them.

17 The name of the fifth is Kasyade: he discovered to the children of men every wicked stroke of spirits and of demons:

18 The stroke of the embryo in the womb, to diminish it;(69) the stroke of the spirit by the bite of the serpent, and the stroke which is given in the mid-day by the offspring of the serpent, the name of which is Tabaet.(70)

19 This is the number of the Kasbel; the principal part of the oath which the Most High, dwelling in glory, revealed to the holy ones.

20 Its name is Beka. He spoke to holy Michael to discover to them the sacred name, that they might understand that secret name, and thus remember the oath; and that those who pointed out every secret thing to the children of men might tremble at that name and oath.

21 This is the power of that oath; for powerful it is, and strong.

22 And he established this oath of Akae by the instrumentality of the holy Michael.

23 These are the secrets of this oath, and by it were they confirmed.

24 Heaven was suspended by it before the world was made, forever.

25 By it has the earth been founded upon the flood; while from the concealed parts of the hills the agitated waters proceed forth from the creation to the end of the world.

26 By this oath the sea has been formed, and the foundation of it.

27 During the period of its fury he established the sand against it, which continues unchanged for ever; and by this oath the abyss has been made

strong; nor is it removable from its station forever and ever.

28 By this oath the sun and moon complete their progress, never swerving from the command given to them forever and ever.

29 By this oath the stars complete their progress;

30 And when their names are called, they return an answer, forever and ever.

31 Thus in the heavens take place the blowings of the winds: all of them have breathings,(71) and effect a complete combination of breathings.

32 There the treasures of thunder are kept, and the splendour of the lightning.

33 There are kept the treasures of hail and of frost, the treasures of snow, the treasures of rain and of dew.

34 All these confess and laud before the Lord of spirits.

35 They glorify with all their power of praise; and he sustains them in all that act of thanksgiving; while they laud, glorify, and exalt the name of the Lord of spirits forever and ever.

36 And with them he establishes this oath, by which they and their paths are preserved; nor does their progress perish.

37 Great was their joy.

38 They blessed, glorified, and exalted, because the name of the Son of man was revealed to them.

39 He sat upon the throne of his glory; and the principal part of the judgment was assigned to him, the Son of man. Sinners shall disappear and perish from the face of the earth, while those who seduced them shall be bound with chains forever.

40 According to their ranks of corruption shall they be imprisoned, and all their works shall disappear from the face of the earth; nor thenceforward shall there be any to corrupt; for the Son of man has been seen, sitting on the throne of his glory.

41 Everything wicked shall disappear, and depart from before his face; and the word of the Son of man shall become powerful in the presence of the Lord of spirits.

42 This is the third parable of Enoch.

(68) Yekun may simply mean "the rebel" (Knibb, p. 160).

(69) The stroke...to diminish it. Or, "the blows (which attack) the embryo in the womb so that it miscarries" (Knibb, p. 162).

(70) Tabaet. Literally, "male" or "strong" (Knibb, p. 162).

(71) Breathings. Or, "spirits" (Laurence, p. 87).

CHAPTER 69

1 After this the name of the Son of man, living with the Lord of spirits, was exalted by the inhabitants of the earth.

2 It was exalted in the chariots of the Spirit; and the name went forth in the midst of them.

3 From that time I was not drawn into the midst of them; but he seated me between two spirits, between the north and the west, where the angels received their ropes, to measure out a place for the elect and the righteous.

4 There I beheld the fathers of the first men, and the saints, who dwell in that place forever.

CHAPTER 70

1 Afterwards my spirit was concealed, ascending into the heavens. I beheld the sons of the holy angels treading on flaming fire, whose garments and robes were white, and whose countenances were transparent as crystal.

2 I saw two rivers of fire glittering like the hyacinth.

3 Then I fell on my face before the Lord of spirits.

4 And Michael, one of the archangels, took me by my right hand, raised me up, and brought me out to where was every secret of mercy and secret of righteousness.

5 He showed me all the hidden things of the extremities of heaven, all the receptacles of the stars, and the splendours of all, from whence they went forth before the face of the holy.

6 And he concealed the spirit of Enoch in the heaven of heavens.

7 There I beheld, in the midst of that light, a building raised with stones of ice;

8 And in the midst of these stone vibrations(72) of living fire. My spirit saw around the circle of this flaming habitation, on one of its extremities, that there were rivers full of living fire, which encompassed it.

9 Then the Seraphim, the Cherubim, and Ophanin(73) surrounded it: these are those who never sleep, but watch the throne of his glory.

10 And I beheld angels innumerable, thousands of thousands, and myriads and myriads, who surrounded that habitation.

11 Michael, Raphael, Gabriel, Phanuel and the holy angels who were in the heavens above, went in and out of it. Michael, Raphael, and Gabriel went out of that habitation, and holy angels innumerable.

12 With them was the Ancient of days, whose head was white as wool, and pure, and his robe was indescribable.

13 Then I fell upon my face, while all my flesh was dissolved, and my spirit became changed.

14 I cried out with a loud voice, with a powerful spirit, blessing, glorifying, and exalting.

15 And those blessings, which proceeded from my mouth, became acceptable in the presence of the Ancient of days.

16 The Ancient of days came with Michael and Gabriel, Raphael and Phanuel, with thousands of thousands, and myriads and myriads, which could not be numbered.

17 Then that angel came to me, and with his voice saluted me, saying, You are the Son of man,(74) who art born for righteousness, and righteousness has rested upon you.

18 The righteousness of the Ancient of days shall not forsake you.

19 He said, On you shall he confer peace in the name of the existing world; for from thence has peace gone forth since the world was created.

20 And thus shall it happen to you forever and ever.

21 All who shall exist, and who shall walk in your path of righteousness, shall not forsake you forever.

22 With you shall be their habitations, with you their lot; nor from you shall they be separated forever and ever.

23 And thus shall length of days be with the Son of man.(75)

24 Peace shall be to the righteous; and the path of integrity shall the righteous pursue, in the name of the Lord of spirits, forever and ever.

(72) Vibrations. Literally, "tongues" (Laurence, p. 90).
(73) Ophanin. The "wheels" of Ezek. 1:15-21 (Charles, p. 162).
(74) Son of man. Laurence's original translation renders this phrase "offspring of man." Knibb (p. 166) and Charles (p. 185) indicate that it should be "Son of man," consistent with the other occurrences of that term in the Book of Enoch.
(75) Son of man. Literally, "offspring of man," or "the Christ who comes from the offspring of man."

CHAPTER 71

1 The book of the revolutions of the luminaries of heaven, according to their respective classes, their respective powers, their respective periods, their respective names, the places where they commence their progress, and their respective months, which Uriel, the holy angel who was with me, explained to me; he who conducted them. The whole account of them, according to every

year of the world for ever, until a new work shall be effected, which will be eternal.

2 This is the first law of the luminaries. The sun and the light arrive at the gates of heaven, which are on the east, and on the west of it at the western gates of heaven.

3 I beheld the gates whence the sun goes forth; and the gates where the sun sets;

4 In which gates also the moon rises and sets; and I beheld the conductors of the stars, among those who precede them; six gates were at the rising, and six at the setting of the sun.

5 All these respectively, one after another, are on a level; and numerous windows are on the right and on the left sides of those gates.

6 First proceeds forth that great luminary, which is called the sun; the orb of which is as the orb of heaven, the whole of it being replete with splendid and flaming fire.

7 Its chariot, where it ascends, the wind blows.

8 The sun sets in heaven, and, returning by the north, to proceed towards the east, is conducted so as to enter by that gate, and illuminate the face of heaven.

9 In the same manner it goes forth in the first month by the great gate.

10 It goes forth through the fourth of those six gates, which are at the rising of the sun.

11 And in the fourth gate, through which the sun with the moon proceeds, in the first part of it,(76) there are twelve open windows; from which issues out a flame, when they are opened in their proper periods.

12 When the sun rises in heaven, it goes forth through this fourth gate thirty days, and by the fourth gate in the west of heaven on a level with it descends.

13 During that period the day is lengthened from the day, and the night curtailed from the night for thirty days. And then the day is longer by two parts than the night.

14 The day is precisely ten parts, and the night is eight.

15 The sun goes forth through this fourth gate, and sets in it, and turns to the fifth gate during thirty days; after which it proceeds from, and sets in, the fifth gate.

16 Then the day becomes lengthened by a second portion, so that it is eleven parts: while the night becomes shortened, and is only seven parts.

17 The sun now returns to the east, entering into the sixth gate, and rising and setting in the sixth gate thirty-one days, on account of its signs.

18 At that period the day is longer than the night, being twice as long as the night; and become twelve parts;

19 But the night is shortened, and becomes six parts. Then the sun rises up, that the day may be shortened, and the night lengthened.

20 And the sun returns toward the east entering into the sixth gate, where it rises and sets for thirty days.

21 When that period is completed, the day becomes shortened precisely one part, so that it is eleven parts, while the night is seven parts.

22 Then the sun goes from the west, from that sixth gate, and proceeds eastwards, rising in the fifth gate for thirty days, and setting again westwards in the fifth gate of the west.

23 At that period the day becomes shortened two parts; and is ten parts, while the night is eight parts.

24 Then the sun goes from the fifth gate, as it sets in the fifth gate of the west; and rises in the fourth gate for thirty-one days, on account of its signs, setting in the west.

25 At that period the day is made equal with the night; and, being equal with it, the night becomes nine parts, and the day nine parts.

26 Then the sun goes from that gate, as it sets in the west; and returning to the east proceeds by the third gate for thirty days, setting in the west at the third gate.

27 At that period the night is lengthened from the day during thirty mornings, and the day is curtailed from the day during thirty days; the night being ten parts precisely, and the day eight parts.

28 The sun now goes from the third gate, as it sets in the third gate in the west; but returning to the east, it proceeds by the second gate of the east for thirty days.

29 In like manner also it sets in the second gate in the west of heaven.

30 At that period the night is eleven parts, and the day seven parts.

31 Then the sun goes at that time from the second gate, as it sets in the second gate in the west; but returns to the east, proceeding by the first gate, for thirty-one days.

32 And sets in the west in the first gate.

33 At that period that night is lengthened as much again as the day.

34 It is twelve parts precisely, while the day is six parts.

35 The sun has thus completed its beginnings, and a second time goes round from these beginnings.

36 Into that first gate it enters for thirty days, and sets in the west, in the opposite part of heaven.

37 At that period the night is contracted in its length a fourth part, that is, one portion, and becomes eleven parts.

38 The day is seven parts.

39 Then the sun returns, and enters into the second gate of the east.

40 It returns by these beginnings thirty days, rising and setting.

41 At that period the night is contracted in its length. It becomes ten parts, and the day eight parts. Then the sun goes from that second gate, and sets in the west; but returns to the east, and rises in the east, in the third gate, thirty-one days, setting in the west of heaven.

42 At that period the night becomes shortened. It is nine parts. And the night is equal with the day. The year is precisely three hundred and sixty-four days.

43 The lengthening of the day and night, and the contraction of the day and night, are made to differ from each other by the progress of the sun.

44 By means of this progress the day is daily lengthened, and the night greatly shortened.

45 This is the law and progress of the sun, and its turning when it turns back, turning during sixty days,(77) and going forth. This is the great everlasting luminary, that which he names the sun forever and ever.

46 This also is that which goes forth a great luminary, and which is named after its peculiar kind, as God commanded.

47 And thus it goes in and out, neither slackening nor resting; but running on in its chariot by day and by night. It shines with a seventh portion of light from the moon;(78) but the dimensions of both are equal.

(76) Through which...part of it. Or, "from which the sun rises in the first month" (Knibb, p. 168).

(77) That is, it is sixty days in the same gates, viz. Thirty days twice every year (Laurence, p. 97).

(78) It shines with...from the moon. Or, "Its light is seven times brighter than that of the moon" (Knibb, p. 171). The Aramaic texts more clearly describe how the moon's light waxes and wanes by a half of a seventh part each day. Here in the Ethiopic version, the moon is thought of as two halves, each half being divided into seven parts. Hence, the "fourteen portions" of 72:9-10 (Knibb, p. 171).

Chapter 72

1 After this law I beheld another law of an inferior luminary, the name of which

is the moon, and the orb of which is as the orb of heaven.

2 Its chariot, which it secretly ascends, the wind blows; and light is given to it by measure.

3 Every month at its exit and entrance it becomes changed; and its periods are as the periods of the sun. And when in like manner its light is to exist,(79) its light is a seventh portion from the light of the sun.

4 Thus it rises, and at its commencement towards the east goes forth for thirty days.

5 At that time it appears, and becomes to you the beginning of the month. Thirty days it is with the sun in the gate from which the sun goes forth.

6 Half of it is in extent seven portions, one half; and the whole of its orb is void of light, except a seventh portion out of the fourteen portions of its light. And in a day it receives a seventh portion, or half that portion, of its light. Its light is by sevens, by one portion, and by the half of a portion. Its sets with the sun.

7 And when the sun rises, the moon rises with it; receiving half a portion of light.

8 On that night, when it commences its period, previously to the day of the month, the moon sets with the sun.

9 And on that night it is dark in its fourteen portions, that is, in each half; but it rises on that day with one seventh portion precisely, and in its progress declines from the rising of the sun.

10 During the remainder of its period its light increases to fourteen portions.

(79) And when in...is to exist. I.e., when the moon is full (Knibb, p. 171).

Chapter 73

1 Then I saw another progress and regulation which He effected in the law of the moon. The progress of the moons, and everything relating to them, Uriel showed me, the holy angel who conducted them all.

2 Their stations I wrote down as he showed them to me.

3 I wrote down their months, as they occur, and the appearance of their light, until it is completed in fifteen days.

4 In each of its two seven portions it completes all its light at rising and at setting.

5 On stated months it changes its settings; and on stated months it makes its progress through each gate. In two gates the moon sets with the sun, viz. in those two gates which are in the midst, in the third and fourth gate. From the

third gate it goes forth for seven days, and makes its circuit.

6 Again it returns to the gate whence the sun goes forth, and in that completes the whole of its light. Then it declines from the sun, and enters in eight days into the sixth gate, and returns in seven days to the third gate, from which the sun goes forth.

7 When the sun proceeds to the fourth gate, the moon goes forth for seven days, until it passes from the fifth gate.

8 Again it returns in seven days to the fourth gate, and completing all its light, declines, and passes on by the first gate in eight days;

9 And returns in seven days to the fourth gate, from which the sun goes forth.

10 Thus I beheld their stations, as according to the fixed order of the months the sun rises and sets.

11 At those times there is an excess of thirty days belonging to the sun in five years; all the days belonging to each year of the five years, when completed, amount to three hundred and sixty-four days; and to the sun and stars belong six days; six days in each of the five years; thus thirty days belonging to them;

12 So that the moon has thirty days less than the sun and stars.

13 The moon brings on all the years exactly, that their stations may come neither too forwards nor too backwards a single day; but that the years may be changed with correct precision in three hundred and sixty-four days. In three years the days are one thousand and ninety-two; in five years they are one thousand eight hundred and twenty; and in eight years two thousand nine hundred and twelve days.

14 To the moon alone belong in three years one thousand and sixty-two days; in five years it has fifty days less than the sun, for an addition being made to the one thousand and sixty-two days, in five years there are one thousand seven hundred and seventy days; and the days of the moon in eight years are two thousand eight hundred and thirty-two days.

15 For its days in eight years are less than those of the sun by eighty days, which eighty days are its diminution in eight years.

16 The year then becomes truly complete according to the station of the moon, and the station of the sun; which rise in the different gates; which rise and set in them for thirty days.

CHAPTER 74

1 These are the leaders of the chiefs of the thousands, those which preside over all creation, and over all the stars; with the four days which are added

and never separated from the place allotted them, according to the complete calculation of the year.

2 And these serve four days, which are not calculated in the calculation of the year.

3 Respecting them, men greatly err, for these luminaries truly serve, in the dwelling place of the world, one day in the first gate, one in the third gate, one in the fourth gate, and one in the sixth gate.

4 And the harmony of the world becomes complete every three hundred and sixty-fourth state of it. For the signs,

5 The seasons,

6 The years,

7 And the days, Uriel showed me; the angel whom the Lord of glory appointed over all the luminaries.

8 Of heaven in heaven, and in the world; that they might rule in the face of the sky, and appearing over the earth, become

9 Conductors of the days and nights: the sun, the moon, the stars, and all the ministers of heaven, which make their circuit with all the chariots of heaven.

10 Thus Uriel showed me twelve gates open for the circuit of the chariots of the sun in heaven, from which the rays of the sun shoot forth.

11 From these proceed heat over the earth, when they are opened in their stated seasons. They are for the winds, and the spirit of the dew, when in their seasons they are opened; opened in heaven at its extremities.

12 Twelve gates I beheld in heaven, at the extremities of the earth, through which the sun, moon, and stars, and all the works of heaven, proceed at their rising and setting.

13 Many windows also are open on the right and on the left.

14 One window at a certain season grows extremely hot. So also are there gates from which the stars go forth as they are commanded, and in which they set according to their number.

15 I saw likewise the chariots of heaven, running in the world above to those gates in which the stars turn, which never set. One of these is greater than all, which goes round the whole world.

CHAPTER 75

1 And at the extremities of the earth I beheld twelve gates open for all the winds, from which they proceed and blow over the earth.

2 Three of them are open in the front of heaven, three in the west, three on the

right side of heaven, and three on the left. The first three are those which are towards the east, three are towards the north, three behind those which are upon the left, towards the south, and three on the west.

3 From four of them proceed winds of blessing, and of health; and from eight proceed winds of punishment; when they are sent to destroy the earth, and the heaven above it, all its inhabitants, and all which are in the waters, or on dry land.

4 The first of these winds proceeds from the gate termed the eastern, through the first gate on the east, which inclines southwards. From this goes forth destruction, drought, heat, and perdition.

5 From the second gate, the middle one, proceeds equity. There issue from it rain, fruitfulness, health, and dew; and from the third gate northwards, proceed cold and drought.

6 After these proceed the south winds through three principal gates; through their first gate, which inclines eastwards, proceeds a hot wind.

7 But from the middle gate proceed grateful odour, dew, rain, health, and life.

8 From the third gate, which is westwards, proceed dew, rain, blight, and destruction.

9 After these are the winds to the north, which is called the sea. They proceed from three gates. The first(80) gate is that which is on the east, inclining southwards; from this proceed dew, rain, blight, and destruction. From the middle direct gate proceed rain, dew, life, and health. And from the third gate, which is westwards, inclining towards the south, proceed mist, frost, snow, rain, dew, and blight.

10 After these in the fourth quarter are the winds to the west. From the first gate, inclining northwards, proceed dew, rain, frost, cold, snow, and chill; from the middle gate proceed rain, health, and blessing;

11 And from the last gate, which is southwards, proceed drought, destruction, scorching, and perdition.

12 The account of the twelve gates of the four quarters of heaven is ended.

13 All their laws, all their infliction of punishment, and the health produced by them, have I explained to you, my son Mathusala.(81)

(80) First. Or, "seventh" (Knibb, p. 178).

(81) Mathusala. Enoch's son, Methuselah. Cp. Gen. 5:21.

CHAPTER 76

1 The first wind is called the eastern, because it is the first.

2 The second is called the south, because the Most High there descends, and frequently there descends he who is blessed forever.

3 The western wind has the name of diminution, because there all the luminaries of heaven are diminished, and descend.

4 The fourth wind, which is named the north, is divided into three parts; one of which is for the habitation of man; another for seas of water, with valleys, woods, rivers, shady places, and snow; and the third part contains paradise.

5 Seven high mountains I beheld, higher than all the mountains of the earth, from which frost proceeds; while days, seasons, and years depart and pass away.

6 Seven rivers I beheld upon earth, greater than all rivers, one of which takes its course from the west; into a great sea its water flows.

7 Two come from the north to the sea, their waters flowing into the Erythraean sea,(82) on the east. And with respect to the remaining four, they take their course in the cavity of the north, two to their sea, the Erythraean sea, and two are poured into a great sea, where also it is said there is a desert.

8 Seven great islands I saw in the sea and on the earth. Seven in the great sea.

(82) The Red Sea.

CHAPTER 77

1 The names of the sun are these: one Aryares, the other Tomas.

2 The moon has four names. The first is Asonya; the second, Ebla; the third, Benase; and the fourth, Erae.

3 These are the two great luminaries, whose orbs are as the orbs of heaven; and the dimensions of both are equal.

4 In the orb of the sun there is a seventh portion of light, which is added to it from the moon.(83) By measure it is put in, until the seventh portion of the light of the sun is departed. They set, enter into the western gate, circuit by the north, and through the eastern gate go forth over the face of heaven.

5 When the moon rises, it appears in heaven; and the half of a seventh portion of light is all which is in it.

6 In fourteen days the whole of its light is completed.

7 By three quintuples light is put into it, until in fifteen days its light is completed, according to the signs of the year; it has three quintuples.

8 The moon has the half of a seventh portion.

9 During its diminution on the first day its light decreases a fourteenth part; on the second day it decreases a thirteenth part; on the third day a twelfth part; on the fourth day an eleventh part; on the fifth day a tenth part; on the sixth day a ninth part; on the seventh day it decreases an eighth part; on the eighth day it decreases a seventh part; on the ninth day it decreases a sixth part; on the tenth day it decreases a fifth part; on the eleventh day it decreases a fourth part; on the twelfth day it decreases third part; on the thirteenth day it decreases a second part; on the fourteenth day it decreases a half of its seventh part; and on the fifteenth day the whole remainder of its light is consumed.

10 On stated months the moon has twenty-nine days.

11 It also has a period of twenty-eight days.

12 Uriel likewise showed me another regulation, when light is poured into the moon, how it is poured into it from the sun.

13 All the time that the moon is in progress with its light, it is poured into it in the presence of the sun, until its light is in fourteen days completed in heaven.

14 And when it is wholly extinguished, its light is consumed in heaven; and on the first day it is called the new moon, for on that day light is received into it.

15 It becomes precisely completed on the day that the sun descends into the west, while the moon ascends at night from the east.

16 The moon then shines all the night, until the sun rises before it; when the moon disappears in turn before the sun.

17 Where light comes to the moon, there again it decreases, until all its light is extinguished, and the days of the moon pass away.

18 Then its orb remains solitary without light.

19 During three months it effects in thirty days each month its period; and during three more months it effects it in twenty-nine days each. These are the times in which it effects its decrease in its first period, and in the first gate, namely, in one hundred and seventy-seven days.

20 And at the time of its going forth during three months it appears thirty days each, and during three more months it appears twenty-nine days each.

21 In the night it appears for each twenty days as the face of a man, and in the day as heaven; for it is nothing else except its light.

(83) A seventh portion...from the moon. Or, "seven parts of light which are added to it more than to the moon" (Knibb, p. 182).

CHAPTER 78

1 And now, my son Mathusala, I have shown you everything; and the account of every ordinance of the stars of heaven is finished.

2 He showed me every ordinance respecting these, which takes place at all times and in all seasons under every influence, in all years, at the arrival and under the rule of each, during every month and every week. He showed me also the decrease of the moon, which is effected in the sixth gate; for in that sixth gate is its light consumed.

3 From this is the beginning of the month; and its decrease is effected in the sixth gate in its period, until a hundred and seventy-seven days are completed; according to the mode of calculation by weeks, twenty-five weeks and two days.

4 Its period is less than that of the sun, according to the ordinance of the stars, by five days in one half year(84) precisely.

5 When that their visible situation is completed. Such is the appearance and likeness of every luminary, which Uriel, the great angel who conducts them, showed to me.

(84) In one half year. Literally, "in one time" (Laurence, p. 110).

CHAPTER 79

1 In those days Uriel answered and said to me, Behold, I have showed you all things, O Enoch;

2 And all things have I revealed to you. You see the sun, the moon, and those which conduct the stars of heaven, which cause all their operations, seasons, and arrivals to return.

3 In the days of sinners the years shall be shortened.

4 Their seed shall be backward in their prolific soil; and everything done on earth shall be subverted, and disappear in its season. The rain shall be restrained, and heaven shall stand still.

5 In those days the fruits of the earth shall be late, and not flourish in their season; and in their season the fruits of the trees shall be withholden.

6 The moon shall change its laws, and not be seen at its proper period. But in those days shall heaven be seen; and barrenness shall take place in the borders of the great chariots in the west. Heaven shall shine more than when illuminated by the orders of light; while many chiefs among the stars of authority shall err, perverting their ways and works.

7 Those shall not appear in their season, who commanded them, and all the classes of the stars shall be shut up against sinners.

8 The thoughts of those who dwell on the earth shall transgress within them; and they shall be perverted in all their ways.

9 They shall transgress, and think themselves(85) gods; while evil shall be multiplied among them.

10 And punishment shall come upon them, so that all of them shall be destroyed.

(85) Themselves. Or, "them" i.e., the chiefs among the stars (vs. 6) (Knibb, p. 186).

CHAPTER 80

1 He said, O Enoch, look on the book which heaven has gradually dropped down;(86) and, reading that which is written in it, understand every part of it.

2 Then I looked on all which was written, and understood all, reading the book and everything written in it, all the works of man;

3 And of all the children of flesh upon earth, during the generations of the world.

4 Immediately after I blessed the Lord, the King of glory, who has thus for ever formed the whole workmanship of the world.

5 And I glorified the Lord, on account of his long-suffering and blessing towards the children of the world.

6 At that time I said, Blessed is the man, who shall die righteous and good, against whom no catalogue of crime has been written, and with whom iniquity is not found.

7 Then those three holy ones caused me to approach, and placed me on the earth, before the door of my house.

8 And they said unto me, Explain everything to Mathusala your son; and inform all your children, that no flesh shall be justified before the Lord; for he is their Creator.

9 During one year we shall leave you with your children, until you shalt again recover your strength, that you may instruct your family, write these things, and explain them to all your children. But in another year they shall take you from the midst of them, and your heart shall be strengthened; for the elect shall point out righteousness to the elect; the righteous with the righteous shall rejoice, congratulating each other; but the sinners with sinners shall die,

10 And the perverted with the perverted shall be drowned.

11 Those likewise who act righteously shall die on account of the works of man, and shall be gathered together on account of the works of the wicked.

12 In those days they finished conversing with me.

13 And I returned to my fellow men, blessing the Lord of worlds.

(86) The book which...dropped down. Or, "the book of the tablets of heaven" (Knibb, p. 186).

Chapter 81

1 Now, my son Mathusala, all these things I speak unto you, and write for you. To you I have revealed all, and have given you books of everything.

2 Preserve, my son Mathusala, the books written by your father; that you may reveal them to future generations.

3 Wisdom have I given you, to your children, and your posterity, that they may reveal to their children, for generations forever, this wisdom in their thoughts; and that those who comprehend it may not slumber, but hear with their ears; that they may learn this wisdom, and be deemed worthy of eating this wholesome food.

4 Blessed are all the righteous; blessed are all who walk in righteousness; in whom no crime is found, as in sinners, when all their days are numbered.

5 With respect to the progress of the sun in heaven, it enters and goes out of each gate for thirty days, with the leaders of the thousand classes of the stars; with four which are added, and appertain to the four quarters of the year, which conduct them, and accompany them at four periods.

6 Respecting these, men greatly err, and do not calculate them in the calculation of every age; for they greatly err respecting them; nor do men know accurately that they are in the calculation of the year. But indeed these are marked down for ever; one in the first gate, one in the third, one in the fourth, and one in the sixth:

7 So that the year is completed in three hundred and sixty-four days.

8 Truly has been stated, and accurately has been calculated that which is marked down; for the luminaries, the months, the fixed periods, the years, and the days, Uriel has explained to me, and communicated to me; whom the Lord of all creation, on my account, commanded (according to the might of heaven, and the power which it possesses both by night and by day) to explain the laws of light to man, of the sun, moon, and stars, and of all the powers of heaven, which are turned with their respective orbs.

9 This is the ordinance of the stars, which set in their places, in their seasons, in their periods, in their days, and in their months.

10 These are the names of the those who conduct them, who watch and enter in their seasons, according to their ordinance in their periods, in their months, in the times of their influence, and in their stations.

11 Four conductors of them first enter, who separate the four quarters of the year. After these, twelve conductors of their classes, who separate the months and the year into three hundred and sixty-four days, with the leaders of a thousand, who distinguish between the days, as well as between the four additional ones; which, as conductors, divide the four quarters of the year.

12 These leaders of a thousand are in the midst of the conductors, and the conductors are added each behind his station, and their conductors make the separation. These are the names of the conductors, who separate the four quarters of the year, who are appointed over them: Melkel, Helammelak,

13 Meliyal, and Narel.

14 And the names of those who conduct them are Adnarel, Jyasusal, and Jyelumeal.

15 These are the three who follow after the conductors of the classes of stars; each following after the three conductors of the classes, which themselves follow after those conductors of the stations, who divide the four quarters of the year.

16 In the first part of the year rises and rules Melkyas, who is named Tamani, and Zahay.(87)

17 All the days of his influence, during which he rules, are ninety-one days.

18 And these are the signs of the days which are seen upon the earth. In the days of his influence there is perspiration, heat, and trouble. All the trees become fruitful; the leaf of every tree comes forth; the corn is reaped; the rose and every species of flowers blossoms in the field; and the trees of winter are dried up.

19 These are the names of the conductors who are under them: Barkel, Zelsabel; and another additional conductor of a thousand is named Heloyalef, the days of those influence have been completed. The other conductor next after them is Helemmelek, whose name they call the splendid Zahay.(88)

20 All the days of his light are ninety-one days.

21 These are the signs of the days upon earth, heat and drought; while the trees bring forth their fruits, warmed and concocted, and give their fruits to dry.

22 The flocks follow and yean.(89) All the fruits of the earth are collected, with

everything in the fields, and the vines are trodden. This takes place during the time of his influence.

23 These are their names and orders, and the names of the conductors who are under them, of those who are chiefs of a thousand: Gedaeyal, Keel, Heel.

24 And the name of the additional leader of a thousand is Asphael.

25 The days of his influence have been completed.

(87) Tamani, and Zahay. Or, "the southern sun" (Knibb, p. 190).
(88) Zahay. Or, "sun" (Knibb, p. 191).
(89) Follow and yean. Mate and bear young.

CHAPTER 82

1 And now I have shown you, my son Mathusala, every sight which I saw prior to your birth. I will relate another vision, which I saw before I was married; they resemble each other.

2 The first was when I was learning a book; and the other before I was married to your mother. I saw a potent vision;

3 And on account of these things besought the Lord.

4 I was lying down in the house of my grandfather Malalel, when I saw in a vision heaven purifying, and snatched away.(90)

5 And falling to the earth,(91) I saw likewise the earth absorbed by a great abyss; and mountains suspended over mountains.

6 Hills were sinking upon hills, lofty trees were gliding off from their trunks, and were in the act of being projected, and of sinking into the abyss.

7 Being alarmed at these things, my voice faltered.(92) I cried out and said, The earth is destroyed. Then my grandfather Malalel raised me up, and said to me: Why do you thus cry out, my son? And wherefore thus do you lament?

8 I related to him the whole vision which I had seen. He said to me, Confirmed is that which you have seen, my son;

9 And potent the vision of your dream respecting every secret sin of the earth. Its substance shall sink into the abyss, and a great destruction take place.

10 Now, my son, rise up; and beseech the Lord of glory (for you are faithful), that a remnant may be left upon earth, and that he would not wholly destroy it. My son, all this calamity upon earth comes down from heaven; upon earth shall there be a great destruction.

11 Then I arose, prayed, and entreated; and wrote down my prayer for the generations of the world, explaining everything to my son Mathusala.

12 When I went down below, and looking up to heaven, beheld the sun proceeding from the east, the moon descending to the west, a few scattered stars, and everything which God has known from the beginning, I blessed the Lord of judgment, and magnified him: because he hath sent forth the sun from the chambers(93) of the east; that, ascending and rising in the face of heaven, it might spring up, and pursue the path which has been pointed out to it.

(90) Purifying, and snatched away. Or, "was thrown down and removed" (Knibb, p. 192).
(91) And falling to the earth. Or, "and when it fell upon the earth" (Knibb, p. 192).
(92) My voice faltered. Literally, "the word fell down in my mouth" (Laurence, p. 118).
(93) Chambers. Literally, "windows" (Laurence, p. 119).

CHAPTER 83

1 I lifted up my hands in righteousness, and blessed the holy, and the Great One. I spoke with the breath of my mouth, and with a tongue of flesh, which God has formed for all the sons of mortal men, that with it they may speak; giving them breath, a mouth, and a tongue to converse with.

2 Blessed are you, O Lord, the King, great and powerful in your greatness, Lord of all the creatures of heaven, King of kings, God of the whole world, whose reign, whose kingdom, and whose majesty endure forever and ever.

3 From generation to generation shall your dominion exist. All the heavens are your throne forever, and all the earth your footstool forever and forever.

4 For you have made them, and over all you reign. No act whatsoever exceeds your power. With your wisdom is unchangeable; nor from your throne and from your presence is it ever averted. You know all things, see and hear them; nor is anything concealed from you; for you perceive all things.

5 The angels of your heavens have transgressed; and on mortal flesh shall your wrath remain, until the day of the great judgment.

6 Now then, O God, Lord and mighty King, I entreat you, and beseech you to grant my prayer, that a posterity may be left to me on earth, and that the whole human race may not perish;

7 That the earth may not be left destitute, and destruction take place for ever.

8 O my Lord, let the race perish from off the earth which has offended you, but a righteous and upright race establish for a posterity(94) forever. Hide not your face, O Lord, from the prayer of your servant.

(94) For a posterity. Literally, "for the plant of a seed" (Laurence, p. 121).

Chapter 84

1 After this I saw another dream, and explained it all to you, my son. Enoch arose and said to his son Mathusala, To you, my son, will I speak. Hear my word; and incline your ear to the visionary dream of your father. Before I married your mother Edna, I saw a vision on my bed;(95)

2 And behold, a cow sprung forth from the earth;

3 And this cow was white.

4 Afterwards a female heifer sprung forth; and with it another heifer:(96) one of them was black, and one was red.(97)

5 The black heifer then struck the red one, and pursued it over the earth.

6 From that period I could see nothing more of the red heifer; but the black one increased in bulk, and a female heifer came with him.

7 After this I saw that many cows proceeded forth, resembling him, and following after him.

8 The first female young one also went out in the presence of the first cow; and sought the red heifer, but found him not.

9 And she lamented with a great lamentation, while she was seeking him.

10 Then I looked until that first cow came to her, from which time she became silent, and ceased to lament.

11 Afterwards she calved another white cow.

12 And again calved many cows and black heifers.

13 In my sleep also I perceived a white bull, which in like manner grew, and became a large white bull.

14 After him many white cows came forth, resembling him.

15 And they began to calve many other white cows, which resembled them and followed each other.

(95) This second vision of Enoch seems to portray in symbolic language the complete history of the world from the time of Adam down to the final judgment and the establishment of the Messianic Kingdom (Charles, p. 227).
(96) Another heifer. The sense seems to require that the passage should read, "two other heifers" (Laurence, p. 121).
(97) Cain and Abel.

Chapter 85

1 Again I looked attentively, while sleeping, and surveyed heaven above.

2 And behold a single star fell from heaven.

3 Which being raised up, ate and fed among those cows.

4 After that I perceived other large and black cows; and behold all of them changed their stalls and pastures, while their young began to lament one with another. Again I looked in my vision, and surveyed heaven; when behold I saw many stars which descended, and projected themselves from heaven to where the first star was,

5 Into the midst of those young ones; while the cows were with them, feeding in the midst of them.

6 I looked at and observed them; when behold, they all acted after the manner of horses, and began to approach the young cows, all of whom became pregnant, and brought forth elephants, camels, and asses.

7 At these all the cows were alarmed and terrified; when they began biting with their teeth, swallowing, and striking with their horns.

8 They began also to devour the cows; and behold all the children of the earth trembled, shook with terror at them, and suddenly fled away.

CHAPTER 86

1 Again I perceived them, when they began to strike and to swallow each other; and the earth cried out. Then I raised my eyes a second time towards heaven, and saw in a vision, that, behold, there came forth from heaven as it were the likeness of white men. One came forth from thence, and three with him.

2 Those three, who came forth last, seized me by my hand; and raising me up from the generations of the earth, elevated me to a high station.

3 Then they showed me a lofty tower on the earth, while every hill became diminished. And they said, Remain here, until you perceive what shall come upon those elephants, camels, and asses, upon the stars, and upon all the cows.

CHAPTER 87

1 Then I looked at that one of the four white men, who came forth first.

2 He seized the first star which fell down from heaven.

3 And, binding it hand and foot, he cast it into a valley; a valley narrow, deep, stupendous, and gloomy.

4 Then one of them drew his sword, and gave it to the elephants, camels, and asses, who began to strike each other. And the whole earth shook on account of them.

5 And when I looked in the vision, behold, one of those four angels, who came forth, hurled from heaven, collected together, and took all the great stars, whose form partly resembles that of horses; and binding them all hand and

foot, cast them into the cavities of the earth.

Chapter 88

1 Then one of those four went to the white cows, and taught them a mystery. While the cow was trembling, it was born, and became a man,(98) and fabricated for himself a large ship. In this he dwelt, and three cows(99) dwelt with him in that ship, which covered them.

(98) Noah.
(99) Shem, Ham, and Japheth

2 Again I lifted up my eyes towards heaven, and saw a lofty roof. Above it were seven cataracts, which poured forth on a certain village much water.
3 Again I looked, and behold there were fountains open on the earth in that large village.
4 The water began to boil up, and rose over the earth; so that the village was not seen, while its whole soil was covered with water.
5 Much water was over it, darkness, and clouds. Then I surveyed the height of this water; and it was elevated above the village.
6 It flowed over the village, and stood higher than the earth.
7 Then all the cows which were collected there, while I looked on them, were drowned, swallowed up, and destroyed in the water.
8 But the ship floated above it. All the cows, the elephants, the camels, and the asses, were drowned on the earth, and all cattle. Nor could I perceive them. Neither were they able to get out, but perished, and sunk into the deep.
9 Again I looked in the vision until those cataracts from that lofty roof were removed, and the fountains of the earth became equalized, while other depths were opened;
10 Into which the water began to descend, until the dry ground appeared.
11 The ship remained on the earth; the darkness receded; and it became light.
12 Then the white cow, which became a man, went out of the ship, and the three cows with him.
13 One of the three cows was white, resembling that cow; one of them was red as blood; and one of them was black. And the white cow left them.
14 Then began wild beasts and birds to bring forth.
15 Of all these the different kinds assembled together, lions, tigers, wolves, dogs, wild boars, foxes, rabbits, and the hanzar.

16 The siset, the avest, kites, the phonkas, and ravens.

17 Then the white cow(100) was born in the midst of them.

(100) Abraham

18 And they began to bite each other; when the white cow, which was born in the midst of them, brought forth a wild ass and a white cow at the same time, and after that many wild asses. Then the white cow,(101) which was born, brought forth a black wild sow and a white sheep.(102)

(101) Isaac.
(102) Esau and Jacob.

19 That wild sow also brought forth many swine.

20 And that sheep brought forth twelve sheep.(103)

(103) The twelve patriarchs.

21 When those twelve sheep grew up, they delivered one of them(104) to the asses(105)

(104) Joseph.
(105) The Midianites.

22 Again those asses delivered that sheep to the wolves,(106)

(106) The Egyptians.

23 And he grew up in the midst of them.

24 Then the Lord brought the eleven other sheep, that they might dwell and feed with him in the midst of the wolves.

25 They multiplied, and there was abundance of pasture for them.

26 But the wolves began to frighten and oppress them, while they destroyed their young ones.

27 And they left their young in torrents of deep water.

28 Now the sheep began to cry out on account of their young, and fled for refuge to their Lord. One(107) however, which was saved, escaped, and went away to the wild asses.

(107) Moses.

29 I beheld the sheep moaning, crying, and petitioning their Lord.

30 With all their might, until the Lord of the sheep descended at their voice from his lofty habitation; went to them; and inspected them.

31 He called to that sheep which had secretly stolen away from the wolves, and told him to make the wolves understand that they were not to touch the sheep.

32 Then that sheep went to the wolves with the word of the Lord, when another met him,(108) and proceeded with him.

(108) Aaron

33 Both of them together entered the dwelling of the wolves; and conversing with them made them understand, that thenceforwards they were not to touch the sheep.

34 Afterwards I perceived the wolves greatly prevailing over the sheep with their whole force. The sheep cried out; and their Lord came to them.

35 He began to strike the wolves, who commenced a grievous lamentation; but the sheep were silent, nor from that time did they cry out.

36 I then looked at them, until they departed from the wolves. The eyes of the wolves were blind, who went out and followed them with all their might. But the Lord of the sheep proceeded with them, and conducted them.

37 All his sheep followed him.

38 His countenance was terrific and splendid, and glorious was his aspect. Yet the wolves began to follow the sheep, until they overtook them in a certain lake of water.(109)

(109) The Red Sea.

39 Then that lake became divided; the water standing up on both sides before their face.

40 And while their Lord was conducting them, he placed himself between them and the wolves.

41 The wolves however perceived not the sheep, but went into the midst of the lake, following them, and running after them into the lake of water.

42 But when they saw the Lord of the sheep, they turned to fly from before his face.

43 Then the water of the lake returned, and that suddenly, according to its nature. It became full, and was raised up, until it covered the wolves. And I saw that all of them which had followed the sheep perished, and were drowned.

44 But the sheep passed over this water, proceeding to a wilderness, which was without both water and grass. And they began to open their eyes and to see.

45 Then I beheld the Lord of the sheep inspecting them, and giving them water and grass.

46 The sheep already mentioned was proceeding with them, and conducting them.

47 And when he had ascended the top of the lofty rock, the Lord of the sheep sent him to them.

48 Afterwards I perceived their Lord standing before them, with an aspect terrific and severe.

49 And when they all beheld him, they were frightened at his countenance.

50 All of them were alarmed, and trembled. They cried out after that sheep; and to the other sheep who had been with him, and who was in the midst of them, saying, We are not able to stand before our Lord, or to look upon him.

51 Then that sheep who conducted them went away, and ascended the top of the rock;

52 When the rest of the sheep began to grow blind, and to wander from the path which he had shown them; but he knew it not.

53 Their Lord however was moved with great indignation against them; and when that sheep had learned what had happened,

54 He descended from the top of the rock, and coming to them, found that there were many,

55 Which had become blind;

56 And had wandered from his path. As soon as they beheld him, they feared, and trembled at his presence;

57 And became desirous of returning to their fold,

58 Then that sheep, taking with him other sheep, went to those which had wandered.

59 And afterwards began to kill them. They were terrified at his countenance. Then he caused those which had wandered to return; who went back to their fold.

60 I likewise saw there in the vision, that this sheep became a man, built a house(110) for the Lord of the sheep, and made them all stand in the house.

(110) A house. A tabernacle (Milik, p. 205).

61 I perceived also that the sheep which proceeded to meet this sheep, their conductor, died. I saw, too, that all the great sheep perished, while smaller ones rose up in their place, entered into a pasture, and approached a river of water. (111)

(111) The river Jordan.

62 Then that sheep, their conductor, who became a man, was separated from them, and died.
63 All the sheep sought after him, and cried for him with bitter lamentation.
64 I saw likewise that they ceased to cry after that sheep, and passed over the river of water.
65 And that there arose other sheep, all of whom conducted them,(112) instead of those who were dead, and who had previously conducted them.

(112) The Judges of Israel.

66 Then I saw that the sheep entered into a goodly place, and a territory delectable and glorious.
67 I saw also that they became satiated; that their house was in the midst of a delectable territory; and that sometimes their eyes were opened, and that sometimes they were blind; until another sheep(113) arose and conducted them. He brought them all back; and their eyes were opened.

(113) Samuel.

68 Then dogs, foxes, and wild boars began to devour them, until again another sheep(114) arose, the master of the flock, one of themselves, a ram, to conduct them. This ram began to butt on every side those dogs, foxes, and wild boars, until they all perished.
(114) Saul.

69 His eyes, and saw the ram in the midst of them, who had laid aside his glory.
70 And he began to strike the sheep, treading upon them, and behaving himself without dignity.

71 Then their Lord sent the former sheep again to a still different sheep,(115) and raised him up to be a ram, and to conduct them instead of that sheep who had laid aside his glory.

(115) David.

72 Going therefore to him, and conversing with him alone, he raised up that ram, and made him a prince and leader of the flock. All the time that the dogs(116) troubled the sheep,

(116) The Philistines.

73 The first ram paid respect to this latter ram.
74 Then the latter ram arose, and fled away from before his face. And I saw that those dogs caused the first ram to fall.
75 But the latter ram arose, and conducted the smaller sheep.
76 That ram likewise begat many sheep, and died.
77 Then there was a smaller sheep,(117) a ram, instead of him, which became a prince and leader, conducting the flock.

(117) Solomon.

78 And the sheep increased in size, and multiplied.
79 And all the dogs, foxes, and wild boars feared, and fled away from him.
80 That ram also struck and killed all the wild beasts, so that they could not again prevail in the midst of the sheep, nor at any time ever snatch them away.
81 And that house was made large and wide; a lofty tower being built upon it by the sheep, for the Lord of the sheep.
82 The house was low, but the tower was elevated and very high.
83 Then the Lord of the sheep stood upon that tower, and caused a full table to approach before him.
84 Again I saw that those sheep wandered, and went various ways, forsaking that their house;
85 And that their Lord called to some among them, whom he sent(118) to them.

(118) The prophets.

86 But these the sheep began to kill. And when one of them was saved from slaughter(119) he leaped, and cried out against those who were desirous of killing him.

(119) Elijah.

87 But the Lord of the sheep delivered him from their hands, and made him ascend to him, and remain with him.

88 He sent also many others to them, to testify, and with lamentations to exclaim against them.

89 Again I saw, when some of them forsook the house of their Lord, and his tower; wandering on all sides, and growing blind,

90 I saw that the Lord of the sheep made a great slaughter among them in their pasture, until they cried out to him in consequence of that slaughter. Then he departed from the place of his habitation, and left them in the power of lions, tigers, wolves, and the zeebt,(120) and in the power of foxes, and of every beast.

(120) Zeebt. Hyenas. (Knibb, p. 209).

91 And the wild beasts began to tear them.

92 I saw, too, that he forsook the house of their fathers, and their tower; giving them all into the power of lions to tear and devour them; into the power of every beast.

93 Then I began to cry out with all my might, imploring the Lord of the sheep, and showing him how the sheep were devoured by all the beasts of prey.

94 But he looked on in silence, rejoicing that they were devoured, swallowed up, and carried off; and leaving them in the power of every beast for food. He called also seventy shepherds, and resigned to them the care of the sheep, that they might overlook them;

95 Saying to them and to their associates, Every one of you henceforwards overlook the sheep, and whatsoever I command you, do; and I will deliver them to you numbered.

96 I will tell you which of them shall be slain; these destroy. And he delivered the sheep to them.

97 Then he called to another, and said, Understand, and watch everything which the shepherds shall do to these sheep; for many more of them shall

perish than I have commanded.

98 Of every excess and slaughter, which the shepherds shall commit, there shall be an account; as, how many may have perished by my command, and how many they may have destroyed of their own heads.

99 Of all the destruction brought about by each of the shepherds there shall be an account; and according to the number I will cause a recital to be made before me, how many they have destroyed of their own heads, and how many they have delivered up to destruction, that I may have this testimony against them; that I may know all their proceedings; and that, delivering the sheep to them, I may see what they will do; whether they will act as I have commanded them, or not.

100 Of this, however, they shall be ignorant; neither shall you make any explanation to them, neither shall you reprove them; but there shall be an account of all the destruction done by them in their respective seasons. Then they began to kill, and destroy more than it was commanded them.

101 And they left the sheep in the power of the lions, so that very many of them were devoured and swallowed up by lions and tigers; and wild boars preyed upon them. That tower they burnt, and overthrew that house.

102 Then I grieved extremely on account of the tower, and because the house of the sheep was overthrown.

103 Neither was I afterwards able to perceive whether they again entered that house.

104 The shepherds likewise, and their associates, delivered them to all the wild beasts, that they might devour them. Each of them in his season, according to his number, was delivered up; each of them, one with another, was described in a book, how many of them, one with another, were destroyed, in a book.

105 More, however, than was ordered, every shepherd killed and destroyed.

106 Then I began to weep, and was greatly indignant, on account of the sheep.

107 In like manner also I saw in the vision him who wrote, how he wrote down one, destroyed by the shepherds, every day. He ascended, remained, and exhibited each of his books to the Lord of the sheep, containing all which they had done, and all which each of them had made away with;

108 And all which they had delivered up to destruction.

109 He took the book up in his hands, read it, sealed it, and deposited it.

110 After this, I saw shepherds overlooking for twelve hours.

111 And behold three of the sheep(121) departed, arrived, went in; and began building all which was fallen down of that house.

(121) Zerubbabel, Joshua, and Nehemiah.

112 But the wild boars(122) hindered them, although they prevailed not.

(122) The Samaritans.

113 Again they began to build as before, and raised up that tower, which was called a lofty tower.

114 And again they began to place before the tower a table, with every impure and unclean kind of bread upon it.

115 Moreover also all the sheep were blind, and could not see, as were the shepherds likewise.

116 Thus were they delivered up to the shepherds for a great destruction, who trod them under foot, and devoured them.

117 Yet was their Lord silent, until all the sheep in the field were destroyed. The shepherds and the sheep were all mixed together; but they did not save them from the power of the beasts.

118 Then he who wrote the book ascended, exhibited it, and read it at the residence of the Lord of the sheep. He petitioned him for them, and prayed, pointing out every act of the shepherds, and testifying before him against them all. Then taking the book, he deposited it with him, and departed.

CHAPTER 89

1 And I observed during the time, that thus thirty-seven(123) shepherds were overlooking, all of whom finished in their respective periods as the first. Others then received them into their hands, that they might overlook them in their respective periods, every shepherd in his own period.

2 Afterwards I saw in the vision, that all the birds of heaven arrived; eagles, the avest, kites and ravens. The eagle instructed them all.

3 They began to devour the sheep, to peck out their eyes, and to eat up their bodies.

4 The sheep then cried out; for their bodies were devoured by the birds.

5 I also cried out, and groaned in my sleep against the shepherd which overlooked the flock.

6 And I looked, while the sheep were eaten up by the dogs, by the eagles, and by the kites. They neither left them their body, nor their skin, nor their muscles, until their bones alone remained; until their bones fell upon the ground. And

the sheep became diminished.

7 I observed likewise during the time, that twenty-tree shepherds(124) were overlooking; who completed in their respective periods fifty-eight periods.

8 Then were small lambs born of those white sheep; who began to open their eyes and to see, crying out to the sheep.

9 The sheep, however, cried not out to them, neither did they hear what they uttered to them; but were deaf, blind, and obdurate in the greatest degrees.

10 I saw in the vision that ravens flew down upon those lambs;

11 That they seized one of them; and that tearing the sheep in pieces, they devoured them.

12 I saw also, that the horns grew upon those lambs; and that the ravens lighted down upon their horns.

13 I saw, too, that a large horn sprouted out on an animal among the sheep, and that their eyes were opened.

14 He looked at them. Their eyes were wide open; and he cried out to them.

15 Then the dabela(125) saw him; all of whom ran to him.

16 And besides this, all the eagles, the avest, the ravens and the kites, were still carrying off the sheep, flying down upon them, and devouring them. The sheep were silent, but the dabela lamented and cried out.

17 Then the ravens contended, and struggled with them.

18 They wished among them to break his horn; but they prevailed not over him.

19 I looked on them, until the shepherds, the eagles, the avest, and the kites came.

20 Who cried out to the ravens to break the horn of the dabela; to contend with him; and to kill him. But he struggled with them, and cried out, that help might come to him.

21 Then I perceived that the man came who had written down the names of the shepherds, and who ascended up before the Lord of the sheep.

22 He brought assistance, and caused everyone to see him descending to the help of the dabela.

23 I perceived likewise that the Lord of the sheep came to them in wrath, while all those who saw him fled away; all fell down in his tabernacle before his face; while all the eagles, the avest, ravens, and kites assembled, and brought with them all the sheep of the field.

24 All came together, and strove to break the horn of the dabela.

25 Then I saw, that the man, who wrote the book at the word of the Lord, opened the book of destruction, of that destruction which the last twelve

shepherds(126) wrought; and pointed out before the Lord of the sheep, that they destroyed more than those who preceded them.

26 I saw also that the Lord of the sheep came to them, and taking in his hand the sceptre of his wrath seized the earth, which became rent asunder; while all the beasts and birds of heaven fell from the sheep, and sunk into the earth, which closed over them.

27 I saw, too, that a large sword was given to the sheep, who went forth against all the beasts of the field to slay them.

28 But all the beasts and birds of heaven fled away from before their face.

29 And I saw a throne erected in a delectable land;

30 Upon this sat the Lord of the sheep, who received all the sealed books;

31 Which were open before him.

32 Then the Lord called the first seven white ones, and commanded them to bring before him the first of the first stars, which preceded the stars whose form partly resembled that of horses; the first star, which fell down first; and they brought them all before him.

33 And he spoke to the man who wrote in his presence, who was one of the seven white ones, saying, Take those seventy shepherds, to whom I delivered up the sheep, and who receiving them killed more of them than I commanded. Behold, I saw them all bound, and standing before him. First came on the trial of the stars, which, being judged, and found guilty, went to the place of punishment. They thrust them into a place, deep, and full of flaming fire, and full of pillars of fire. Then the seventy shepherds were judged, and being found guilty, were thrust into the flaming abyss.

34 At that time likewise I perceived, that one abyss was thus opened in the midst of the earth, which was full of fire.

35 And to this were brought the blind sheep; which being judged, and found guilty, were all thrust into that abyss of fire on the earth, and burnt.

36 The abyss was on the right of that house.

37 And I saw the sheep burning, and their bones consuming.

38 I stood beholding him immerge that ancient house, while they brought out its pillars, every plant in it, and the ivory infolding it. They brought it out, and deposited it in a place on the right side of the earth.

39 I also saw, that the Lord of the sheep produced a new house, great, and loftier than the former, which he bound by the former circular spot. All its pillars were new, and its ivory new, as well as more abundant than the former ancient ivory, which he had brought out.

40 And while all the sheep which were left were in the midst of it, all the beasts of the earth, and all the birds of heaven, fell down and worshipped them, petitioning them, and obeying them in everything.

41 Then those three, who were clothed in white, and who, holding me by my hand, had before caused me to ascend, while the hand of him who spoke held me; raised me up, and placed me in the midst of the sheep, before the judgment took place.

42 The sheep were all white, with wool long and pure. Then all who had perished, and had been destroyed, every beast of the field, and every bird of heaven, assembled in that house: while the Lord of the sheep rejoiced with great joy, because all were good, and had come back again to his dwelling.

43 And I saw that they laid down the sword which had been given to the sheep, and returned it to his house, sealing it up in the presence of the Lord.

44 All the sheep would have been inclosed in that house, had it been capable of containing them; and the eyes of all were open, gazing on the good One; nor was there one among them who did not behold him.

45 I likewise perceived that the house was large, wide, and extremely full. I saw, too, that a white cow was born, whose horns were great; and that all the beasts of the field, and all the birds of heaven, were alarmed at him, and entreated him at all times.

46 Then I saw that the nature of all of them was changed, and that they became white cows;

47 And that the first, who was in the midst of them, spoke, when that word became(127) a large beast, upon the head of which were great and black horns;

48 While the Lord of the sheep rejoiced over them, and over all the cows.

49 I lay down in the midst of them: I awoke; and saw the whole. This is the vision which I saw, lying down and waking. Then I blessed the Lord of righteousness, and gave glory to Him.

50 Afterwards I wept abundantly, nor did my tears cease, so that I became incapable of enduring it. While I was looking on, they flowed on account of what I saw; for all was come and gone by; every individual circumstance respecting the conduct of mankind was seen by me.

51 In that night I remembered my former dream; and therefore wept and was troubled, because I had seen that vision.

(123) Thirty-seven. An apparent error for thirty-five (see verse 7). The kings of Judah and Israel (Laurence, p. 139).

(124) The kings of Babylon, etc., during and after the captivity. The numbers thirty-five and twenty-three make fifty-eight; and not thirty-seven, as erroneously put in the first verse (Laurence, p. 139).
(125) Dabela. The ibex, probably symbolizing Alexander the Great (Laurence, p. 140).
(126) The native princes of Judah after its delivery from the Syrian yoke.
(127) Spoke, when that word came. Or "was a wild-ox, and that wild-ox was..." (Knibb, p. 216).

Chapter 90

1 And now, my son Mathusala, call to me all your brethren, and assemble for me all the children of your mother; for a voice calls me, and the spirit is poured out upon me, that I may show you everything which shall happen to you forever.
2 Then Mathusala went, called to him all his brethren, and assembled his kindred.
3 And conversing with all his children in truth,
4 Enoch said, Hear, my children, every word of your father, and listen in uprightness to the voice of my mouth; for I would gain your attention, while I address you. My beloved, be attached to integrity, and walk in it.
5 Approach not integrity with a double heart; nor be associated with double-minded men: but walk, my children, in righteousness, which will conduct you in good paths; and be truth your companion.
6 For I know, that oppression will exist and prevail on earth; that on earth great punishment shall in the end take place; and that there shall be a consummation of all iniquity, which shall be cut off from its root, and every fabric raised by it shall pass away. Iniquity, however, shall again be renewed, and consummated on earth. Every act of crime, and every act of oppression and impiety, shall be a second time embraced.
7 When therefore iniquity, sin, blasphemy, tyranny, and every evil work, shall increase, and when transgression, impiety, and uncleanness also shall increase, then upon them all shall great punishment be inflicted from heaven.
8 The holy Lord shall go forth in wrath, and upon them all shall great punishment from heaven be inflicted.
9 The holy Lord shall go forth in wrath, and with punishment, that he may execute judgment upon earth.
10 In those days oppression shall be cut off from its roots, and iniquity with fraud shall be eradicated, perishing from under heaven.
11 Every place of strength(128) shall be surrendered with its inhabitants; with fire shall it be burnt. They shall be brought from every part of the earth, and

be cast into a judgment of fire. They shall perish in wrath, and by a judgment overpowering them forever.

12 Righteousness shall be raised up from slumber; and wisdom shall be raised up, and conferred upon them.

13 Then shall the roots of iniquity be cut off; sinners perish by the sword; and blasphemers be annihilated everywhere.

14 Those who meditate oppression, and those who blaspheme, by the sword shall perish.

15 And now, my children, I will describe and point out to you the path of righteousness and the path of oppression.

16 I will again point them out to you, that you may know what is to come.

17 Hear now, my children, and walk in the path of righteousness, but shun that of oppression; for all who walk in the path of iniquity shall perish forever.

(128) Every place of strength. Or, "all the idols of the nations" (Knibb, p. 218).

CHAPTER 91

1 That which was written by Enoch. He wrote all this instruction of wisdom for every man of dignity, and every judge of the earth; for all my children who shall dwell upon earth, and for subsequent generations, conducting themselves uprightly and peaceably.

2 Let not your spirit be grieved on account of the times; for the holy, the Great One, has prescribed a period to all.

3 Let the righteous man arise from slumber; let him arise, and proceed in the path of righteousness, in all its paths; and let him advance in goodness and eternal clemency. Mercy shall be showed to the righteous man; upon him shall be conferred integrity and power forever. In goodness and in righteousness shall he exist, and shall walk in everlasting light; but sin shall perish in eternal darkness, nor be seen from that time forward for evermore.

CHAPTER 92

1 After this, Enoch began to speak from a book.

2 And Enoch said, Concerning the children of righteousness, concerning the elect of the world, and concerning the plant of righteousness and integrity.

3 Concerning these things will I speak, and these things will I explain to you, my children: I who am Enoch. In consequence of that which has been shown to me, from my heavenly vision and from the voice of the holy angels(129)

have I acquired knowledge; and from the tablet of heaven have I acquired understanding.

4 Enoch then began to speak from a book, and said, I have been born the seventh in the first week, while judgment and righteousness wait with patience.

5 But after me, in the second week, great wickedness shall arise, and fraud shall spring forth.

6 In that week the end of the first shall take place, in which mankind shall be safe.(130)

7 But when the first is completed, iniquity shall grow up; and during the second week he shall execute the decree(131) upon sinners.

8 Afterwards, in the third week, during its completion, a man(132) of the plant of righteous judgment shall be selected; and after him the Plant(133) of righteousness shall come forever.

9 Subsequently, in the fourth week, during its completion, the visions of the holy and the righteous shall be seen, the order of generation after generation shall take place, and a habitation shall be made for them. Then in the fifth week, during its completion, the house of glory and of dominion(134) shall be erected forever.

10 After that, in the sixth week, all those who are in it shall be darkened, the hearts of all of them shall be forgetful of wisdom, and in it shall a Man(135) arise and come forth.

11 And during its completion He shall burn the house of dominion with fire, and all the race of the elect root shall be dispersed.(136)

12 Afterwards, in the seventh week, a perverse generation shall arise; abundant shall be its deeds, and all its deeds perverse. During its completion, the righteous shall be selected from the everlasting plant of righteousness; and to them shall be given the sevenfold doctrine of his whole creation.

13 Afterwards there shall be another week, the eighth(137) of righteousness, to which shall be given a sword to execute judgment and justice upon all oppressors.

14 Sinners shall be delivered up into the hands of the righteous, who during its completion shall acquire habitations by their righteousness; and the house of the great King shall be established for celebrations forever. After this, in the ninth week, shall the judgment of righteousness be revealed to the whole world.

15 Every work of the ungodly shall disappear from the whole earth; the world shall be marked for destruction; and all men shall be on the watch for the path

of integrity.

16 And after this, on the seventh day of the tenth week, there shall be an everlasting judgment, which shall be executed upon the Watchers; and a spacious eternal heaven shall spring forth in the midst of the angels.

17 The former heaven shall depart and pass away; a new heaven shall appear; and all the celestial powers shall shine with sevenfold splendour forever. Afterwards likewise shall there be many weeks, which shall externally exist in goodness and in righteousness.

18 Neither shall sin be named there forever and forever.

19 Who is there of all the children of men, capable of hearing the voice of the Holy One without emotion?

20 Who is there capable of thinking his thoughts? Who capable of contemplating all the workmanship of heaven? Who of comprehending the deeds of heaven?

21 He may behold its animation, but not its spirit. He may be capable of conversing respecting it, but not of ascending to it. He may see all the boundaries of these things, and meditate upon them; but he can make nothing like them.

22 Who of all men is able to understand the breadth and length of the earth?

23 By whom have been seen the dimensions of all these things? Is it every man who is capable of comprehending the extent of heaven; what its elevation is, and by what it is supported?

24 How many are the numbers of the stars; and where all the luminaries remain at rest?

(129) Holy angels. A Qumran text reads, "Watchers and Holy Ones," clearly denoting heavenly Watchers who did not fall along with the wicked ones (Milik, p. 264). See also Dan. 4:13, "a watcher and a holy one came down from heaven"; 4:17, "watchers, and... holy ones."
(130) Mankind shall be safe. Or, "a man will be saved" (Knibb, p. 224).
(131) The Deluge after the first (in the middle of the second) Millennium (2500 B.C.).
(132) King David at the end of the third Millennium (1000 B.C.).
(133) The Messiah at the end of the fourth Millennium (4 B.C. to 30 A.D.).
(134) The establishment (30 A.D.) and building of the Church through the fifth (and sixth) Millennium.
(135) The Messiah at the end of the sixth Millennium.
(136) The destruction of Jerusalem and the disbursement of those who dwell in that land at the end of the sixth (and the beginning of the seventh) Millennium.
(137) The beginning of the eighth Millennium.

CHAPTER 93

1 And now let me exhort you, my children, to love righteousness, and to walk in it; for the paths of righteousness are worthy of acceptation; but the paths of iniquity shall suddenly fail, and be diminished.

2 To men of note in their generation the paths of oppression and death are revealed; but they keep far from them, and do not follow them.

3 Now, too, let me exhort you who are righteous, not to walk in the paths of evil and oppression, nor in the paths of death. Approach them not, that you may not perish; but covet,

4 And choose for yourselves righteousness, and a good life.

5 Walk in the paths of peace, that you may live, and be found worthy. Retain my words in your inmost thoughts, and obliterate them not from your hearts; for I know that sinners counsel men to commit crime craftily. They are not found in every place, nor does every counsel possess a little of them.

6 Woe to those who build iniquity and oppression, and who lay the foundation of fraud; for suddenly shall they be subverted, and never obtain peace.

7 Woe to those who build up their houses with crime; for from their very foundations shall their houses be demolished, and by the sword shall they themselves fall. Those, too, who acquire gold and silver, shall justly and suddenly perish. Woe to you who are rich, for in your riches have you trusted; but from your riches you shall be removed; because you have not remembered the Most High in the days of your prosperity.

8 You have committed blasphemy and iniquity; and are destined to the day of the effusion of blood, to the day of darkness, and to the day of the great judgment.

9 This I will declare and point out to you, that he who created you will destroy you.

10 When you fall, he will not show you mercy; but your Creator will rejoice in your destruction.

11 Let those, then, who shall be righteous among you in those days, detest sinners, and the ungodly.

CHAPTER 94

1 O that my eyes were clouds of water, that I might weep over you, and pour forth my tears like rain, and rest from the sorrow of my heart!

2 Who has permitted you to hate and to transgress? Judgment shall overtake you, ye sinners.

3 The righteous shall not fear the wicked; because God will again bring them into your power, that you may avenge yourselves of them according to your pleasure.

4 Woe to you who shall be so bound by execrations, that you cannot be released from them; the remedy being far removed from you on account of your sins. Woe to you who recompense your neighbour with evil; for you shall be recompensed according to your works.

5 Woe to you, false witnesses, you who aggravate iniquity; for you shall suddenly perish.

6 Woe to you, sinners; for you reject the righteous; for you receive or reject at pleasure those who commit iniquity; and their yoke shall prevail over you.

CHAPTER 95

1 Wait in hope, you righteous; for suddenly shall sinners perish from before you, and you shall exercise dominion over them, according to your will.

2 In the day of the sufferings of sinners your offspring shall be elevated, and lifted up like eagles. Your nest shall be more exalted than that of the avest; you shall ascend, and enter into the cavities of the earth, and into the clefts of the rocks forever, like conies, from the sight of the ungodly;

3 Who shall groan over you, and weep like sirens.

4 You shall not fear those who trouble you; for restoration shall be yours; a splendid light shall shine around you, and the voice of tranquility shall be heard from heaven. Woe to you, sinners; for your wealth makes you resemble saints, but your hearts reproach you, knowing that you are sinners. This word shall testify against you, for the remembrance of crime.

5 Woe to you who feed upon the glory of the corn, and drink the strength of the deepest spring, and in the pride of your power tread down the humble.

6 Woe to you who drink water at pleasure; for suddenly shall you be recompensed, consumed, and withered, because you have forsaken the foundation of life.

7 Woe to you who act iniquitously, fraudulently, and blasphemously; there shall be a remembrance against you for evil.

8 Woe to you, powerful, who with power strike down righteousness; for the day of your destruction shall come; while at that very time many and good days shall be the portion of the righteous, even at the period of your judgment.

CHAPTER 96

1 The righteous are confident that sinners will be disgraced, and perish in the day of iniquity.

2 You shall yourselves be conscious of it; for the Most High will remember your destruction, and the angels shall rejoice over it. What will you do sinners? And where will you fly in the day of judgment, when you shall hear the words of the prayer of the righteous?

3 You are not like them who in this respect witness against you; you are associates of sinners.

4 In those days shall the prayers of the righteous come up before the Lord. When the day of your judgment shall arrive; and every circumstance of your iniquity be related before the great and the holy One;

5 Your faces shall be covered with shame; while every deed, strengthened by crime, shall be rejected.

6 Woe unto you, sinners, who in the midst of the sea, and on dry land, are those against whom an evil record exists. Woe to you who squander silver and gold, not obtained in righteousness, and say, We are rich, possess wealth, and have acquired everything which we can desire.

7 Now then will we do whatsoever we are disposed to do; for we have amassed silver; our barns are full, and the husbandmen of our families are like overflowing water.

8 Like water shall your falsehood pass away; for your wealth will not be permanent, but shall suddenly ascend from you, because you have obtained it all iniquitously; to extreme malediction shall you be delivered up.

9 And now I swear to you, crafty, as well as simple ones; that you, often contemplating the earth, you who are men, clothe yourselves more elegantly that married women, and both together more so than unmarried ones,(138) everywhere arraying yourselves in majesty, in magnificence, in authority, and in silver: but gold, purple, honour, and wealth, like water, flow away.

10 Erudition therefore and wisdom are not theirs. Thus shall they perish, together with their riches, with all their glory, and with their honours;

11 While with disgrace, with slaughter, and in extreme penury, shall their spirits be thrust into a furnace of fire.

12 I have sworn to you, sinners, that neither mountain nor hill has been or shall be subservient(139) to woman.

13 Neither in this way has crime been sent down to us upon earth, but men of their own heads have invented it; and greatly shall those who give it efficiency

be execrated.

14 Barrenness shall not be previously inflicted on woman; but on account of the work of her hands shall she die childless.

15 I have sworn to you, sinners, by the holy and the Great One, that all your evil deeds are disclosed in the heavens; and that none of your oppressive acts are concealed and secret.

16 Think not in your minds, neither say in your hearts, that every crime is not manifested and seen. In heaven it is daily written down before the Most High. Henceforwards shall it be manifested; for every act of oppression which you commit shall be daily recorded, until the period of your condemnation.

17 Woe to you, simple ones, for you shall perish in your simplicity. To the wise you will not listen, and that which is good you shall not obtain.

18 Now therefore know that you are destined to the day of destruction; nor hope that sinners shall live; but in process of time you shall die; for you are not marked for redemption;

19 But are destined to the day of the great judgment, to the day of distress, and the extreme ignominy of your souls.

20 Woe to you, obdurate in heart, who commit crime, and feed on blood. Whence is it that you feed on good things, drink, and are satiated? Is it not because our Lord, the Most High, has abundantly supplied every good thing upon earth? To you there shall not be peace.

21 Woe to you who love the deeds of iniquity. Why do you hope for that which is good? Know that you shall be given up into the hands of the righteous; who shall cut off your necks, slay you, and show you no compassion.

22 Woe to you who rejoice in the trouble of the righteous; for a grave shall not be dug for you.

23 Woe to you who frustrate the word of the righteous; for to you there shall be no hope of life.

24 Woe to you who write down the word of falsehood, and the word of the wicked; for their falsehood they record, that they may hear and not forget folly.

25 To them there shall be no peace; but they shall surely die suddenly.

(138) Than married women...unmarried ones. Or, "than a woman and more coloured (garments) than a girl..." (Knibb, p. 230).
(139) Subservient. Literally, "a servant." Perhaps in furnishing them with treasures for ornaments (Laurence, p. 159).

CHAPTER 97

1 Woe to them who act impiously, who laud and honour the word of falsehood. You have been lost in perdition; and have never led a virtuous life.

2 Woe to you who change the words of integrity. They transgress against the everlasting decree;(140)

3 And cause the heads of those who are not sinners to be trodden down upon the earth.

4 In those days you, O righteous, shall have been deemed worthy of having your prayers rise up in remembrance; and shall have deposited them in testimony before the angels, that they might records the sins of the sinners in the presence of the Most High.

5 In those days the nations shall be overthrown; but the families of the nations shall rise again in the day of perdition.

6 In those days they who become pregnant shall go forth, carry off their children, and forsake them. Their offspring shall slip from them, and while suckling them shall they forsake them; they shall never return to them, and never instruct their beloved.

7 Again I swear to you, sinners, that crime has been prepared for the day of blood, which never ceases.

8 They shall worship stones, and engrave golden, silver, and wooden images. They shall worship impure spirits, demons, and every idol, in temples; but no help shall be obtained for them. Their hearts shall become impious through their folly, and their eyes be blinded with mental superstition.(141) In their visionary dreams shall they be impious and superstitious, lying in all their actions, and worshipping a stone. Altogether shall they perish.

9 But in those days blessed shall they be, to whom the word of wisdom is delivered; who point out and pursue the path of the Most High; who walk in the way of righteousness, and who act not impiously with the impious.

10 They shall be saved.

11 Woe to you who expand the crime of your neighbour; for in hell shall you be slain.

12 Woe to you who lay the foundation of sin and deceit, and who are bitter on earth; for on it shall you be consumed.

13 Woe to you who build your houses by the labour of others, every part of which is constructed with brick, and with the stone of crime; I tell you, that you shall not obtain peace.

14 Woe to you who despise the extent of the everlasting inheritance of

your fathers, while your souls follow after idols; for to you there shall be no tranquillity.

15 Woe to them who commit iniquity, and give aid to blasphemy, who slay their neighbour until the day of the great judgment; for your glory shall fall; malevolence shall He put into your hearts, and the spirit of his wrath shall stir you up, that every one of you may perish by the sword.

16 Then shall all the righteous and the holy remember your crimes.

(140) They transgress...the everlasting decree. Or, "they distort the eternal law" (Knibb, p. 232).

(141) Mental superstition. Literally, "with the fear of their hearts" (Laurence, p. 162).

CHAPTER 98

1 In those days shall fathers be struck down with their children in the presence of each other; and brethren with their brethren shall fall dead: until a river shall flow from their blood.

2 For a man shall not restrain his hand from his children, nor from his children's children; his mercy will be to kill them.

3 Nor shall the sinner restrain his hand from his honoured brother. From the dawn of day to the setting sun shall the slaughter continue. The horse shall wade up to his breast, and the chariot shall sink to its axle, in the blood of sinners.

CHAPTER 99

1 In those days the angels shall descend into places of concealment, and gather together in one spot all who have assisted in crime.

2 In that day shall the Most High rise up to execute the great judgment upon all sinners, and to commit the guardianship of all the righteous and holy to the holy angels, that they may protect them as the apple of an eye, until every evil and every crime be annihilated.

3 Whether or not the righteous sleep securely, wise men shall then truly perceive.

4 And the sons of the earth shall understand every word of that book, knowing that their riches cannot save them in the ruin of their crimes.

5 Woe to you, sinners, when you shall be afflicted on account of the righteous in the day of the great trouble; shall be burnt in the fire; and be recompensed according to your deeds.

6 Woe to you, perverted in heart, who are watchful to obtain an accurate knowledge of evil, and to discover terrors. No one shall assist you.

7 Woe to you, sinners; for with the words of your mouths, and with the work of your hands, have you acted impiously; in the flame of a blazing fire shall you be burnt.

8 And now know, that the angels shall inquire into your conduct in heaven; of the sun, the moon, and the stars, shall they inquire respecting your sins; for upon earth you exercise jurisdiction over the righteous.

9 Every cloud shall bear witness against you, the snow, the dew, and the rain: for all of them shall be withholden from you, that they may not descend upon you, nor become subservient to your crimes.

10 Now then bring gifts of salutation to the rain; that, not being withholden, it may descend upon you; and to the dew, if it has received from you gold and silver. But when the frost, snow, cold, every snowy wind, and every suffering belonging to them, fall upon you, in those days you will be utterly incapable of standing before them.

CHAPTER 100

1 Attentively consider heaven, all you progeny of heaven, and all the works of the Most High; fear him, nor conduct yourselves criminally before him.

2 If He shut up the windows of heaven, restraining the rain and dew, that it may not descend upon the earth on your account, what will you do?

3 And if He send his wrath upon you, and upon all your deeds, you are not they who can supplicate him; you who utter against his righteousness, language proud and powerful. To you there shall be no peace.

4 Do you not see the commanders of ships, how their vessels are tossed about by the waves, torn to pieces by the winds, and exposed to the greatest peril?

5 That they therefore fear, because their whole property is embarked with them on the ocean; and that they forbode evil in their hearts, because it may swallow them up, and they may perish in it?

6 Is not the whole sea, all its waters, and all its commotion, the work of him, the Most High; of him who has sealed up all its exertions, and girded it on every side with sand?

7 Is it not at his rebuke dried up, and alarmed; while all its fish with everything contained in it die? And will not you, sinners, who are on earth, fear him? Is not He the maker of heaven and earth, and of all things which are in them?

8 And who has given erudition and wisdom to all that move progressive upon

the earth, and over the sea?

9 Are not the commanders of ships terrified at the ocean? And shall not sinners be terrified at the Most High?

(NO CHAPTER 101)

CHAPTER 102

1 In those days, when He shall cast the calamity of fire upon you, whither will you fly, and where will you be safe?

2 And when He sends forth his word against you, are you not spared, and terrified?

3 All the luminaries are agitated with great fear; and all the earth is spared, while it trembles, and suffers anxiety.

4 All the angels fulfill the commands received by them, and are desirous of being concealed from the presence of the great Glory; while the children of the earth are alarmed and troubled.

5 But you, sinners, are forever accursed; to you there shall be no peace.

6 Fear not, souls of the righteous; but wait with patient hope for the day of your death in righteousness. Grieve not, because your souls descend in great trouble, with groaning, lamentation, and sorrow, to the receptacle of the dead. In your lifetime your bodies have not received a recompense in proportion to your goodness, but in the period of your existence have sinners existed; in the period of execration and of punishment.

7 And when you die, sinners say concerning you, As we die, the righteous die. What profit have they in their works? Behold, like us, they expire in sorrow and in darkness. What advantage have they over us? Henceforward are we equal. What will be within their grasp, and what before their eyes forever? For behold they are dead; and never will they again perceive the light. I say unto you, sinners, You have been satisfied with meat and drink, with human plunder and rapine, with sin, with the acquisition of wealth and with the sight of good days. Have you not marked the righteous, how their end is in peace? For no oppression is found in them even to the day of their death. They perish, and are as if they were not, while their souls descend in trouble to the receptacle of the dead.

CHAPTER 103

1 But now I swear to you, righteous, by the greatness of his splendour and

his glory; by his illustrious kingdom and by his majesty, to you I swear, that I comprehend this mystery; that I have read the tablet of heaven, have seen the writing of the holy ones, and have discovered what is written and impressed on it concerning you.

2 I have seen that all goodness, joy, and glory has been prepared for you, and been written down for the spirits of them who die eminently righteous and good. To you it shall be given in return for your troubles; and your portion of happiness shall far exceed the portion of the living.

3 The spirits of you who die in righteousness shall exist and rejoice. Their spirits shall exult; and their remembrance shall be before the face of the Mighty One from generation to generation. Nor shall they now fear disgrace.

4 Woe to you, sinners, when you die in your sins; and they, who are like you, say respecting you, Blessed are these sinners. They have lived out their whole period; and now they die in happiness and in wealth. Distress and slaughter they knew not while alive; in honour they die; nor ever in their lifetime did judgment overtake them.

5 But has it not been shown to them, that, when to the receptacle of the dead their souls shall be made to descend, their evil deeds shall become their greatest torment? Into darkness, into the snare, and into the flame, which shall burn to the great judgment, shall their spirits enter; and the great judgment shall take effect for ever and forever.

6 Woe to you; for to you there shall be no peace. Neither can you say to the righteous, and to the good who are alive, In the days of our trouble have we been afflicted; every manner of trouble have we seen, and many evil things have suffered.

7 Our spirits have been consumed, lessened, and diminished.

8 We have perished; nor has there been a possibility of help for us in word or in deed: we have found none, but have been tormented and destroyed.

9 We have not expected to live day after day.

10 We hoped indeed to have been the head;

11 But we have become the tail. We have been afflicted, when we have exerted ourselves; but we have been devoured by sinners and the ungodly; their yoke has been heavy upon us.

12 Those have exercised dominion over us who detest and who goad us; and to those who hate us have we humbled our neck; but they have shown no compassion towards us.

13 We have been desirous of escaping from them, that we might fly away and

be at rest; but we have found no place to which we could fly, and be secure from them. We have sought an asylum with princes in our distress, and have cried out to those who were devouring us; but our cry has not been regarded, nor have they been disposed to hear our voice;

14 But rather to assist those who plunder and devour us; those who diminish us, and hide their oppression; who remove not their yoke from us, but devour, enervate, and slay us; who conceal our slaughter, nor remember that they have lifted up their hands against us.

CHAPTER 104

1 I swear to you, righteous, that in heaven the angels record your goodness before the glory of the Mighty One.

2 Wait with patient hope; for formerly you have been disgraced with evil and with affliction; but now shall you shine like the luminaries of heaven. You shall be seen, and the gates of heaven shall be opened to you. Your cries have cried for judgment; and it has appeared to you; for an account of all your sufferings shall be required from the princes, and from everyone who has assisted your plunderers.

3 Wait with patient hope; nor relinquish your confidence; for great joy shall be yours, like that of the angels in heaven. Conduct yourselves as you may, still you shall not be concealed in the day of the great judgment. You shall not be found like sinners; and eternal condemnation shall be far from you, so long as the world exists.

4 And now fear not, righteous, when you see sinners flourishing and prosperous in their ways.

5 Be not associates with them; but keep yourselves at a distance from their oppression; be you associated with the host of heaven. You, sinners, say, All our transgressions shall not be taken account of, and be recorded. But all your transgressions shall be recorded daily.

6 And be assured by me, that light and darkness, day and night, behold all your transgressions. Be not impious in your thoughts; lie not; surrender not the word of uprightness; lie not against the word of the holy and the mighty One; glorify not your idols; for all your lying and all your impiety is not for righteousness, but for great crime.

7 Now will I point out a mystery: Many sinners shall turn and transgress against the word of uprightness.

8 They shall speak evil things; they shall utter falsehood; execute great

undertakings;(142) and compose books in their own words. But when they shall write all my words correctly in their own languages,

9 They shall neither change or diminish them; but shall write them all correctly; all which from the first I have uttered concerning them.(143)

10 Another mystery also I point out. To the righteous and the wise shall be given books of joy, of integrity, and of great wisdom. To them shall books be given, in which they shall believe;

11 And in which they shall rejoice. And all the righteous shall be rewarded, who from these shall acquire the knowledge of every upright path.

(142) Execute great undertakings. Literally, "create a great creation" (Laurence, p. 173).
(143) Despite Enoch's mandate, his book was most certainly "changed" and "diminished" by later editors, though these fragments of it have survived.

CHAPTER 104A

1 In those days, saith the Lord, they shall call to the children of the earth, and make them listen to their wisdom. Show them that you are their leaders;

2 And that remuneration shall take place over the whole earth; for I and my Son will forever hold communion with them in the paths of uprightness, while they are still alive. Peace shall be yours. Rejoice, children of integrity, in the truth.

CHAPTER 105

1 After a time, my son Mathusala took a wife for his son Lamech.

2 She became pregnant by him, and brought forth a child, the flesh of which was as white as snow, and red as a rose; the hair of whose head was white like wool, and long; and whose eyes were beautiful. When he opened them, he illuminated all the house, like the sun; the whole house abounded with light.

3 And when he was taken from the hand of the midwife, Lamech his father became afraid of him; and flying away came to his own father Mathusala, and said, I have begotten a son, unlike to other children. He is not human; but, resembling the offspring of the angels of heaven, is of a different nature from ours, being altogether unlike to us.

4 His eyes are bright as the rays of the sun; his countenance glorious, and he looks not as if he belonged to me, but to the angels.

5 I am afraid, lest something miraculous should take place on earth in his days.

6 And now, my father, let me entreat and request you to go to our progenitor Enoch, and learn from him the truth; for his residence is with the angels.

7 When Mathusala heard the words of his son, he came to me at the extremities of the earth; for he had been informed that I was there: and he cried out.

8 I heard his voice, and went to him saying, Behold, I am here, my son; since you have come to me.

9 He answered and said, On account of a great event have I come to you; and on account of a sight difficult to be comprehended have I approached you.

10 And now, my father, hear me; for to my son Lamech a child has been born, who resembles not him; and whose nature is not like the nature of man. His colour is whiter than snow; he is redder than the rose; the hair of his head is whiter than white wool; his eyes are like the rays of the sun; and when he opened them he illuminated the whole house.

11 When also he was taken from the hand of the midwife,

12 His father Lamech feared, and fled to me, believing not that the child belonged to him, but that he resembled the angels of heaven. And behold I am come to you, that you might point out to me the truth.

13 Then I, Enoch, answered and said, The Lord will effect a new thing upon the earth. This have I explained, and seen in a vision. I have shown you that in the generations of Jared my father, those who were from heaven disregarded the word of the Lord. Behold they committed crimes; laid aside their class, and intermingled with women. With them also they transgressed; married with them, and begot children.(144)

14 A great destruction therefore shall come upon all the earth; a deluge, a great destruction, shall take place in one year.

15 This child which is born to your son shall survive on the earth, and his three sons shall be saved with him. When all mankind who are on the earth shall die, he shall be safe.

16 And his posterity shall beget on the earth giants, not spiritual, but carnal. Upon the earth shall a great punishment be inflicted, and it shall be washed from all corruption. Now therefore inform your son Lamech, that he who is born is his child in truth; and he shall call his name Noah, for he shall be to you a survivor. He and his children shall be saved from the corruption which shall take place in the world; from all the sin and from all the iniquity which shall be consummated on earth in his days. Afterwards shall greater impiety take place than that which had been before consummated on the earth; for I am acquainted with holy mysteries, which the Lord himself has discovered and explained to me; and which I have read in the tablets of heaven.

17 In them I saw it written, that the generation after generation shall transgress,

until a righteous race shall arise; until transgression and crime perish from off the earth; until all goodness come upon it.

18 And now, my son, go tell your son Lamech,

19 That the child which is born is his child in truth; and that there is no deception.

20 When Mathusala heard the word of his father Enoch, who had shown him every secret thing, he returned with understanding, and called the name of that child Noah; because he was to console the earth on account of all its destruction.

21 Another book, which Enoch wrote for his son Mathusala, and for those who should come after him, and preserve their purity of conduct in the latter days. You, who have laboured, shall wait in those days, until the evil doers be consumed, and the power of the guilty be annihilated. Wait, until sin pass away; for their names shall be blotted out of the holy books; their seed shall be destroyed, and their spirits slain. They shall cry out and lament in the invisible waste, and in the bottomless fire shall they burn.(145) There I perceived, as it were, a cloud which could not be seen through; for from the depth of it I was unable to look upwards. I beheld also a flame of fire blazing brightly, and, as it were, glittering mountains whirled around, and agitated from side to side.

22 Then I inquired of one of the holy angels who was with me, and said, What is this splendid object? For it is not heaven, but a flame of fire alone which blazes; and in it there is the clamour of exclamation, of woe, and of great suffering.

23 He said, There, into that place which you behold, shall be thrust the spirits of sinners and blasphemers; of those who shall do evil, and who shall pervert all which God has spoken by the mouth of the prophets; all which they ought to do. For respecting these things there shall be writings and impressions above in heaven, that the angels may read them and know what shall happen both to sinners and to the spirits of the humble; to those who have suffered in their bodies, but have been rewarded by God; who have been injuriously treated by wicked men; who have loved God; who have been attached neither to gold nor silver, nor to any good thing in the world, but have given their bodies to torment;

24 To those who from the period of their birth have not been covetous of earthly riches; but have regarded themselves as a breath passing away.

25 Such has been their conduct; and much has the Lord tried them; and their spirits have been found pure, that they might bless his name. All their blessings have I related in a book; and He has rewarded them; for they have been found to love heaven with an everlasting aspiration. God has said, While they have

been trodden down by wicked men, they have heard from them revilings and blasphemies; and have been ignominiously treated, while they were blessing me. And now will I call the spirits of the good from the generation of light, and will change those who have been born in darkness; who have not in their bodies been recompensed with glory, as their faith may have merited.

26 I will bring them into the splendid light of those who love my holy name: and I will place each of them on a throne of glory, of glory peculiarly his own, and they shall be at rest during unnumbered periods. Righteous is the judgment of God;

27 For to the faithful shall he give faith in the habitations of uprightness. They shall see those, who have been born in darkness unto darkness shall be cast; while the righteous shall be at rest. Sinners shall cry out, beholding them, while they exist in splendour and proceed forwards to the days and periods prescribed to them.

(144) After this verse, one Greek papyrus adds, "who are not like spiritual beings, but creatures of flesh" (Milik, p. 210).
(145) In the bottomless fire shall they burn. Literally, "in the fire shall they burn, where there is no earth" (Laurence, p. 178).

THE TESTAMENT OF MOSES

CHAPTER 1

The Testament of Moses even the things which he commanded in the one hundred and twentieth year of his life, that is the two thousand five hundredth year from the creation of the world: [But according to oriental reckoning the two thousand and seven hundredth, and the four hundredth after the departure from Phoenicia], when the people had gone forth after the Exodus that was made by Moses to Amman beyond the Jordan, in the prophecy that was made by Moses in the book Deuteronomy: and he called to him Joshua the son of Nun, a man approved of the Lord, that he might be the minister of the people and of the tabernacle of the testimony with all its holy things, and that he might bring the people into the land given to their fathers, that it should be given to them according to the covenant and the oath, which He spoke in the tabernacle to give (it) by Joshua: saying to Joshua these words: '(Be strong) and of a good courage so as to do with thy might all that has been commanded that you may be blameless unto God.' So says the Lord of the world. For He has created the world on behalf of His people. But He was not pleased to manifest this purpose of creation from the foundation of the world, in order that the Gentiles might thereby be convicted, yea to their own humiliation might by (their) arguments convict one another. Accordingly He designed and devised me, and He prepared me before the foundation of the world, that I should be the mediator of His covenant. And now I declare unto you that the time of the years of my life is fulfilled and I am passing away to sleep with my fathers even in the presence of all the people. And receive this writing that you may know how to preserve the books which I shall deliver unto you: and you shall set these in order and anoint them with oil of cedar and put them away in earthen vessels in the place which He made from the beginning of the creation of the world, that His name should be called upon until the day of repentance in the visitation wherewith the Lord will visit them in the consummation of the end of the days.

CHAPTER 2

And now they shall go by means of you into the land which He determined and promised to give to their fathers, in the which you shall bless and give to them individually and confirm unto them their inheritance in me and establish for them the kingdom, and you shall appoint them local magistrates according to the good pleasure of their Lord in judgment and righteousness. And five years after they enter into the land, that thereafter they shall be ruled by chiefs and kings for eighteen years, and during nineteen years the ten tribes shall break away. And the twelve tribes shall go down and transfer the tabernacle of the testimony. Then the God of heaven will make the court of His tabernacle and the tower of His sanctuary, and the two holy tribes shall be (there) established: but the ten tribes shall establish kingdoms for themselves according to their own ordinances. And they shall offer sacrifices throughout twenty years: and seven shall entrench the walls, and I will protect nine, but four shall transgress the covenant of the Lord, and profane the oath which the Lord made with them. And they shall sacrifice their sons to strange gods, and they shall set up idols in the sanctuary, to worship them. And in the house of the Lord they shall work impiety and engrave every form of beast, even many abominations.

CHAPTER 3

And in those days a king from the east shall come against them and his cavalry shall cover their land. And he shall burn their colony with fire together with the holy temple of the Lord, and he shall carry away all the holy vessels. And he shall cast forth all the people, and he shall take them to the land of his nativity, yea he shall take the two tribes with him. Then the two tribes shall call upon the ten tribes, and shall march as a lioness on the dusty plains, being hungry and thirsty. And they shall cry aloud: 'Righteous and holy is the Lord, for, inasmuch as ye have sinned, we too, in like manner, have been carried away with you, together with our children.' Then the ten tribes shall mourn on hearing the reproaches of the two tribes, and they shall say: 'What have we done unto you, brethren Has not this tribulation come on all the house of Israel' And all the tribes shall mourn, crying unto heaven and saying: 'God of Abraham God of Isaac and God of Jacob, remember Thy covenant which You made with them, and the oath which You didst swear unto them by Yourself, that their seed should never fail from the land which You hast given them.' Then they shall remember me, saying, in that day, tribe unto tribe and each man unto his neighbor: 'Is not this that which Moses did then declare unto us in prophecies, who suffered many things in Egypt and in the Red Sea and in the wilderness during forty years: and assuredly called heaven and earth to witness against us, that we should not transgress His commandments, in the which he was a mediator unto us Behold these things have befallen us after his death according to his declaration, as he declared to us at that time, yes, behold these have taken place even to our being carried away captive into the country of the east.' Who shall be also in bondage for about seventy and seven years.

CHAPTER 4

Then there shall enter one who is over them, and he shall spread forth his hands, and kneel upon his knees and pray on their behalf saying: 'Lord of all, King on the lofty throne, who rules the world, and did will that this people should be Your elect people, then (indeed) You didst will that You should be called their God, according to the covenant which You didst make with their fathers. And yet they have gone in captivity in another land with their wives and their children, and around the gates of strange peoples and where there is great vanity. Regard and have compassion on them, O Lord of heaven.' Then God will remember them on account of the covenant which He made with their fathers. and He will manifest His compassion in those times also. And He will put it into the mind of a king to have compassion on them, and he shall send them off to their land and country. Then some portions of the tribes shall go up and they shall come to their appointed place, and they shall anew surround the place with walls. And the two tribes shall continue in their prescribed faith, sad and lamenting because they will not be able to offer sacrifices to the Lord of their fathers. And the ten tribes shall increase and multiply among the Gentiles during the time of their captivity.

CHAPTER 5

And when the times of chastisement draw nigh and vengeance arises through the kings who share in their guilt and punish them, they themselves also shall be divided as to the truth. Wherefore it hath been said: 'They shall turn aside from righteousness and approach iniquity, and they shall defile with pollutions the house of their worship,' and [because] 'they shall prostitute themselves with strange gods.' For they shall not follow the truth of God, but some shall pollute the altar with the (very) gifts which they offer to the Lord, who are not priests but slaves, sons of slaves. And many in those times shall have respect unto desirable persons and receive gifts, and pervert judgment [on receiving presents]. And on this account the colony and the borders of their habitation shall be filled with lawless deeds and iniquities: those who wickedly depart from the Lord shall be judges: they shall be ready to judge for money as each may wish.

CHAPTER 6

Then there shall be raised up unto them kings bearing rule, and they shall call themselves priests of the Most High God: they shall assuredly work iniquity in the holy of holies. And an insolent king shall succeed them, who will not be of the race of the priests, a man bold and shameless, and he shall judge them as they shall deserve. And he shall cut off their chief men with the sword, and shall destroy them in secret places, so that no one may know where their bodies are. He shall slay the old and the young, and he shall not spare. Then the fear of him shall be bitter unto them in their land. And he shall execute judgments on them as the Egyptians executed upon them, during thirty and four years, and he shall punish them. And he shall beget children, (who) succeeding him shall rule for shorter periods. Into their parts cohorts and a powerful king of the west shall come, who shall conquer them: and he shall take them captive, and burn a part of their temple with fire, (and) shall crucify some around their colony.

CHAPTER 7

And when this is done the times shall be ended, in a moment the (second) course shall be (ended), the four hours shall come. They shall be forced ... And, in the time of these, destructive and impious men shall rule, saying that they are just. And these shall stir up the poison of their minds, being treacherous men, self-pleasers, dissemblers in all their own affairs and lovers of banquets at every hour of the day. gluttons, gourmands... Devourers of the goods of the (poor) saying that they do so on the ground of their justice, but in reality to destroy them, complainers, deceitful, concealing themselves lest they should be recognized, impious, filled with lawlessness and iniquity from sunrise to sunset: saying: 'We shall have feastings and luxury, eating and drinking, and we shall esteem ourselves as princes.' And though their hands and their minds touch unclean things, yet their mouth shall speak great things, and they shall say furthermore: 'Do not touch me lest you should pollute me in the place (where I stand')...

CHAPTER 8

And there shall come upon them a second visitation and wrath, such as has not befallen them from the beginning until that time, in which He will stir up against them the king of the kings of the earth and one that rules with great power, who shall crucify those who confess to their circumcision: and those who conceal (it) he shall torture and deliver them up to be bound and led into prison. And their wives shall be given to the gods among the Gentiles, and their young sons shall be operated on by the physicians in order to bring forward their foreskin. And others amongst them shall be punished by tortures and fire and sword, and they shall be forced to bear in public their idols, polluted as they are like those who keep. them. And they shall likewise be forced by those who torture them to enter their inmost sanctuary, and they shall be forced by goads to blaspheme with insolence the word, finally after these things the laws and what they had above their altar.

CHAPTER 9

Then in that day there shall be a man of the tribe of Levi, whose name shall be Taxo, who having seven sons shall speak to them exhorting (them): 'Observe, my sons, behold a second ruthless (and) unclean visitation has come upon the people, and a punishment merciless and far exceeding the first. For what nation or what region or what people of those who are impious towards the Lord, who have done many abominations, have suffered as great calamities as have befallen us Now, therefore, my sons, hear me: for observe and know that neither did the fathers nor their forefathers tempt God, so as to transgress His commands. And you know that this is our strength, and thus we will do. Let us fast for the space of three days and on the fourth let us go into a cave which is in the field, and let us die rather than transgress the commands of the Lord of Lords, the God of our fathers. For if we do this and die, our blood shall be avenged before the Lord.

CHAPTER 10

And then His kingdom shall appear throughout all His creation,

And then Satan shall be no more,

And sorrow shall depart with him.

Then the hands of the angel shall be filled

Who has been appointed chief,

And he shall forthwith avenge them of their enemies.

For the Heavenly One will arise from His royal throne,

And He will go forth from His holy habitation

With indignation and wrath on account of His sons.

And the earth shall tremble: to its confines shall it be shaken:

And the high mountains shall be made low

And the hills shall be shaken and fall.

And the horns of the sun shall be broken and he shall be turned into darkness;

And the moon shall not give her light, and be turned wholly into blood.

And the circle of the stars shall be disturbed.

And the sea shall retire into the abyss,

And the fountains of waters shall fail,

And the rivers shall dry up.

For the Most High will arise, the Eternal God alone,

And He will appear to punish the Gentiles,

And He will destroy all their idols.

Then you, O Israel, shall be happy,

And you shall mount upon the necks and wings of the eagle,

And they shall be ended.

And God will exalt you,

And He will cause you to approach to the heaven of the stars,

In the place of their habitation.

And you will look from on high and see your enemies in Ge(henna)

And you shall recognize them and rejoice,

And you shall give thanks and confess thy Creator.

And do you; Joshua (the son of) Nun, keep these words and this book; For from my death [assumption] until His advent there shall be 250 times [= year-weeks = 1750 years]. And this is the course of the times which they shall pursue till they are consummated. And I shall go to sleep with my fathers.

Wherefore, Joshua you (son of) Nun, (be strong and) be of good courage; (for) God has chosen (you) to be minister in the same covenant.

CHAPTER 11

And when Joshua had heard the words of Moses that were so written in his writing all that he had before said, he rent his clothes and cast himself at Moses' feet. And Moses comforted him and wept with him. And Joshua answered him and said: 'Why do you comfort me, (my) lord Moses And how shall I be comforted in regard to the bitter word which you hast spoken which has gone forth from thy mouth, which is full of tears and lamentation, in that you depart from this people (But now) what place shall receive you Or what shall be the sign that marks (your) sepulcher Or who shall dare to move your body from there as that of a mere man from place to place For all men when they die have according to their age their sepulchers on earth; but your sepulcher is from the rising to the setting sun, and from the south to the confines of the north: all the world is your sepulcher. My lord, you are departing, and who shall feed this people Or who is there that shall have compassion on them and who shall be their guide by the way Or who shall pray for them, not omitting a single day, in order that I may lead them into the land of their forefathers How therefore am I to foster this people as a father (his) only son, or as a mistress her daughter, a virgin who is being prepared to be given to the husband whom she will revere, while she guards her person from the sun and (takes care) that her feet are not unshod for running upon the ground. (And how) shall I supply them with food and drink according to the pleasure of their will For of them, there shall be 600,000 (men), for these have multiplied to this degree through your prayers, (my) lord Moses. And what wisdom or understanding have I that I should judge or answer by word in the house (of the Lord) And the kings of the Amorites also when they hear that we are attacking them, believing that there is no longer among them the holy spirit who was worthy of the Lord, manifold and incomprehensible, the lord of the word, who was faithful in all things, God's chief prophet throughout the earth, the most perfect teacher in the world, [that he is no longer among them], shall say "Let us go against them. If the enemy have but once wrought impiously against their Lord, they have no advocate to offer prayers on their behalf to the Lord, like Moses the great messenger, who every hour day and night had his knees fixed to the earth, praying and looking for help to Him that rules all the world with compassion and righteousness, reminding Him of the covenant of the fathers and propitiating the Lord with the oath." For they shall say: "He is not with them: let us go therefore and destroy them from off the face of the earth." What shall then become of this people, my lord Moses.'

CHAPTER 12

And when Joshua had finished (these) words, he cast himself again at the feet of Moses. And Moses took his hand and raised him into the seat before him, and answered and said unto him: Joshua, do not despise yourself; but set your mind at ease, and hear my words. All the nations which are in the earth God has created and us, He has foreseen them and us from the beginning of the creation of the earth unto the end of the age, and nothing has been neglected by Him even to the least thing, but all things He hath foreseen and caused all to come forth. (Yes) all things which are to be in this earth the Lord has foreseen and, look, they are brought forward (into the light ... The Lord,) has on their behalf appointed me to (pray) for their sins and (make intercession) for them. For not for any virtue or strength of mine, but of His good pleasure have His compassion and longsuffering fallen to my lot. For I say unto you, Joshua: it is not on account of the godliness of this people that you shall root out the nations. The lights of the heaven, the foundations of the earth have been made and approved by God and are under the signet ring of His right hand. Those, therefore, who do and fulfill the commandments of God shall increase and be prospered: but those who sin and set at naught the commandments shall be without the blessings before mentioned, and they shall be punished with many torments by the nations. But wholly to root out and destroy them is not permitted. For God will go forth who has foreseen all things for ever, and His covenant has been established and by the oath which . . .

Translation adapted from R. H. Charles, *The Apocrypha and Pseudepigrapha of the Old Testament* (Oxford: University Press, 1913) 2: 407-424.

Chapters 6 & 7 are widely held to be a first century AD interpolation (referring to the Herodian family) into a second century BC document (referring to events precipitated by the persecution of Jews by Antiochus IV Epiphanes).